Nonfiction Writing

Grade 3

Writing: Jennifer Kroll
Content Editing: Robin Kelly
Leslie Sorg
James Spears
Andrea Weiss
Copy Editing: Carrie Gwynne
Art Direction: Cheryl Puckett
Cover Design: Liliana Potigian
Illustration: John Aardema
Design/Production: Carolina Caird
Susan Lovell

EMC 6013

Congratulations on your purchase of some of the finest teaching materials in the world.

For information about other Evan-Moor products, call 1-800-777-4362, fax 1-800-777-4332, or visit our Web site, www.evan-moor.com.

18 Lower Ragsdale Drive, Monterey, CA 93940-5746. Printed in USA.

Correlated to State Standards Visit *teaching-standards.com* to view a correlation of this book's activities to your state's standards. This is a free service.

CPSIA: Printed by McNaughton & Gunn, Saline, MI USA. [7/2011]

Contents

Persuasive Writing

Narrative Writing

How to Use This Book

Nonfiction Writing provides 17 units of instruction and practice activities. Each unit focuses on a basic element or specific form of nonfiction writing and includes guided lessons and accompanying student pages. Each lesson targets a skill essential to that element or form. The units are grouped into four sections: basics of nonfiction writing, expository writing, persuasive writing, and narrative writing.

Teacher Pages

Use the lesson plans to provide guided instruction and modeling of the targeted skills in each unit.

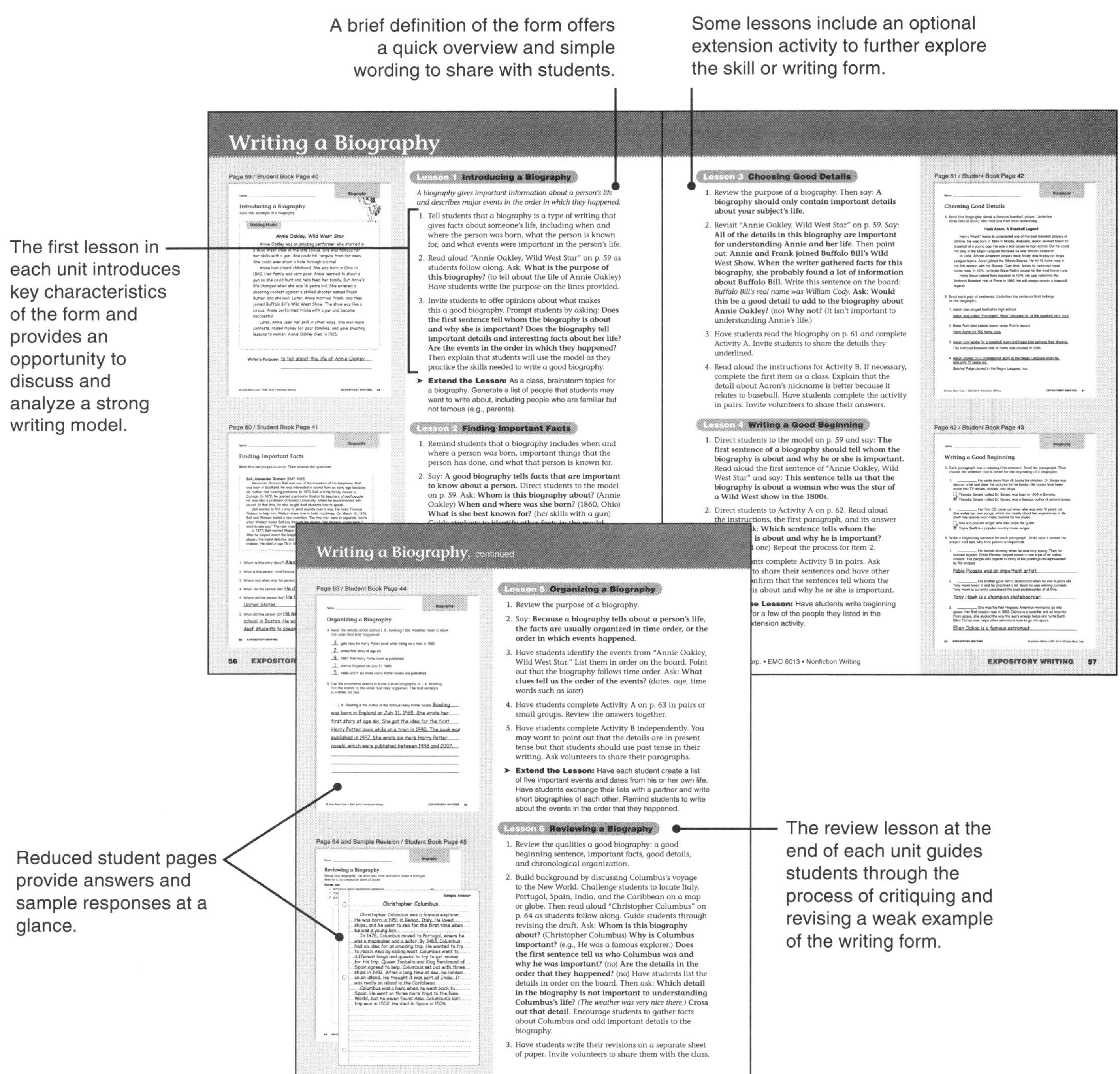

Student Activity Pages

In each unit, students apply the skills they are learning by analyzing a writing model and completing a variety of focused activity pages.

Writing Model

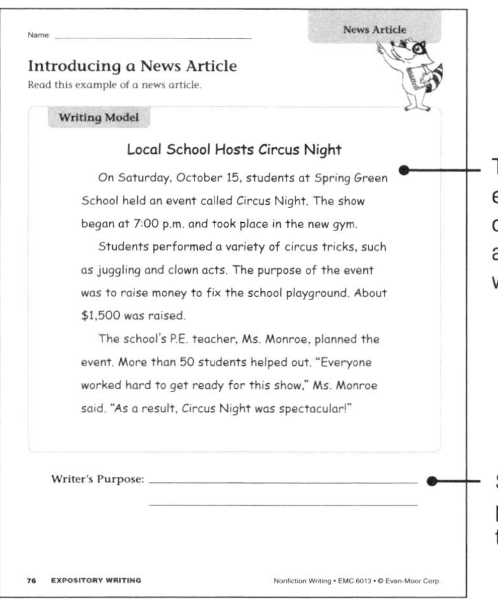
Name: ______

News Article

Introducing a News Article

Read this example of a news article.

Writing Model

Local School Hosts Circus Night

On Saturday, October 15, students at Spring Green School held an event called Circus Night. The show began at 7:00 p.m. and took place in the new gym.

Students performed a variety of circus tricks, such as juggling and clown acts. The purpose of the event was to raise money to fix the school playground. About $1,500 was raised.

The school's P.E. teacher, Ms. Monroe, planned the event. More than 50 students helped out. "Everyone worked hard to get ready for this show," Ms. Monroe said. "As a result, Circus Night was spectacular!"

Writer's Purpose: ______

76 EXPOSITORY WRITING — Nonfiction Writing • EMC 6013 • © Evan-Moor Corp

The writing model contains examples of key elements of the form and provides an opportunity to study the writer's craft.

Students connect the purpose for writing with the writing form.

Review

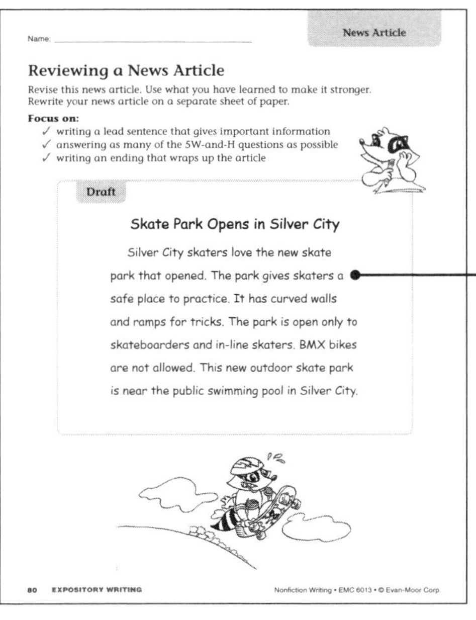
Name: ______

News Article

Reviewing a News Article

Revise this news article. Use what you have learned to make it stronger. Rewrite your news article on a separate sheet of paper.

Focus on:

- ✓ writing a lead sentence that gives important information
- ✓ answering as many of the 5W-and-H questions as possible
- ✓ writing an ending that wraps up the article

Draft

Skate Park Opens in Silver City

Silver City skaters love the new skate park that opened. The park gives skaters a safe place to practice. It has curved walls and ramps for tricks. The park is open only to skateboarders and in-line skaters. BMX bikes are not allowed. This new outdoor skate park is near the public swimming pool in Silver City.

80 EXPOSITORY WRITING — Nonfiction Writing • EMC 6013 • © Evan-Moor Corp

At the end of the unit, a weak model of the writing form is provided for students to revise, giving them the opportunity to review and apply all the skills they have learned.

Activity Pages

Students practice skills in a variety of activity formats designed to deepen students' understanding of the form and craft.

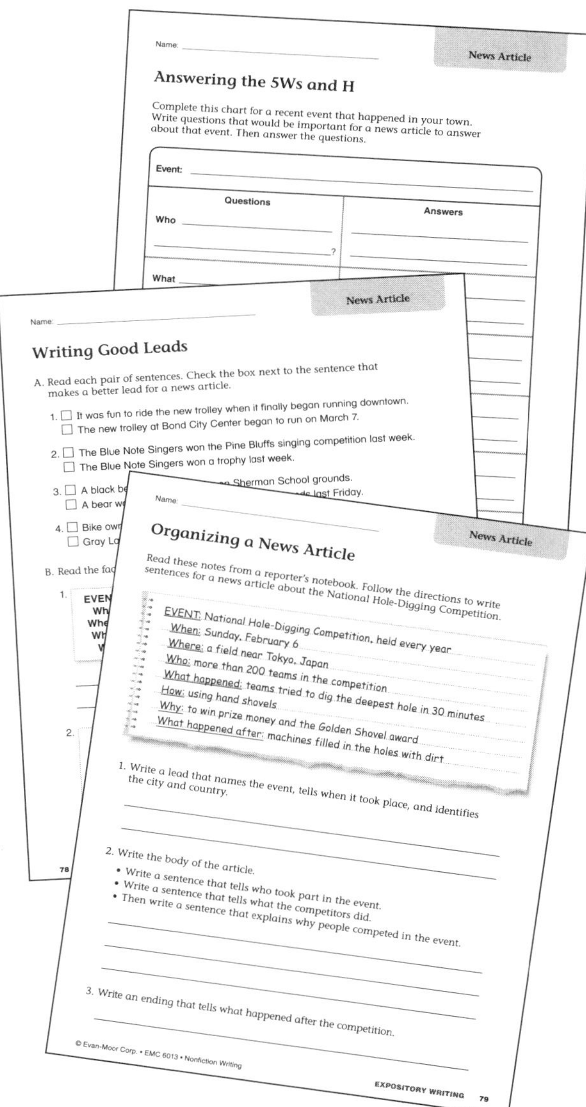
Name: ______

News Article

Answering the 5Ws and H

Complete this chart for a recent event that happened in your town. Write questions that would be important for a news article to answer about that event. Then answer the questions.

Event: ______

Questions	Answers
Who ______?	
What	

Name: ______

News Article

Writing Good Leads

A. Read each pair of sentences. Check the box next to the sentence that makes a better lead for a news article.

1. ☐ It was fun to ride the new trolley when it finally began running downtown.
   ☐ The new trolley at Bond City Center began to run on March 7.
2. ☐ The Blue Note Singers won the Pine Bluffs singing competition last week.
   ☐ The Blue Note Singers won a trophy last week.
3. ☐ A black b... Sherman School grounds.
   ☐ A bear w... last Friday.
4. ☐ Bike own...
   ☐ Gray Lo...

B. Read the fa...

Name: ______

News Article

Organizing a News Article

Read these notes from a reporter's notebook. Follow the directions to write sentences for a news article about the National Hole-Digging Competition.

EVENT: National Hole-Digging Competition, held every year
When: Sunday, February 6
Where: a field near Tokyo, Japan
Who: more than 200 teams in the competition
What happened: teams tried to dig the deepest hole in 30 minutes
How: using hand shovels
Why: to win prize money and the Golden Shovel award
What happened after: machines filled in the holes with dirt

1. Write a lead that names the event, tells when it took place, and identifies the city and country.
2. Write the body of the article.
   - Write a sentence that tells who took part in the event.
   - Write a sentence that tells what the competitors did.
   - Then write a sentence that explains why people competed in the event.
3. Write an ending that tells what happened after the competition.

© Evan-Moor Corp. • EMC 6013 • Nonfiction Writing — EXPOSITORY WRITING 79

Additional Student Pages

Three of the units in this book have unique pages that are necessary to provide the appropriate modeling and support for the writing form.

Response to Literature

The first and last lessons of the *Response to Literature* unit begin with a reading selection to give students practice analyzing a writing prompt and responding to it—just as they would on a test or homework assignment.

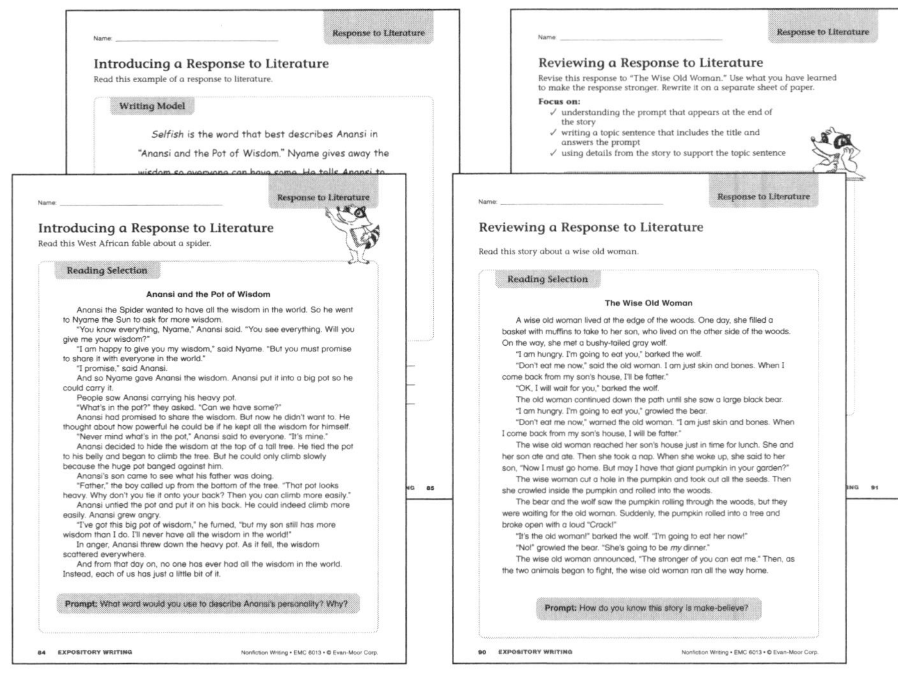

Name: ______ Response to Literature

Introducing a Response to Literature

Read this example of a response to literature.

Writing Model

Selfish is the word that best describes Anansi in "Anansi and the Pot of Wisdom." Nyame gives away the

Name: ______ Response to Literature

Reviewing a Response to Literature

Revise this response to "The Wise Old Woman." Use what you have learned to make the response stronger. Rewrite it on a separate sheet of paper.

Focus on:
- ✓ understanding the prompt that appears at the end of the story
- ✓ writing a topic sentence that includes the title and answers the prompt
- ✓ using details from the story to support the topic sentence

Name: ______ Response to Literature

Introducing a Response to Literature

Read this West African fable about a spider.

Reading Selection

Anansi and the Pot of Wisdom

Anansi the Spider wanted to have all the wisdom in the world. So he went to Nyame the Sun to ask for more wisdom.

"You know everything, Nyame," Anansi said. "You see everything. Will you give me your wisdom?"

"I am happy to give you my wisdom," said Nyame. "But you must promise to share it with everyone in the world."

"I promise," said Anansi.

And so Nyame gave Anansi the wisdom. Anansi put it into a big pot so he could carry it.

People saw Anansi carrying his heavy pot.

"What's in the pot?" they asked. "Can we have some?"

Anansi had promised to share the wisdom. But now he didn't want to. He thought about how powerful he could be if he kept all the wisdom for himself.

"Never mind what's in the pot," Anansi said to everyone. "It's mine."

Anansi decided to hide the wisdom at the top of a tall tree. He tied the pot to his belly and began to climb the tree. But he could only climb slowly because the huge pot banged against him.

Anansi's son came to see what his father was doing.

"Father," the boy called up from the bottom of the tree. "That pot looks heavy. Why don't you tie it onto your back? Then you can climb more easily."

Anansi untied the pot and put it on his back. He could indeed climb more easily. Anansi grew angry.

"I've got this big pot of wisdom," he fumed, "but my son still has more wisdom than I do. I'll never have all the wisdom in the world!"

In anger, Anansi threw down the heavy pot. As it fell, the wisdom scattered everywhere.

And from that day on, no one has ever had all the wisdom in the world. Instead, each of us has just a little bit of it.

Prompt: What word would you use to describe Anansi's personality? Why?

84 EXPOSITORY WRITING Nonfiction Writing • EMC 6013 • © Evan-Moor Corp.

Name: ______ Response to Literature

Reviewing a Response to Literature

Read this story about a wise old woman.

Reading Selection

The Wise Old Woman

A wise old woman lived at the edge of the woods. One day, she filled a basket with muffins to take to her son, who lived on the other side of the woods. On the way, she met a bushy-tailed gray wolf.

"I am hungry. I'm going to eat you," barked the wolf.

"Don't eat me now," said the old woman. I am just skin and bones. When I come back from my son's house, I'll be fatter."

"OK, I will wait for you," barked the wolf.

The old woman continued down the path until she saw a large black bear.

"I am hungry. I'm going to eat you," growled the bear.

"Don't eat me now," warned the old woman. "I am just skin and bones. When I come back from my son's house, I will be fatter."

The wise old woman reached her son's house just in time for lunch. She and her son ate and ate. Then she took a nap. When she woke up, she said to her son, "Now I must go home. But may I have that giant pumpkin in your garden?"

The wise woman cut a hole in the pumpkin and took out all the seeds. Then she crawled inside the pumpkin and rolled into the woods.

The bear and the wolf saw the pumpkin rolling through the woods, but they were waiting for the old woman. Suddenly, the pumpkin rolled into a tree and broke open with a loud "Crack!"

"It's the old woman!" barked the wolf. "I'm going to eat her now!"

"No!" growled the bear. "She's going to be *my* dinner."

The wise old woman announced, "The stronger of you can eat me." Then, as the two animals began to fight, the wise old woman ran all the way home.

Prompt: How do you know this story is make-believe?

90 EXPOSITORY WRITING Nonfiction Writing • EMC 6013 • © Evan-Moor Corp.

Summary

The first and last lessons of the *Summary* unit begin with a reading selection for students to summarize.

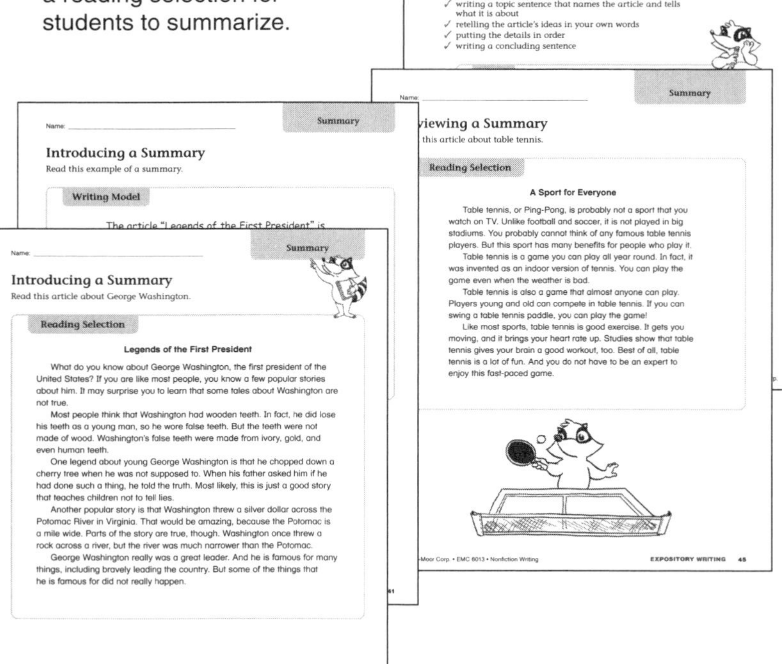

Name: ______ Summary

Reviewing a Summary

Revise this summary of the article "A Sport for Everyone." Use what you have learned to make it stronger. Rewrite the summary on a separate sheet of paper.

Focus on:
- ✓ writing a topic sentence that names the article and tells what it is about
- ✓ retelling the article's ideas in your own words
- ✓ putting the details in order
- ✓ writing a concluding sentence

Name: ______ Summary

Reviewing a Summary

Read this article about table tennis.

Reading Selection

A Sport for Everyone

Table tennis, or Ping-Pong, is probably not a sport that you watch on TV. Unlike football and soccer, it is not played in big stadiums. You probably cannot think of any famous table tennis players. But this sport has many benefits for people who play it.

Table tennis is a game you can play all year round. In fact, it was invented as an indoor version of tennis. You can play the game even when the weather is bad.

Table tennis is also a game that almost anyone can play. Players young and old can compete in table tennis. If you can swing a table tennis paddle, you can play the game!

Like most sports, table tennis is good exercise. It gets you moving, and it brings your heart rate up. Studies show that table tennis gives your brain a good workout, too. Best of all, table tennis is a lot of fun. And you do not have to be an expert to enjoy this fast-paced game.

© Evan-Moor Corp. • EMC 6013 • Nonfiction Writing EXPOSITORY WRITING 45

Name: ______ Summary

Introducing a Summary

Read this example of a summary.

Writing Model

The article "Legends of the First President" is

Name: ______ Summary

Introducing a Summary

Read this article about George Washington.

Reading Selection

Legends of the First President

What do you know about George Washington, the first president of the United States? If you are like most people, you know a few popular stories about him. It may surprise you to learn that some tales about Washington are not true.

Most people think that Washington had wooden teeth. In fact, he did lose his teeth as a young man, so he wore false teeth. But the teeth were not made of wood. Washington's false teeth were made from ivory, gold, and even human teeth.

One legend about young George Washington is that he chopped down a cherry tree when he was not supposed to. When his father asked him if he had done such a thing, he told the truth. Most likely, this is just a good story that teaches children not to tell lies.

Another popular story is that Washington threw a silver dollar across the Potomac River in Virginia. That would be amazing, because the Potomac is a mile wide. Parts of the story are true, though. Washington once threw a rock across a river, but the river was much narrower than the Potomac.

George Washington really was a great leader. And he is famous for many things, including bravely leading the country. But some of the things that he is famous for did not really happen.

40 EXPOSITORY WRITING Nonfiction Writing • EMC 6013 • © Evan-Moor Corp.

Research Report

The *Research Report* unit provides a model outline and bibliography in addition to the writing model.

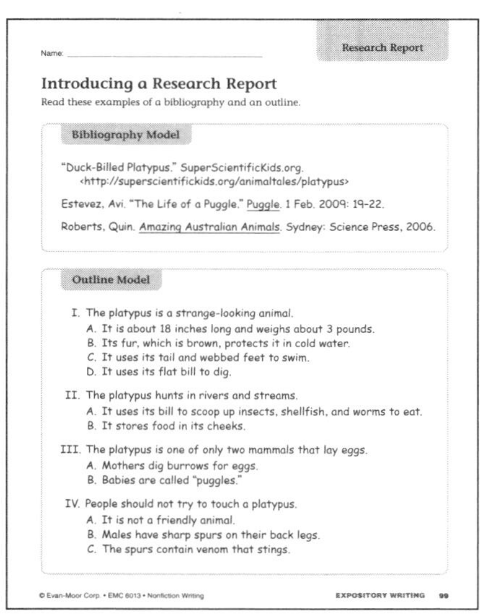

Name: ______ Research Report

Introducing a Research Report

Read these examples of a bibliography and an outline.

Bibliography Model

"Duck-Billed Platypus." SuperScientificKids.org. <http://superscientifickids.org/animaltales/platypus>

Estevez, Avi. "The Life of a Puggle." Puggle. 1 Feb. 2009: 19–22.

Roberts, Quin. Amazing Australian Animals. Sydney: Science Press, 2006.

Outline Model

I. The platypus is a strange-looking animal.
   A. It is about 18 inches long and weighs about 3 pounds.
   B. Its fur, which is brown, protects it in cold water.
   C. It uses its tail and webbed feet to swim.
   D. It uses its flat bill to dig.

II. The platypus hunts in rivers and streams.
   A. It uses its bill to scoop up insects, shellfish, and worms to eat.
   B. It stores food in its cheeks.

III. The platypus is one of only two mammals that lay eggs.
   A. Mothers dig burrows for eggs.
   B. Babies are called "puggles."

IV. People should not try to touch a platypus.
   A. It is not a friendly animal.
   B. Males have sharp spurs on their back legs.
   C. The spurs contain venom that stings.

© Evan-Moor Corp. • EMC 6013 • Nonfiction Writing EXPOSITORY WRITING 99

Forms of Nonfiction Writing

The following writing forms are presented in this book to provide students with a variety of real-world and academic formats and purposes for writing.

Expository Writing

Biography: a true story about a person's life, giving important information about the person and describing major events in the order in which they happened

Descriptive Paragraph: a paragraph that describes a person, place, thing, or event, using vivid details so the reader can easily imagine it

How-to Instructions: a paragraph that tells readers how to make or do something

News Article: a report that gives factual information about a current event and answers *who, what, where, when, why,* and *how* about the event

Research Report: a report that gives details and facts about a topic, using information gathered from different sources

Response to Literature: writing that responds to a prompt, or question, about a specific reading selection

Summary: a short piece of writing that gives the main idea and the most important details about a longer piece of writing, such as a story or book

Persuasive Writing

Persuasive Letter: a letter written to persuade someone to agree with a certain idea or to take a specific action

Persuasive Paragraph: a paragraph written to persuade others to agree with the writer or to take a specific action

Review: a piece of writing that gives important information and expresses an opinion about a book, movie, show, restaurant, or product

Narrative Writing

Creative Nonfiction: a true story that a writer tells, using some of the same strategies writers use when they write fiction

Friendly Letter: a letter that tells about something personal in the writer's life and that is written to someone the writer knows

Personal Narrative: a true story that a writer tells about a specific event or experience from his or her own life

Page 10 / Student Book Page 2

Name: ____________________

Paragraph

Introducing a Paragraph

Read this example of a paragraph.

Writing Model

Beach Fun

When the ocean is too cold for swimming, you can still have fun at the beach. You can look for animals that live on the shore or in the ocean. You might see gulls and crabs, or even dolphins and seals. It is fun to collect shells and stones at the beach. The beach is a great place for flying kites and playing volleyball, too. You can also play catch or tag. And, of course, you can always build a sand castle. So, even if the cold water sends you running, you won't run out of fun!

Writer's Purpose: to tell about fun things to do at the beach besides swimming

10 BASICS OF NONFICTION WRITING Nonfiction Writing • EMC 6013 • © Evan-Moor Corp.

Page 11 / Student Book Page 3

Name: ____________________

Paragraph

Writing a Topic Sentence

A. Read each paragraph and then underline the topic sentence.

1. **Topic:** ostriches
   The ostrich is an interesting bird. Even though it has feathers, it cannot fly. But ostriches have very long legs and can run fast. In fact, they are the fastest runners of all birds.
2. **Topic:** storing fresh foods
   What would it be like to live with no refrigerator? It's hard even to imagine! Long ago, people found ways to keep fresh food cold so it didn't spoil. Some people kept food in an icebox, which was a box with a large block of ice that melted slowly.
3. **Topic:** fossils
   If you like rocks, you probably like fossils, too. Fossils are the hardened remains of plants or animals that lived long ago. They are found buried in rock. Fossils tell us how life on Earth has changed.

B. Read each paragraph. Revise the underlined sentence so it tells the main idea of the paragraph.

1. **Topic:** an ancient game
   The game of Senet might be fun to play today. Players moved game pieces around a game board. The board had three rows, each with ten squares. Ancient Egyptians really liked the game. People have found many Senet game sets in mummy tombs in Egypt.
   Senet was a board game played in Egypt long ago.
2. **Topic:** the dangers of cycling
   When you think of a dangerous sport, do you think of hockey or football? What about cycling? Cycling is a popular sport. More cyclists than hockey players end up in the hospital. Also, kids are more likely to get hurt from cycling than from playing football. Wearing a bike helmet is the best way for cyclists to stay safe.
   Cycling can be a dangerous sport.

© Evan-Moor Corp. • EMC 6013 • Nonfiction Writing BASICS OF NONFICTION WRITING 11

Lesson 1 Introducing a Paragraph

A paragraph expresses one main idea. A topic sentence clearly states that idea. Other sentences add supporting details.

1. Display the model on p. 10, "Beach Fun," and say: **A paragraph is a group of sentences about the same topic.** Ask: **Based on the title, what do you think this paragraph is about?** (having fun at the beach)
2. Read aloud the paragraph as students follow along. Then ask: **What is the purpose of this paragraph?** (to tell about fun things to do at the beach besides swimming) Have students write the purpose on the lines provided.
3. Invite students to offer opinions about what makes this a good paragraph. Prompt students by asking: **Is it clear that this paragraph is about fun things to do at the beach? Are all of the sentences about fun things to do?**
4. Explain that students will use the model as they practice the skills needed to write a good paragraph.

Lesson 2 Writing a Topic Sentence

1. Say: **All of the sentences in a paragraph should be about one main idea. A *topic sentence* tells the main idea, or what the paragraph is mostly about. It is often, but not always, the first sentence of a paragraph.**
2. Revisit "Beach Fun" and ask: **Which sentence tells the main idea of this paragraph?** (the first one) Explain that this is the topic sentence. Have students underline it.
3. Read aloud the directions for Activity A on p. 11. Then read the first paragraph and ask: **What are all of the sentences about?** (ostriches) **Which sentence tells the main idea?** (the first one) Have students underline it. Read the second paragraph and ask: **Is the first sentence of this paragraph the topic sentence?** (no) Then have students complete the activity independently.
4. Complete the first item of Activity B as a group. Have students complete the second item independently.

➤ **Extend the Lesson:** List a few paragraph topics such as rainy-day activities, different kinds of rocks, and seasonal sports. Brainstorm additional topics as a class. Then have partners choose a topic and write a topic sentence for a possible paragraph on that topic.

Lesson 3 Adding Good Details

1. Review the concept of a main idea and details in a paragraph. Say: **The topic sentence tells the main idea. Other sentences in the paragraph add details.**
2. Explain that details tell more about the main idea, usually by giving additional information or examples. Read aloud this sentence from "Beach Fun": *You can look for animals that live on the shore or in the ocean.* Ask: **How does this sentence add a detail about the topic?** (It gives an example of something fun to do at the beach.) Say: **Good details tell only about the main idea of your paragraph. If you see any details in your paragraph that do *not* tell about the main idea, you should cross them out.**
3. Have students complete Activity A on p. 12 in pairs. Invite volunteers to share their answers.
4. Model Activity B. Read aloud the topic sentence in the first item and say: **Fantasy books are an example of a kind of book that kids like to read.** Help students turn this fact into a detail sentence. Then have students complete the activity independently. Invite volunteers to share their sentences.

➤ **Extend the Lesson:** Have each student write one or two detail sentences for the topic sentence composed in the Lesson 2 extension activity.

Lesson 4 Reviewing a Paragraph

1. Review the qualities of a paragraph: a topic sentence that states the main idea, and sentences that add details about that main idea.
2. Read aloud "Kickball" on p. 13 as students follow along. Then guide students through revising the draft. Ask: **What is the main idea of the paragraph?** (playing kickball) **Is there one sentence that tells what kickball is?** (no) Say: **This paragraph needs a topic sentence.** (e.g., Kickball is a popular playground game.) Then ask: **What detail does the first sentence tell us about kickball?** (that it can be dangerous) **Does this detail fit the main idea of the paragraph?** (no) **Which other sentence does *not* tell about the main idea?** *(Usually, the bases on the field are white.)* Suggest that students cross out those sentences. Then ask: **What details could you add about kickball?** Guide students to add sentences with good details.
3. Have students write their revisions on a separate sheet of paper. Invite volunteers to read them aloud.

Page 12 / Student Book Page 4

Name: ______________________ Paragraph

Adding Good Details

A. Read each paragraph. Cross out the sentence that does not tell more about the main idea. Then check the box next to the detail that *does* tell more about the main idea.

1. The World Cup is a soccer tournament held every four years. A different country hosts the World Cup each time the games are held. ~~The goalie is an important member of a soccer team.~~ In 2010, the World Cup was held in South Africa.
   - ☑ Millions of people watch the World Cup.
   - ☐ The Summer Olympics are also held every four years.
2. The first pencil sharpener was made in 1828. ~~Some pencils do not need to be sharpened.~~ Before 1828, people used knives to sharpen pencils. Pencil sharpeners made the task easier and safer.
   - ☐ Some pencils have an eraser on the end.
   - ☑ Many pencil sharpeners today use electricity.
3. Monkeys are different from apes. Monkeys have tails, but apes do not. Monkeys are also smaller than apes. ~~Most states do not allow people to keep apes or monkeys as pets.~~
   - ☑ Apes can walk on two legs for a while, but monkeys cannot.
   - ☐ Monkeys like many of the same fruits that humans like.

B. Read each topic sentence. Write a detail sentence to go with it.

1. Kids like to read all kinds of books.
   Fantasy books are some of the most popular books.
2. Painting is fun, but there are many other kinds of art to make.
   You can make sculptures or pots out of clay.
3. Parks are great places for families to visit.
   Most parks have a playground where kids can play.

12 BASICS OF NONFICTION WRITING — Nonfiction Writing • EMC 6013 • © Evan-Moor Corp.

Page 13 and Sample Revision / Student Book Page 5

Name: ______________________ Paragraph

Reviewing a Paragraph

Revise this paragraph. Use what you have learned to make it stronger. Rewrite the paragraph on a separate sheet of paper.

Focus on:
- ✓ writing a good topic sentence
- ✓ leaving out details that do not belong
- ✓ adding details that support the main idea

Draft

Kickball

Kickball can be dangerous. It is like baseball. In fact, it was first called "kick

Sample Answer

Kickball

Kickball is a fun game to play at recess. The game is a lot like baseball. In fact, it was first called "kick baseball." Kickball uses a large, soft rubber ball that players kick. The pitcher on one team rolls the ball to a kicker on the other team. That player kicks the ball as far as possible and runs around the field. If the kicker reaches home plate, the team gets a point. Kickball is popular at school because teams can be large or small. Almost anyone can play this game.

Name: ______________________________

Introducing a Paragraph

Read this example of a paragraph.

Writing Model

Beach Fun

When the ocean is too cold for swimming, you can still have fun at the beach. You can look for animals that live on the shore or in the ocean. You might see gulls and crabs, or even dolphins and seals. It is fun to collect shells and stones at the beach. The beach is a great place for flying kites and playing volleyball, too. You can also play catch or tag. And, of course, you can always build a sand castle. So, even if the cold water sends you running, you won't run out of fun!

Writer's Purpose: ______________________________

____

Name: ______________________________

Writing a Topic Sentence

A. Read each paragraph and then underline the topic sentence.

1. **Topic:** ostriches

The ostrich is an interesting bird. Even though it has feathers, it cannot fly. But ostriches have very long legs and can run fast. In fact, they are the fastest runners of all birds.

2. **Topic:** storing fresh foods

What would it be like to live with no refrigerator? It's hard even to imagine! Long ago, people found ways to keep fresh food cold so it didn't spoil. Some people kept food in an icebox, which was a box with a large block of ice that melted slowly.

3. **Topic:** fossils

If you like rocks, you probably like fossils, too. Fossils are the hardened remains of plants or animals that lived long ago. They are found buried in rock. Fossils tell us how life on Earth has changed.

B. Read each paragraph. Revise the underlined sentence so it tells the main idea of the paragraph.

1. **Topic:** an ancient game

The game of Senet might be fun to play today. Players moved game pieces around a game board. The board had three rows, each with ten squares. Ancient Egyptians really liked the game. People have found many Senet game sets in mummy tombs in Egypt.

____

2. **Topic:** the dangers of cycling

When you think of a dangerous sport, do you think of hockey or football? What about cycling? Cycling is a popular sport. More cyclists than hockey players end up in the hospital. Also, kids are more likely to get hurt from cycling than from playing football. Wearing a bike helmet is the best way for cyclists to stay safe.

____

Name: ____________________

Adding Good Details

A. Read each paragraph. Cross out the sentence that does not tell more about the main idea. Then check the box next to the detail that *does* tell more about the main idea.

1. The World Cup is a soccer tournament held every four years. A different country hosts the World Cup each time the games are held. The goalie is an important member of a soccer team. In 2010, the World Cup was held in South Africa.

   ☐ Millions of people watch the World Cup.

   ☐ The Summer Olympics are also held every four years.

2. The first pencil sharpener was made in 1828. Some pencils do not need to be sharpened. Before 1828, people used knives to sharpen pencils. Pencil sharpeners made the task easier and safer.

   ☐ Some pencils have an eraser on the end.

   ☐ Many pencil sharpeners today use electricity.

3. Monkeys are different from apes. Monkeys have tails, but apes do not. Monkeys are also smaller than apes. Most states do not allow people to keep apes or monkeys as pets.

   ☐ Apes can walk on two legs for a while, but monkeys cannot.

   ☐ Monkeys like many of the same fruits that humans like.

B. Read each topic sentence. Write a detail sentence to go with it.

1. Kids like to read all kinds of books.

   ____

2. Painting is fun, but there are many other kinds of art to make.

   ____

3. Parks are great places for families to visit.

   ____

Name: ______________________________

Reviewing a Paragraph

Revise this paragraph. Use what you have learned to make it stronger. Rewrite the paragraph on a separate sheet of paper.

Focus on:

✓ writing a good topic sentence
✓ leaving out details that do not belong
✓ adding details that support the main idea

Draft

Kickball

Kickball can be dangerous. It is like baseball. In fact, it was first called "kick baseball." Kickball uses a large, soft rubber ball that players kick. The pitcher on one team rolls the ball to a kicker on the other team. That player kicks the ball as far as possible and runs around the field. Usually, the bases on the field are white. Kickball is popular at school because teams can be large or small.

Writing to Show Sequence

Page 16 / Student Book Page 7

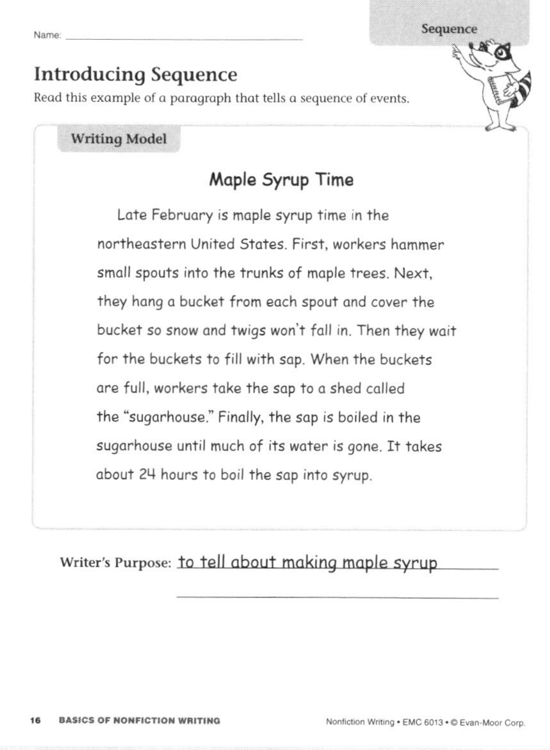

Name: ____________

Sequence

Introducing Sequence

Read this example of a paragraph that tells a sequence of events.

Writing Model

Maple Syrup Time

Late February is maple syrup time in the northeastern United States. First, workers hammer small spouts into the trunks of maple trees. Next, they hang a bucket from each spout and cover the bucket so snow and twigs won't fall in. Then they wait for the buckets to fill with sap. When the buckets are full, workers take the sap to a shed called the "sugarhouse." Finally, the sap is boiled in the sugarhouse until much of its water is gone. It takes about 24 hours to boil the sap into syrup.

Writer's Purpose: to tell about making maple syrup

16 BASICS OF NONFICTION WRITING — Nonfiction Writing • EMC 6013 • © Evan-Moor Corp.

Page 17 / Student Book Page 8

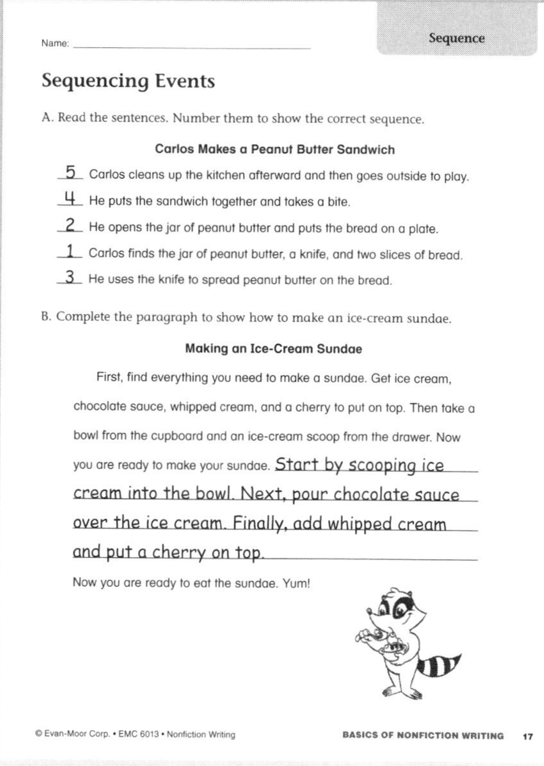

Name: ____________

Sequence

Sequencing Events

A. Read the sentences. Number them to show the correct sequence.

Carlos Makes a Peanut Butter Sandwich

5 Carlos cleans up the kitchen afterward and then goes outside to play.
4 He puts the sandwich together and takes a bite.
2 He opens the jar of peanut butter and puts the bread on a plate.
1 Carlos finds the jar of peanut butter, a knife, and two slices of bread.
3 He uses the knife to spread peanut butter on the bread.

B. Complete the paragraph to show how to make an ice-cream sundae.

Making an Ice-Cream Sundae

First, find everything you need to make a sundae. Get ice cream, chocolate sauce, whipped cream, and a cherry to put on top. Then take a bowl from the cupboard and an ice-cream scoop from the drawer. Now you are ready to make your sundae. Start by scooping ice cream into the bowl. Next, pour chocolate sauce over the ice cream. Finally, add whipped cream and put a cherry on top.

Now you are ready to eat the sundae. Yum!

© Evan-Moor Corp. • EMC 6013 • Nonfiction Writing — BASICS OF NONFICTION WRITING 17

Lesson 1 Introducing Sequence

Writing that shows sequence usually identifies steps in a process or tells about a series of events using chronological order and order words.

1. Read aloud "Maple Syrup Time" on p. 16 as students follow along. Ask: **What is the purpose of this paragraph?** (to tell about making maple syrup) Have students write the purpose on the lines provided. Then have them identify the topic sentence of the paragraph. *(Late February is maple syrup time in the northeastern United States.)*
2. Invite students to offer opinions about what makes this a good example of writing that shows sequence. Prompt students by asking: **Does the paragraph tell the events in order? Does it include words that tell what happened first, next, and last?**
3. Explain that students will use the model as they practice the skills needed for writing to show sequence.

➤ **Extend the Lesson:** Have students make a comic strip that illustrates the events described in "Maple Syrup Time." Tell students to include captions.

Lesson 2 Sequencing Events

1. Say: **When you write to show sequence, you tell about the events in time order, or the order in which things happen.** Point out that "Maple Syrup Time" uses time order. Have students identify each step in the process by asking: **What do workers do first?** (hammer spouts into the tree trunks) **Then what happens?** (They hang buckets from the spouts to collect sap.) Continue to ask questions about the process.
2. Read aloud the directions for Activity A on p. 17. Invite volunteers to read aloud the sentences. Then have students complete the activity in pairs. To confirm the sequence, encourage students to act out the steps for making a peanut butter sandwich. Review the answers together and give students an opportunity to explain their reasoning.
3. Read aloud the directions for Activity B. Explain that the first three sentences name everything you need to make an ice-cream sundae. Say: **Imagine that you are making a sundae. Think about how you would get started. Then think about what you would do next.** Have students complete the activity independently. Invite volunteers to share their paragraphs with the class.

Lesson 3 Using Order Words and Phrases

1. Say: **Writing that shows a sequence of events often includes words that tell the order in which events happened. *First, next, then,* and *finally* are examples of order words.** Have students underline the order words from the model on p. 16. *(First, Next, Then, Finally)*
2. Point out that some events are signaled by phrases such as *soon after, a year ago,* or *at last,* or even more specific phrases. Ask: **When do workers take the tree sap to the sugarhouse?** (when the buckets are full)
3. Read aloud the directions for Activity A on p. 18. As needed, clarify the meaning of the order words and phrases in the box. Explain that the paragraph is about a boy looking for his baseball cap. Say: **The words that you add will make the order of events clearer.** Then have students complete the activity in pairs, or conduct it with the class.
4. Read the directions for Activity B and model completing the first two sentences. Say: **I can write about the last time I gave a present to my best friend, Alda. First, I remembered that Alda likes to read. Then I went to the bookstore to find a book that she might enjoy.** Have students complete Activity B independently.

➤ **Extend the Lesson:** Have students write about a simple, familiar game such as hide-and-seek or "freeze tag," using order words and phrases.

Lesson 4 Reviewing Sequence

1. Review the qualities of a paragraph that shows sequence: a topic sentence, sentences that show time order, and order words and phrases.
2. Read aloud "From Caterpillar to Butterfly" on p. 19 as students follow along. Review the stages in the life cycle of a monarch butterfly. Then guide students through revising the draft. Ask: **What is this paragraph about?** (the life cycle of a monarch butterfly) **Is there one sentence that tells the main idea of the paragraph?** (no) Help students improve the topic sentence. Then ask: **Which stage is best to tell about first?** (laying eggs) **Which sentences are out of sequence?** *(The egg hatches. The chrysalis opens.)* Prompt students to add words or phrases to signal the order of events (e.g., *soon* or *next*).
3. Have students write their revisions on a separate sheet of paper. Invite volunteers to share their paragraphs.

Page 18 / Student Book Page 9

Name: ____________________ Sequence

Using Order Words and Phrases

A. Complete the paragraph to show when things happened. Use the words in the box.

as soon as	at last	first	next

Yesterday I lost my special baseball cap, so I decided to look for it. ___First___, I looked on the porch. I looked in the kitchen, too, but I didn't find my cap there. I looked in my room ___next___. My cap wasn't there, but I found a clue. My little sister Gloria had left her sparkly shoes on my bedroom floor. ___As soon as___ I saw Gloria's shoes, I ran to check her room. Her stuffed animals were on her bed, and each one was wearing a hat. Gloria's teddy bear was wearing a baseball cap—my special baseball cap! I had found my missing cap ___at last___!

B. Think about the last time you gave someone a present. Complete the sentences to describe the steps you followed.

First, I thought about what I should get for Mark.

Then I went to the toy store with my mom and bought a rocket kit that he might like.

Next, I wrapped the kit in some striped paper.

Finally, I made a card with my stamp set and colored markers and taped it to the package.

18 BASICS OF NONFICTION WRITING Nonfiction Writing • EMC 6013 • © Evan-Moor Corp.

Page 19 and Sample Revision / Student Book Page 10

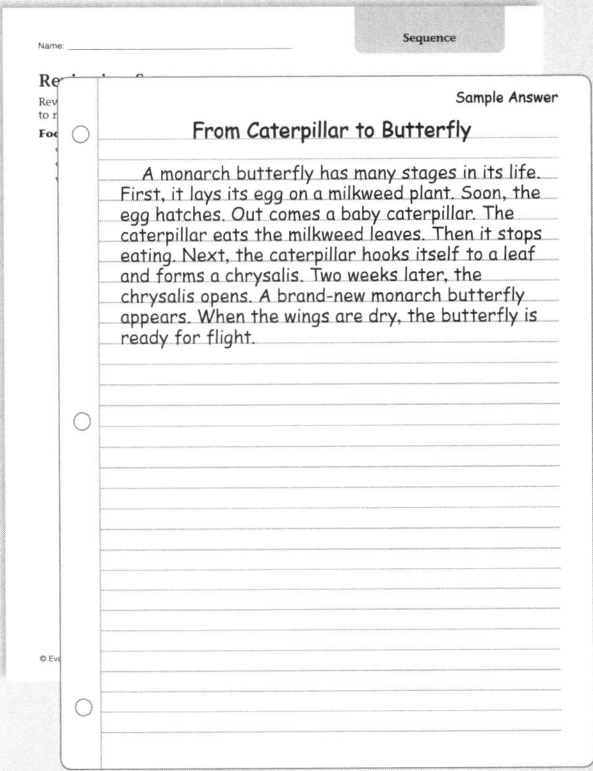
Name: ____________________ Sequence

Sample Answer

From Caterpillar to Butterfly

A monarch butterfly has many stages in its life. First, it lays its egg on a milkweed plant. Soon, the egg hatches. Out comes a baby caterpillar. The caterpillar eats the milkweed leaves. Then it stops eating. Next, the caterpillar hooks itself to a leaf and forms a chrysalis. Two weeks later, the chrysalis opens. A brand-new monarch butterfly appears. When the wings are dry, the butterfly is ready for flight.

Name: ____________________

Introducing Sequence

Read this example of a paragraph that tells a sequence of events.

Writing Model

Maple Syrup Time

Late February is maple syrup time in the northeastern United States. First, workers hammer small spouts into the trunks of maple trees. Next, they hang a bucket from each spout and cover the bucket so snow and twigs won't fall in. Then they wait for the buckets to fill with sap. When the buckets are full, workers take the sap to a shed called the "sugarhouse." Finally, the sap is boiled in the sugarhouse until much of its water is gone. It takes about 24 hours to boil the sap into syrup.

Writer's Purpose: ____________________

____

Name: ______________________________

Sequencing Events

A. Read the sentences. Number them to show the correct sequence.

Carlos Makes a Peanut Butter Sandwich

____ Carlos cleans up the kitchen afterward and then goes outside to play.

____ He puts the sandwich together and takes a bite.

____ He opens the jar of peanut butter and puts the bread on a plate.

____ Carlos finds the jar of peanut butter, a knife, and two slices of bread.

____ He uses the knife to spread peanut butter on the bread.

B. Complete the paragraph to show how to make an ice-cream sundae.

Making an Ice-Cream Sundae

First, find everything you need to make a sundae. Get ice cream, chocolate sauce, whipped cream, and a cherry to put on top. Then take a bowl from the cupboard and an ice-cream scoop from the drawer. Now you are ready to make your sundae. ______________________________

____

____

____

Now you are ready to eat the sundae. Yum!

Name: ______________________________

Using Order Words and Phrases

A. Complete the paragraph to show when things happened.
Use the words in the box.

as soon as	at last	first	next

Yesterday I lost my special baseball cap, so I decided to look for it. ______________, I looked on the porch. I looked in the kitchen, too, but I didn't find my cap there. I looked in my room ______________. My cap wasn't there, but I found a clue. My little sister Gloria had left her sparkly shoes on my bedroom floor. ______________ I saw Gloria's shoes, I ran to check her room. Her stuffed animals were on her bed, and each one was wearing a hat. Gloria's teddy bear was wearing a baseball cap—my special baseball cap! I had found my missing cap ______________!

B. Think about the last time you gave someone a present. Complete the sentences to describe the steps you followed.

First, ____.

Then ____

____.

Next, ____.

Finally, ____

____.

Name: ______________________________

Reviewing Sequence

Revise this paragraph to show sequence. Use what you have learned to make it stronger. Rewrite the paragraph on a separate sheet of paper.

Focus on:

- ✓ writing a sentence that tells the main idea
- ✓ putting events in the correct order
- ✓ using words and phrases to clearly show the order

Draft

From Caterpillar to Butterfly

A monarch butterfly comes from a caterpillar. The egg hatches. The butterfly lays its egg on a milkweed plant. Out comes a baby caterpillar. The caterpillar eats the milkweed leaves. It stops eating. The caterpillar hooks itself onto a leaf and forms a chrysalis. Two weeks later, a brand-new monarch butterfly appears. The chrysalis opens. When the wings are dry, the butterfly is ready for flight.

Page 23 / Student Book Page 12

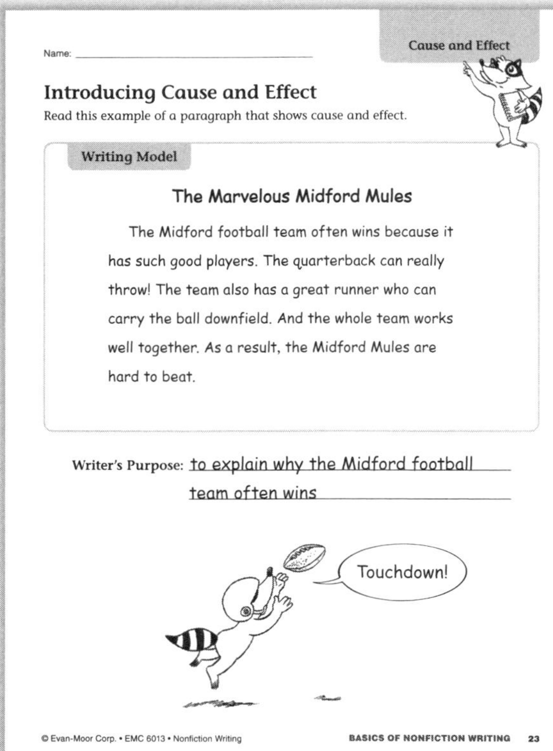
Name: ______

Cause and Effect

Introducing Cause and Effect

Read this example of a paragraph that shows cause and effect.

Writing Model

The Marvelous Midford Mules

The Midford football team often wins because it has such good players. The quarterback can really throw! The team also has a great runner who can carry the ball downfield. And the whole team works well together. As a result, the Midford Mules are hard to beat.

Writer's Purpose: to explain why the Midford football team often wins

© Evan-Moor Corp. • EMC 6013 • Nonfiction Writing   BASICS OF NONFICTION WRITING 23

Lesson 1 Introducing Cause and Effect

A cause-and-effect paragraph tells what happens and why it happens. The topic sentence tells the cause-and-effect relationship. Details support the topic sentence and tell more about the cause or the effect.

1. Draw two boxes, side by side, on the board, with an arrow connecting them. Label the first box *cause* and the second box *effect*. Demonstrate the concept of cause and effect by inflating a party balloon and holding the opening tight. Ask: **What happened to the balloon?** (It got bigger.) **What caused it to get bigger?** (filling it with air) Write each response in the appropriate box on the board. Repeat with other simple actions.

2. Then explain: **An *effect* is something that happens. A *cause* is why it happens.**

3. Read aloud "The Marvelous Midford Mules" on p. 23 as students follow along. Ask: **What is the purpose of this paragraph?** (to explain why the Midford football team often wins) Have students write the purpose on the lines provided.

4. Invite students to offer opinions about what makes this a good example of writing to show cause and effect. Prompt students by asking: **Does the paragraph tell about something that happens? Does it explain why it happens and then give details?**

5. Explain that students will use the model as they practice the skills needed to write a good paragraph that shows cause and effect.

➤ **Extend the Lesson:** Have students record in graphic organizers at least one specific thing that happened to them recently (an effect) and the reason it happened (the cause). Suggest possibilities such as getting a good report card or missing the school bus.

Lesson 2 Identifying Causes and Effects

1. Remind students that an *effect* is something that happens and a *cause* is why it happens.

2. Read aloud the topic sentence of the model on p. 23: *The Midford football team often wins because it has such good players.* Explain that the sentence introduces the cause-and-effect relationship that the paragraph is about. Ask: **Why does the team win?** (because the players are good) **What is the effect of having good players?** (The team often wins.)

3. Read aloud the directions for Activity A on p. 24. Use the first item to model. Say: **The morning rain is the cause of something. I ask myself, What is likely to happen because of the rain? One possibility is that the streets will be wet.** Ask: **What else is likely to happen?** You may want to record students' suggestions on the board. Then have students complete the activity in pairs. Invite partners to share their answers.
4. Read the directions for Activity B and clarify that students are looking for the likely *cause* this time. Have students complete the activity in pairs. Invite partners to share their answers with the class.

➤ **Extend the Lesson:** Have students complete these sentences to show cause and effect: *When I hear ____, it makes me smile. When I feel sad, it makes me ____.*

Lesson 3 Using Cause-and-Effect Signal Words

1. Say: **Writers can use words like *so* and *because* to signal a cause or an effect.** Write a list of cause-and-effect signal words and phrases on the board. (e.g., *because, as a result, for this reason, if … then, due to, therefore*)
2. Read aloud this sentence from p. 23, stressing the signal word: *The Midford football team often wins because it has such good players.* Say: **The word *because* signals a cause.** Ask: **Why did the team win?** (because it has such good players) Challenge students to find another sentence on p. 23 that uses a signal phrase. *(As a result, the Midford Mules are hard to beat.)* Have students underline *because* and *as a result*. Then explain: **Some cause-and-effect signal words, like *therefore* or *as a result*, usually come at the beginning of a sentence. Others, like *so* and *because*, often are in the middle.**
3. Read aloud the directions for Activity A on p. 25. Explain that there may be more than one way to rewrite the sentences to show cause and effect. Model using the first item. Then have students complete the activity independently or in pairs.
4. Have students complete Activity B in pairs. Ask volunteers to share their sentences with the class.

➤ **Extend the Lesson:** Review the list of signal words and phrases on the board. Then have students rewrite their sentences from Activity B, using different signal words or phrases. Model by replacing *so* in the first item with *As a result.*

Page 24 / Student Book Page 13

Name: __________ Cause and Effect

Identifying Causes and Effects

A. Read each cause. Check the box next to the effect that makes the most sense. Then write another possible effect.

1. **Cause:** It rained this morning. That is why ____.
   - ☐ I left my umbrella at home
   - ☑ the streets are wet

   Another possible effect: the sidewalks have puddles
2. **Cause:** Jesse's bicycle has a flat tire. That is why ____.
   - ☑ he walked to school
   - ☐ he rode his bicycle to school

   Another possible effect: he took the bus
3. **Cause:** Maria could not find clean socks to wear. That is why ____.
   - ☑ she wore sandals
   - ☐ she wore her favorite hat

   Another possible effect: she wore dirty socks

B. Read each effect. Check the box next to the cause that makes the most sense. Then write another possible cause.

1. **Effect:** Whales often swim to the ocean surface. That is because ____.
   - ☑ the fish that they eat live mainly near the surface
   - ☐ they can swim about 30 miles an hour

   Another possible cause: they come to the surface to breathe
2. **Effect:** Mom was late for work this morning. That is because ____.
   - ☐ she packed my lunch as usual
   - ☑ the neighbor's car was blocking our driveway

   Another possible cause: she forgot to set her alarm clock

24 BASICS OF NONFICTION WRITING Nonfiction Writing • EMC 6013 • © Evan-Moor Corp.

Page 25 / Student Book Page 14

Name: __________ Cause and Effect

Using Cause-and-Effect Signal Words

A. Rewrite each pair of sentences, using the signal word in bold.

1. The elm tree grew tall. The garden is now shaded all day. (**so**)
   The elm tree grew tall, so the garden is now shaded all day.
2. Cats do not like water. It is hard to give cats a bath. (**because**)
   Because cats do not like water, it is hard to give them a bath.
3. Eli had a toothache. Eli went to the dentist. (**therefore**)
   Eli had a toothache. Therefore, he went to the dentist.

B. Circle each signal word or phrase. Then complete the sentence to show cause and effect.

1. Our basketball team practiced a lot, (so) we won many games.
2. We played in a muddy yard. (Therefore) we got dirty.
3. The neighbors' dog got loose. That is (because) the neighbors left the gate open.
4. This morning I made my bed and cleaned my room. (As a result) Mom was in a good mood.
5. (Because) Irina lost her jacket, she can't go outside during recess.

© Evan-Moor Corp. • EMC 6013 • Nonfiction Writing BASICS OF NONFICTION WRITING 25

Page 26 / Student Book Page 15

Name: ______________________ Cause and Effect

Adding Details

Complete each sentence. Then add two details that tell more about the cause and its effect.

Example
I am good at math, because I like to play number games.
Details: I play Sudoku every day. Also, when I visit my grandma, I play math games on her computer.

1. I am good at swimming, because I practice a lot.
Details: My dad taught me to swim when I was 5 years old.
I go to swim camp every summer.

2. I do not like thunderstorms, because they are scary.
Details: Loud claps of thunder surprise me.
Bright flashes of lightning make me nervous.

3. My favorite season is spring, because that's when flowers bloom.
Details: Bluebonnets bloom on the sides of the roads.
Tulips of all colors bloom in the park.

4. If I lived in France, then I probably would speak French.
Details: Most people in France speak French.
I can say a few things in French.

26 BASICS OF NONFICTION WRITING — Nonfiction Writing • EMC 6013 • © Evan-Moor Corp.

Page 27 and Sample Revision / Student Book Page 16

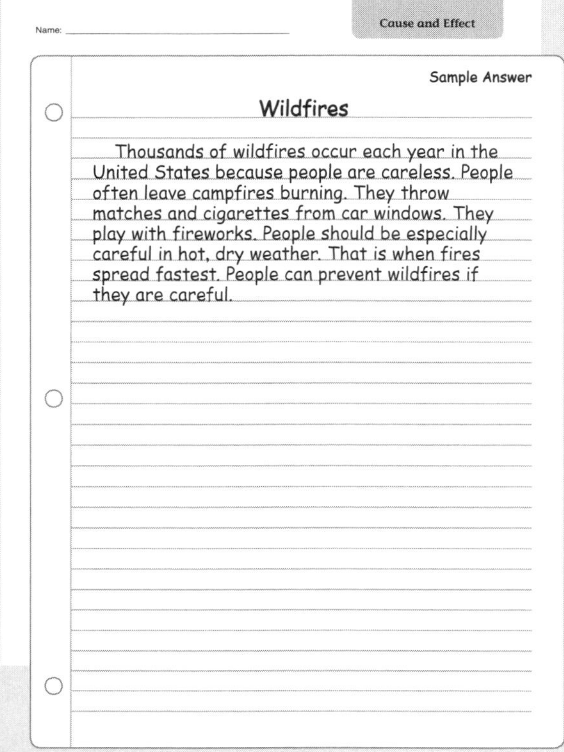

Name: ______________________ Cause and Effect

Sample Answer

Wildfires

Thousands of wildfires occur each year in the United States because people are careless. People often leave campfires burning. They throw matches and cigarettes from car windows. They play with fireworks. People should be especially careful in hot, dry weather. That is when fires spread fastest. People can prevent wildfires if they are careful.

Lesson 4 Adding Details

1. Remind students that a good cause-and-effect paragraph has a topic sentence that names a cause and its effect. Say: **Other sentences in the paragraph give details about the topic and relate to either the cause or the effect.**

2. Revisit the model on p. 23 and ask: **Which sentences give details about Midford's successful football team?** *(The quarterback can really throw! The team also has a great runner … And the whole team works well together.)* Point out that the concluding sentence sums up the ideas in the paragraph.

3. Read aloud the directions for the activity on p. 26. Explain that the first sentence in the example identifies a cause and its effect and that the next two sentences give details that tell more about the cause-and-effect relationship. Ask: **How could playing math games make you better at math?** (It gives you practice with math skills.) Complete the first item as a class. Then preview items 2, 3, and 4 and give examples as needed. Have students complete the activity in pairs or small groups. Invite volunteers to share their sentences.

➤ **Extend the Lesson:** Point out sentences on p. 25 that express a cause-and-effect relationship. Have students write two details for one of those sentences.

Lesson 5 Reviewing Cause and Effect

1. Review the qualities of a paragraph that shows cause and effect: a topic sentence that tells something that happened and explains why, details that tell more, and words that signal cause and effect.

2. Read aloud "Wildfires" on p. 27 as students follow along. Invite students to share ideas about how people can cause wildfires. Then guide students through revising the draft. Ask: **What is the main idea of this paragraph?** (that people can cause wildfires) **What causes many wildfires?** (being careless) **Is there one sentence that tells the cause and its effect?** (no) Read this sentence aloud: *They often leave campfires burning.* Ask: **What is another careless activity that often causes wildfires?** (e.g., tossing lighted matches or cigarettes, using fireworks) List related details on the board and suggest that students add one or two of them when they revise their paragraphs.

3. Have students write their revisions on a separate sheet of paper. Invite volunteers to share their paragraphs.

Name: ______________________________

Introducing Cause and Effect

Read this example of a paragraph that shows cause and effect.

Writing Model

The Marvelous Midford Mules

The Midford football team often wins because it has such good players. The quarterback can really throw! The team also has a great runner who can carry the ball downfield. And the whole team works well together. As a result, the Midford Mules are hard to beat.

Writer's Purpose: ______________________________

____

Name: ______________________________

Identifying Causes and Effects

A. Read each cause. Check the box next to the effect that makes the most sense. Then write another possible effect.

1. **Cause:** It rained this morning. That is why ________.

   ☐ I left my umbrella at home

   ☐ the streets are wet

   Another possible effect: ______________________________

2. **Cause:** Jesse's bicycle has a flat tire. That is why ________.

   ☐ he walked to school

   ☐ he rode his bicycle to school

   Another possible effect: ______________________________

3. **Cause:** Maria could not find clean socks to wear. That is why ________.

   ☐ she wore sandals

   ☐ she wore her favorite hat

   Another possible effect: ______________________________

B. Read each effect. Check the box next to the cause that makes the most sense. Then write another possible cause.

1. **Effect:** Whales often swim to the ocean surface. That is because ________.

   ☐ the fish that they eat live mainly near the surface

   ☐ they can swim about 30 miles an hour

   Another possible cause: ______________________________

2. **Effect:** Mom was late for work this morning. That is because ________.

   ☐ she packed my lunch as usual

   ☐ the neighbor's car was blocking our driveway

   Another possible cause: ______________________________

Name: ______________________________

Using Cause-and-Effect Signal Words

A. Rewrite each pair of sentences, using the signal word in bold.

1. The elm tree grew tall. The garden is now shaded all day. (**so**)

____

____

2. Cats do not like water. It is hard to give cats a bath. (**because**)

____

____

3. Eli had a toothache. Eli went to the dentist. (**therefore**)

____

____

B. Circle each signal word or phrase. Then complete the sentence to show cause and effect.

1. Our basketball team practiced a lot, so ______________________________.

2. We played in a muddy yard. Therefore, ______________________________.

3. The neighbors' dog got loose. That is because ______________________________

______________________________.

4. This morning I made my bed and cleaned my room. As a result, ______________

______________________________.

5. Because Irina lost her jacket, ______________________________

______________________________.

Name: ______________________________

Adding Details

Complete each sentence. Then add two details that tell more about the cause and its effect.

Example

I am good at math, because I like to play number games.

Details: I play Sudoku every day. Also, when I visit my grandma, I play math games on her computer.

1. I am good at ____________________, because ____________________.

   Details: ____

   ____

2. I do not like ____________________, because ____________________.

   Details: ____

   ____

3. My favorite season is ____________________, because ____________________.

   Details: ____

   ____

4. If I lived in ____________________, then ____________________.

   Details: ____

   ____

Name: ______________________________

Reviewing Cause and Effect

Revise this cause-and-effect paragraph. Use what you have learned to make it stronger. Rewrite the paragraph on a separate sheet of paper.

Focus on:

- ✓ writing a topic sentence that tells a cause and an effect
- ✓ using a word or phrase to signal a cause or an effect
- ✓ adding details that tell more

Draft

Wildfires

Thousands of wildfires occur each year in the United States. People are too careless! They often leave campfires burning. People should be especially careful in hot, dry weather. That is when fires spread fastest. People can prevent wildfires if they are careful.

Writing to Compare and Contrast

Page 31 / Student Book Page 18

Name: ____________________

Compare and Contrast

Introducing Writing to Compare and Contrast

Read this example of writing that compares and contrasts.

Writing Model

Two Favorite Snacks

Popcorn and potato chips have a lot in common. Both are crunchy, salty snack foods that people love. They are also foods that people pick up with their fingers. Another way that popcorn and potato chips are similar is that they are made from vegetables.

However, these two snacks are not the same in every way. Popcorn is made by heating kernels of corn until they pop. Most potato chips, on the other hand, are made by frying or baking thinly sliced potatoes. These snacks are different in another way. Lots of people eat popcorn at the movies. But people do not usually eat potato chips in a movie theater.

Writer's Purpose: to tell how popcorn and potato chips are alike and different

© Evan-Moor Corp. • EMC 6013 • Nonfiction Writing BASICS OF NONFICTION WRITING 31

Page 32 / Student Book Page 19

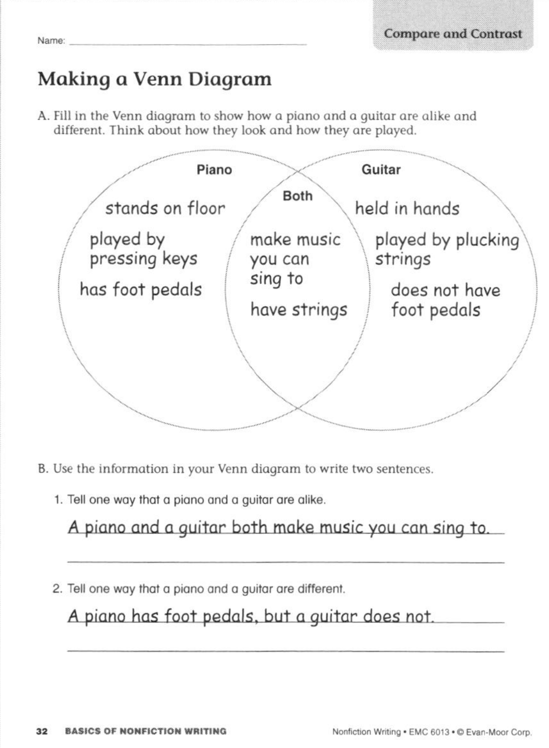
Name: ____________________

Compare and Contrast

Making a Venn Diagram

A. Fill in the Venn diagram to show how a piano and a guitar are alike and different. Think about how they look and how they are played.

B. Use the information in your Venn diagram to write two sentences.

1. Tell one way that a piano and a guitar are alike.
   A piano and a guitar both make music you can sing to.
2. Tell one way that a piano and a guitar are different.
   A piano has foot pedals, but a guitar does not.

32 BASICS OF NONFICTION WRITING Nonfiction Writing • EMC 6013 • © Evan-Moor Corp.

Lesson 1 Introducing Writing to Compare and Contrast

Writing that compares and contrasts shows how two or more things are alike or different.

1. Say: **If you wanted to tell how two things, such as a truck and a car, are alike and different, you would compare and contrast them.** Remind students that *compare* means to tell how things are alike, and *contrast* means to tell how they are different.
2. Read "Two Favorite Snacks" on p. 31 as students follow along. Have students identify the topic sentence of each paragraph. *(Popcorn and potato chips have a lot in common. However, these two snacks are not the same in every way.)* Point out that the sentences name what the composition compares and contrasts.
3. Ask: **What is the purpose of this composition?** (to tell how popcorn and potato chips are alike and different) Have students write the purpose on the lines provided.
4. Invite students to offer opinions about what makes this a good example of writing that compares and contrasts. Prompt students by asking: **Does the first sentence tell what the paragraphs will compare and contrast? Does the composition give specific examples of how potato chips and popcorn are alike and different?** Then explain that students will use the model as they practice the skills needed for writing to compare and contrast.

➤ **Extend the Lesson:** Have students name things that would be fun or interesting to compare in writing (e.g., a movie and a TV show).

Lesson 2 Making a Venn Diagram

1. Draw a Venn diagram on the board. Label the circles *Popcorn* and *Potato chips* and the overlapping area *Both*. Revisit p. 31 and ask: **How are popcorn and potato chips alike?** Record responses on the board. (Both: crunchy, salty snacks; picked up using your fingers; made from vegetables) Ask: **How are they different?** (Popcorn: made from corn kernels, heated until popped, eaten in movie theaters; Potato chips: made from sliced potatoes, are fried or baked, not usually eaten in theaters)
2. Say: **You can use a Venn diagram like this one to record your ideas when you compare and contrast two things.** Read the directions for Activity A on p. 32 and have students complete the activity in pairs. If possible, display pictures of a piano and a guitar.

3. After discussing the completed Venn diagrams, have students complete Activity B independently.

➤ **Extend the Lesson:** Have each student choose a topic from the Lesson 1 extension activity and create a Venn diagram for it.

Lesson 3 Using Signal Words

1. Read aloud this sentence from the writing model: *Both are crunchy, salty snack foods that people love.* Say: **The word *both* tells me that this sentence is making a comparison. It shows one way that popcorn and potato chips are alike.** Write the signal words *alike, similar, both,* and *also* on the board and discuss how they signal comparisons.
2. Read aloud this sentence from the model: *Most potato chips, on the other hand, are made by frying or baking thinly sliced potatoes.* Say: **The phrase *on the other hand* tells me that this sentence is contrasting the snacks.** Write *but, however, different,* and *on the other hand* on the board and explain: **You can use these signal words to contrast two or more things.** Have students circle all of the signal words in the model.
3. Read aloud the directions for Activity A on p. 33. Have students work in small groups to fill in the signal words.
4. Have students complete Activity B independently. Invite volunteers to share their sentences.

➤ **Extend the Lesson:** Have students answer the questions in Activity B, using different signal words.

Lesson 4 Writing Transition Sentences

1. Say: **Good writing flows smoothly and is easy to follow. Writers can use a sentence at the end of one paragraph or the beginning of the next paragraph to connect ideas. This is called a *transition sentence.* Transition sentences often use signal words such as *however* and *although*.**
2. Point out the main idea of each paragraph in the writing model on p. 31. Then read aloud this sentence: *However, these two snacks are not the same in every way.* Ask: **What are the two ideas that this sentence links together?** (the idea that popcorn and potato chips are similar, with the idea that they are different)
3. Read aloud the directions for Activity A on p. 34. Model using item 1. Then have students complete the second item independently. Review the answers.

Page 33 / Student Book Page 20

Name: ______________________ Compare and Contrast

Using Signal Words

A. Complete the paragraphs by writing the correct signal words from the box.

also	but	different	however	similar

You may think that a vulture and a Tyrannosaurus rex, or T. rex, have little in common. A vulture is a bird, __but__ a T. rex was a dinosaur. Many vultures live in North and South America. The T. rex, __however__, is extinct. The T. rex was huge. Vultures are much smaller. So size is another way these animals are __different__.

These two animals are __similar__ in some ways, though. Scientists think that the T. rex was mostly a scavenger, an animal that finds and eats dead animals. Like the T. rex, vultures __also__ are scavengers.

B. Answer each question by writing a sentence that uses the signal word in bold.

1. What is the same about crayons and watercolor paints? (**both**)
   Crayons and watercolor paints are both used for coloring.
2. How are crayons and watercolor paints different? (**however**)
   You use a brush with watercolor paints. However, you do not use a brush to color with crayons.
3. What is the same about gloves and mittens? (**both**)
   Both gloves and mittens keep hands warm.
4. How are gloves and mittens different? (**but**)
   Gloves have separate fingers, but mittens do not.

© Evan-Moor Corp. • EMC 6013 • Nonfiction Writing BASICS OF NONFICTION WRITING 33

Page 34 / Student Book Page 21

Name: ______________________ Compare and Contrast

Writing Transition Sentences

A. Read each pair of paragraphs. Choose the transition sentence that best connects the two paragraphs.

1. Bats and flying squirrels have many things in common. Because both are mammals, they have fur. Both eat insects by swooping down on them.
   __________ Bats have wings, so they can fly. Flying squirrels can only glide from tree to tree. They cannot move as far or as fast as bats can.
   - ☐ Both look strange.
   - ☑ Bats and flying squirrels move in different ways, though.
2. Chinese checkers is not the same game as checkers. It uses a star-shaped game board. Checkers uses a square game board.
   __________ Players move the pieces across the game board. Each player can jump the other player's pieces.
   - ☑ In both games, though, the players move game pieces.
   - ☐ Neither dominoes nor marbles needs a game board.

B. Complete each transition sentence to connect the paragraphs.

1. Valleys and canyons are both landforms. They are formed by flowing water. Over time, rivers or glaciers carve out rock and soil.
   Although valleys and canyons are similar, they are not the same. Canyons are deeper than valleys. The walls of a canyon are high and steep.
2. Our solar system has eight planets. All planets orbit the sun. Some take longer than others to make one complete orbit.
   In a similar way, the moon orbits Earth. The moon's orbit is about 28 days. That means it takes about 28 days for the moon to go completely around Earth.

34 BASICS OF NONFICTION WRITING Nonfiction Writing • EMC 6013 • © Evan-Moor Corp.

Page 35 / Student Book Page 22

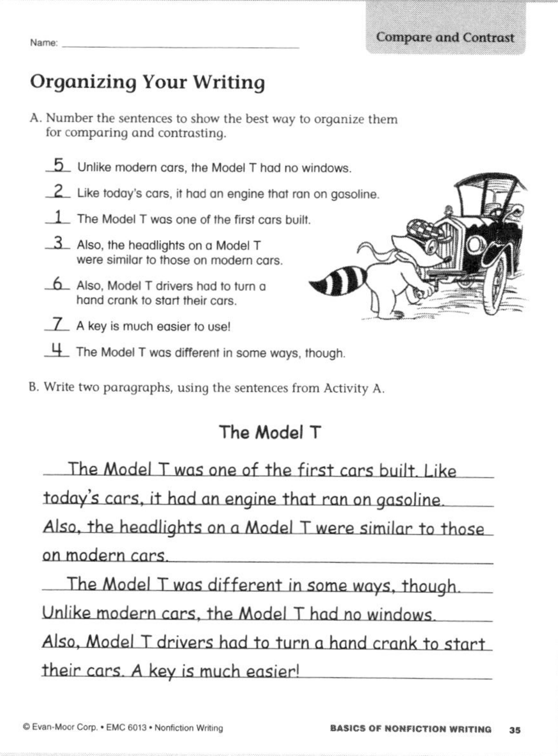
Name: ______________________

Compare and Contrast

Organizing Your Writing

A. Number the sentences to show the best way to organize them for comparing and contrasting.

5 Unlike modern cars, the Model T had no windows.
2 Like today's cars, it had an engine that ran on gasoline.
1 The Model T was one of the first cars built.
3 Also, the headlights on a Model T were similar to those on modern cars.
6 Also, Model T drivers had to turn a hand crank to start their cars.
7 A key is much easier to use!
4 The Model T was different in some ways, though.

B. Write two paragraphs, using the sentences from Activity A.

The Model T

The Model T was one of the first cars built. Like today's cars, it had an engine that ran on gasoline. Also, the headlights on a Model T were similar to those on modern cars.

The Model T was different in some ways, though. Unlike modern cars, the Model T had no windows. Also, Model T drivers had to turn a hand crank to start their cars. A key is much easier!

© Evan-Moor Corp. • EMC 6013 • Nonfiction Writing BASICS OF NONFICTION WRITING 35

Page 36 Sample Revision / Student Book Page 23

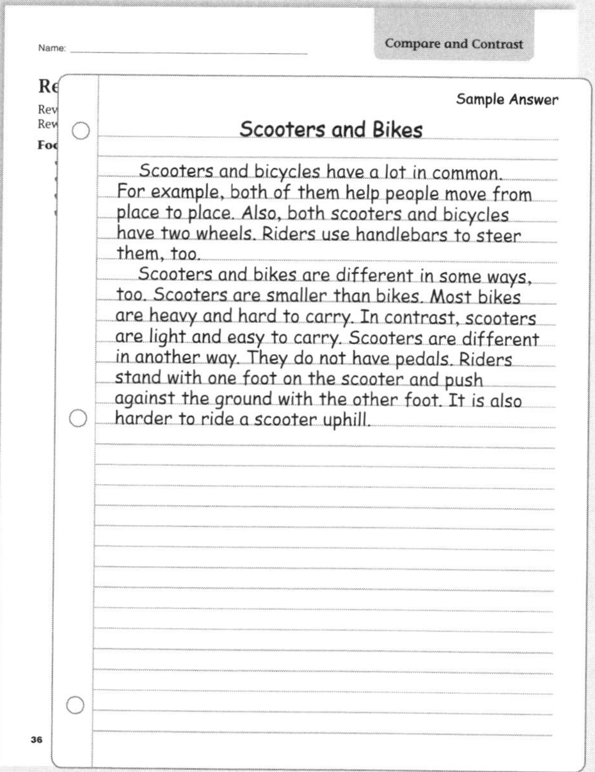
Name: ______________________

Compare and Contrast

Sample Answer

Scooters and Bikes

Scooters and bicycles have a lot in common. For example, both of them help people move from place to place. Also, both scooters and bicycles have two wheels. Riders use handlebars to steer them, too.

Scooters and bikes are different in some ways, too. Scooters are smaller than bikes. Most bikes are heavy and hard to carry. In contrast, scooters are light and easy to carry. Scooters are different in another way. They do not have pedals. Riders stand with one foot on the scooter and push against the ground with the other foot. It is also harder to ride a scooter uphill.

36

4. Have students complete Activity B in pairs. Invite volunteers to share their sentences.

➤ **Extend the Lesson:** Have students look for transition sentences in their science and social studies texts.

Lesson 5 Organizing Your Writing

1. Say: **One way to organize writing that compares and contrasts two or more things is to tell about the similarities in one paragraph and then tell about the differences in another.** Remind students that a good paragraph has a topic sentence, sentences that give details, and usually a concluding sentence.
2. Refer to the model on p. 31 and ask: **What are the sentences in the first paragraph about?** (the similarities of popcorn and potato chips) **What are the sentences in the second paragraph about?** (the differences) Point out that the topic sentence in each paragraph tells what the paragraph is about.
3. Read aloud the directions for Activity A on p. 35. Explain that the sentences are about an old car called a Model T. Guide students by asking: **Which sentence would make the best beginning? Which one tells what a Model T is?** Have students complete the activity in small groups.
4. Then have students complete Activity B independently. Ask a volunteer to read aloud the paragraphs.

➤ **Extend the Lesson:** Have students write and organize sentences based on the Venn diagrams they created in the Lesson 2 extension activity.

Lesson 6 Reviewing Writing to Compare and Contrast

1. Review the qualities of writing that compares and contrasts: a topic sentence that tells what is being compared and contrasted, signal words, transition sentences, and organization that makes sense.
2. Read aloud "Scooters and Bikes" on p. 36 as students follow along. Then guide students through the revision. Ask: **What is the main idea of the composition?** (that scooters and bikes are alike but different) **Do all of the sentences in the first paragraph go with the topic sentence?** (no) Use a Venn diagram to organize the details. Then help students organize the sentences. Prompt them to add signal words and transitions.
3. Have students write their revisions on a separate sheet of paper. Invite volunteers to share their writing.

Name: ______________________________

Introducing Writing to Compare and Contrast

Read this example of writing that compares and contrasts.

Writing Model

Two Favorite Snacks

Popcorn and potato chips have a lot in common. Both are crunchy, salty snack foods that people love. They are also foods that people pick up with their fingers. Another way that popcorn and potato chips are similar is that they are made from vegetables.

However, these two snacks are not the same in every way. Popcorn is made by heating kernels of corn until they pop. Most potato chips, on the other hand, are made by frying or baking thinly sliced potatoes. These snacks are different in another way. Lots of people eat popcorn at the movies. But people do not usually eat potato chips in a movie theater.

Writer's Purpose: ______________________________

____

Name: ____________________

Making a Venn Diagram

A. Fill in the Venn diagram to show how a piano and a guitar are alike and different. Think about how they look and how they are played.

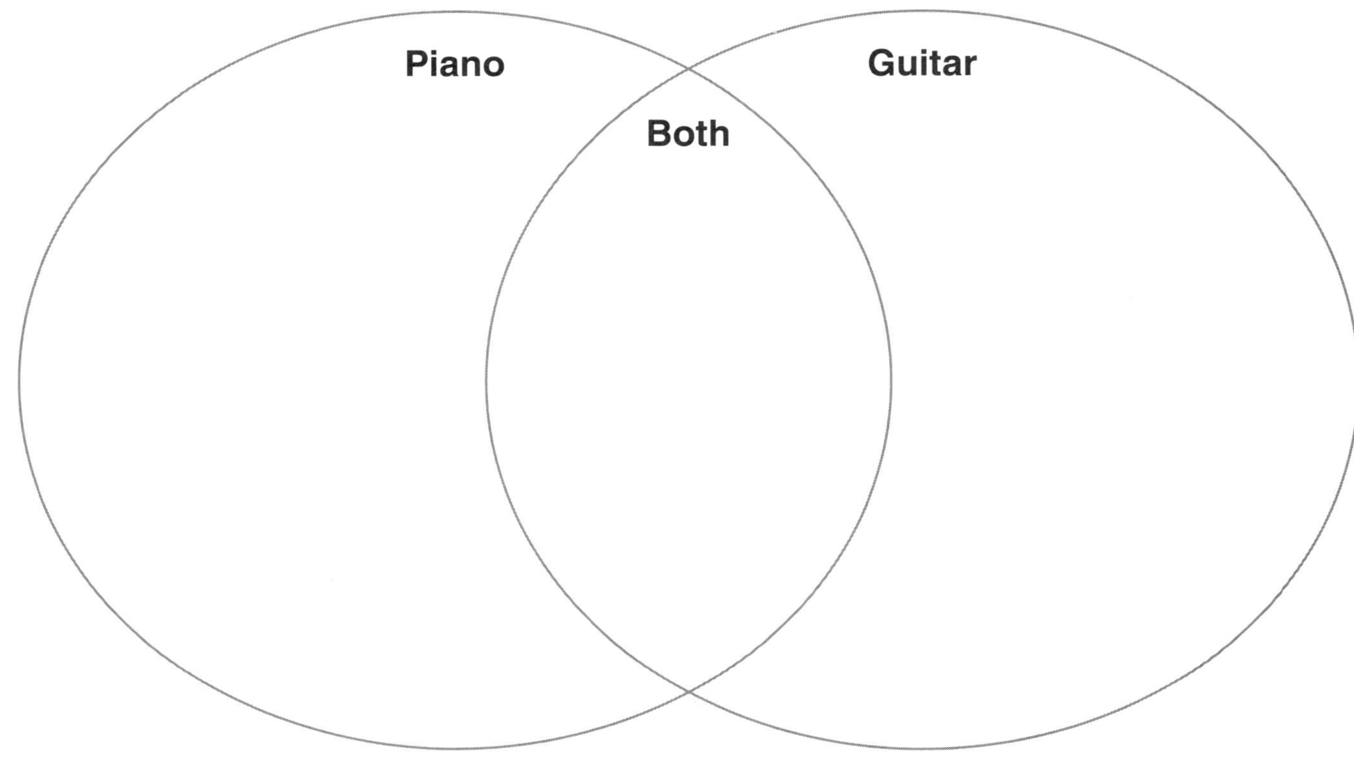

B. Use the information in your Venn diagram to write two sentences.

1. Tell one way that a piano and a guitar are alike.

____

____

2. Tell one way that a piano and a guitar are different.

____

____

Name: ______________________________

Using Signal Words

A. Complete the paragraphs by writing the correct signal words from the box.

also	but	different	however	similar

You may think that a vulture and a Tyrannosaurus rex, or T. rex, have little in common. A vulture is a bird, ____________ a T. rex was a dinosaur. Many vultures live in North and South America. The T. rex, ____________, is extinct. The T. rex was huge. Vultures are much smaller. So size is another way these animals are ____________.

These two animals are ____________ in some ways, though. Scientists think that the T. rex was mostly a scavenger, an animal that finds and eats dead animals. Like the T. rex, vultures ____________ are scavengers.

B. Answer each question by writing a sentence that uses the signal word in bold.

1. What is the same about crayons and watercolor paints? (**both**)

   ____

2. How are crayons and watercolor paints different? (**however**)

   ____

   ____

3. What is the same about gloves and mittens? (**both**)

   ____

4. How are gloves and mittens different? (**but**)

   ____

Name: ______________________________

Writing Transition Sentences

A. Read each pair of paragraphs. Choose the transition sentence that best connects the two paragraphs.

1. Bats and flying squirrels have many things in common. Because both are mammals, they have fur. Both eat insects by swooping down on them.

   __________ Bats have wings, so they can fly. Flying squirrels can only glide from tree to tree. They cannot move as far or as fast as bats can.

   ☐ Both look strange.

   ☐ Bats and flying squirrels move in different ways, though.

2. Chinese checkers is not the same game as checkers. It uses a star-shaped game board. Checkers uses a square game board.

   __________ Players move the pieces across the game board. Each player can jump the other player's pieces.

   ☐ In both games, though, the players move game pieces.

   ☐ Neither dominoes nor marbles needs a game board.

B. Complete each transition sentence to connect the paragraphs.

1. Valleys and canyons are both landforms. They are formed by flowing water. Over time, rivers or glaciers carve out rock and soil.

   Although ____.

   Canyons are deeper than valleys. The walls of a canyon are high and steep.

2. Our solar system has eight planets. All planets orbit the sun. Some take longer than others to make one complete orbit.

   In a similar way, ______________________________. The moon's orbit is about 28 days. That means it takes about 28 days for the moon to go completely around Earth.

Name: ______________________________

Organizing Your Writing

A. Number the sentences to show the best way to organize them for comparing and contrasting.

____ Unlike modern cars, the Model T had no windows.

____ Like today's cars, it had an engine that ran on gasoline.

____ The Model T was one of the first cars built.

____ Also, the headlights on a Model T were similar to those on modern cars.

____ Also, Model T drivers had to turn a hand crank to start their cars.

____ A key is much easier to use!

____ The Model T was different in some ways, though.

B. Write two paragraphs, using the sentences from Activity A.

The Model T

____

____

____

____

____

____

____

____

Name: ______________________________

Reviewing Writing to Compare and Contrast

Revise these paragraphs. Use what you have learned to make them stronger. Rewrite the paragraphs on a separate sheet of paper.

Focus on:

- ✓ writing topic sentences that tell what is compared and contrasted
- ✓ using words to signal similarities and differences
- ✓ connecting the ideas with transition sentences
- ✓ putting the sentences in order so they make sense

Draft

Scooters and Bikes

Scooters and bicycles have a lot in common. For example, both help people move from place to place. Scooters are smaller than bikes. Most bikes are heavy and hard to carry. Scooters are light and easy to carry.

Both scooters and bicycles have two wheels. Riders use handlebars to steer them, too. Scooters do not have pedals. Riders stand with one foot on the scooter and push against the ground with the other foot. It is harder to ride a scooter uphill.

Writing a Summary

Lesson 1 Introducing a Summary

A summary gives the main idea and the most important details about a longer piece of writing, such as a story, article, or book.

1. Ask students to think of their favorite sport. Say: **If you had less than a minute to tell about it, you probably would tell the most important thing about the sport or why you like it. You may include a few interesting details so listeners understand the sport.** Explain that a written summary does the same thing: It tells the most important information, such as the main idea and supporting details, of a longer piece of writing.
2. Direct students to the article on p. 40, "Legends of the First President." If necessary, define *legend*. Have volunteers read aloud the article, paragraph by paragraph. Then invite a volunteer to read aloud the summary on p. 41.
3. Ask: **What is the purpose of this summary?** (to tell the most important information from an article about George Washington) Have students write the purpose on the lines provided.
4. Invite students to offer opinions about what makes this a good summary. Prompt them by asking: **Is the summary shorter than the article? Is there one sentence that tells the article's title and main idea? Did the writer tell the ideas in his own words?**
5. Explain that students will use "Legends of the First President" and the model as they practice the skills needed to write a good summary.

➤ **Extend the Lesson:** Provide short summaries of children's books from online bookstores. Have students name books that interest them, based on the summaries.

Lesson 2 Marking Up an Article

1. Say: **Before you begin writing a summary, it's a good idea to mark up the text you are going to summarize. This helps you focus on the most important things to include in your summary.**
2. Help students mark up "Legends of the First President." Have them draw a box around the title and a wavy line under the sentence that tells what the article is mostly about. *(It may surprise you ...)* Explain: **The next three paragraphs give examples of stories about Washington that are not true.** Prompt students to find and underline the topic sentence in each of the three paragraphs. *(Most people think ... One legend about young George ... Another popular story ...)*

Page 40 / Student Book Pages 25

Name: ______________________

Summary

Introducing a Summary

Read this article about George Washington.

Reading Selection

Legends of the First President

What do you know about George Washington, the first president of the United States? If you are like most people, you know a few popular stories about him. It may surprise you to learn that some tales about Washington are not true.

Most people think that Washington had wooden teeth. In fact, he did lose his teeth as a young man, so he wore false teeth. But the teeth were not made of wood. Washington's false teeth were made from ivory, gold, and even human teeth.

One legend about young George Washington is that he chopped down a cherry tree when he was not supposed to. When his father asked him if he had done such a thing, he told the truth. Most likely, this is just a good story that teaches children not to tell lies.

Another popular story is that Washington threw a silver dollar across the Potomac River in Virginia. That would be amazing, because the Potomac is a mile wide. Parts of the story are true, though. Washington once threw a rock across a river, but the river was much narrower than the Potomac.

George Washington really was a great leader. And he is famous for many things, including bravely leading the country. But some of the things that he is famous for did not really happen.

40 EXPOSITORY WRITING Nonfiction Writing • EMC 6013 • © Evan-Moor Corp.

Page 41 / Student Book Page 26

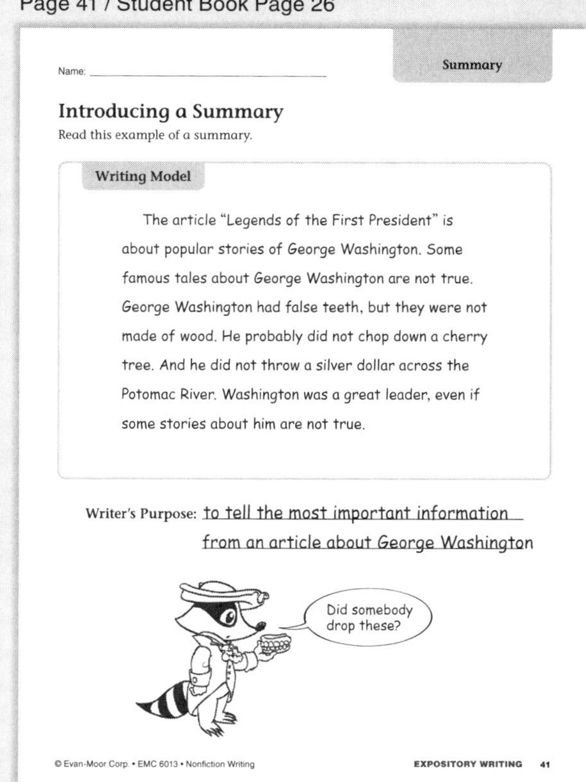

Name: ______________________

Summary

Introducing a Summary

Read this example of a summary.

Writing Model

The article "Legends of the First President" is about popular stories of George Washington. Some famous tales about George Washington are not true. George Washington had false teeth, but they were not made of wood. He probably did not chop down a cherry tree. And he did not throw a silver dollar across the Potomac River. Washington was a great leader, even if some stories about him are not true.

Writer's Purpose: to tell the most important information from an article about George Washington

© Evan-Moor Corp. • EMC 6013 • Nonfiction Writing EXPOSITORY WRITING 41

Page 42 / Student Book Page 27

Name: ____________________ Summary

Marking Up an Article

Read this article about cave art. Do the following:

- Draw a box around the title.
- Draw a wavy line under the sentence that tells the main idea of the article.
- Draw a straight line under the topic sentence of each paragraph.

Maria's Discovery

In 1879, an eight-year-old girl named Maria made an important discovery. She wandered into a cave near her home in northern Spain. Maria found paintings of animals on the walls and ceiling of the cave. She shouted for her father, who was nearby. She wanted him to see the cave art.

Maria's father knew right away that the paintings were special. The artists who made them had lived thousands of years ago. That was long before people could write. In a way, cave art is like writing.

Cave art can tell us how people lived long ago. These paintings show herds of large wild animals with horns. They also show deer and wild pigs. These were the kinds of animals that people hunted long ago. The animals were important to the cave artists.

42 EXPOSITORY WRITING Nonfiction Writing • EMC 6013 • © Evan-Moor Corp.

Page 43 / Student Book Page 28

Name: ____________________ Summary

Retelling in Your Own Words

A. Read each paragraph. Check the box next to the sentence that retells the paragraph best.

1. Someone who is afraid of high places has acrophobia. The word part *acro* means "top." The word part *phobia* means "fear."
   - ☑ Acrophobia is the fear of heights.
   - ☐ The word *acrophobia* comes from two Greek words.
2. The Great Lakes include five main lakes and many smaller ones. Together, they form the largest cluster of freshwater lakes in the world.
   - ☑ The Great Lakes make up the world's largest group of freshwater lakes.
   - ☐ Some of the Great Lakes are larger than others.
3. Diwali is a national holiday throughout the country of India. During the five days of Diwali, people light lamps or candles.
   - ☑ People light candles to celebrate Diwali, a five-day holiday in India.
   - ☐ Diwali is a holiday that takes place in India in autumn.

B. Read each paragraph. Then retell the paragraph's ideas in your own words.

1. Mix, color, and shine. Those are a few of the steps it takes to make candy corn, a colorful candy that looks like kernels of corn. Huge machines do all the work to make this autumn treat.

   Candy corn is made using big machines. There are many steps in making it.
2. Granny Smith and Red Delicious are two types of apples. A ripe Granny Smith apple is green even when it is ripe. It is crunchy and tart. A Red Delicious apple is soft, sweet, and red.

   Granny Smith apples are green, crunchy, and tart. Red Delicious apples are soft and sweet.

© Evan-Moor Corp. • EMC 6013 • Nonfiction Writing EXPOSITORY WRITING 43

3. Read aloud the article on p. 42. Ask: **Which sentence tells what the article is mostly about?** *(Maria found paintings of animals on the walls ...)* Have students complete the activity in pairs. Invite them to share the sentences they underlined and to explain their choices.
4. Ask: **How could the underlined sentences help you write a summary of the article?** (They show the most important information to include.)

➤ **Extend the Lesson:** Have students mark up another piece of nonfiction writing such as an article from a children's magazine or a passage from a textbook.

Lesson 3 Retelling in Your Own Words

1. Review the purpose of a summary. Point out that a summary is shorter than the piece of writing it summarizes. Say: **One way to keep your summary short is to combine some details from two or more sentences into one or two sentences.**
2. Explain that when you summarize, you should use your own words to express ideas from the original text. Say: **When you use your own words, be careful not to change the meaning of what you are retelling.**
3. Read aloud this sentence from p. 40: *It may surprise you to learn that some tales about Washington are not true.* Then ask: **Which sentence in the summary on p. 41 retells that idea?** *(Some famous tales about George ...)*
4. Read aloud the directions for Activity A on p. 43. Model the activity, using item 1. Say: **The second choice is not the best retelling of the paragraph because it leaves out something important—the definition of *acrophobia*. The second choice gives information that isn't in the original paragraph—the fact that the word parts in *acrophobia* are from Greek words.** Have students complete items 2 and 3 in pairs. Discuss the answers.
5. Read the directions for Activity B. Explain: **Write one or two short sentences that tell what the paragraph is about. Include only the important details.** Have students complete the activity independently or in pairs. Remind them that there is more than one way to retell the ideas. Invite volunteers to share their revisions.

➤ **Extend the Lesson:** Have students play a game of "pass the message." Each player writes a short message and passes it to another player, who retells the message in his or her own words.

Lesson 4 Organizing a Summary

1. Explain that a summary has three parts: The first part is the topic sentence, which names the longer piece of writing that is being summarized; the second part gives important details about the topic based on the original text; and the third part is a concluding sentence, which brings the summary to a close.
2. Display the writing model on p. 41 and draw attention to the topic sentence and the four detail sentences that follow. Point out that the detail sentences follow the order of information in the article. Then read aloud the concluding sentence from the model. Explain that this sentence brings the summary to a close.
3. Read aloud the directions for Activity A on p. 44. Have volunteers take turns reading aloud the sentences. Prompt students to find the topic sentence for the summary. Then have students complete the activity in small groups. Review the answers and have students explain how they determined the order of the sentences. Note that some answers may vary.
4. Have students complete Activity B independently.

➤ **Extend the Lesson:** Have students identify the three parts of a summary, using the samples from the Lesson 1 extension activity.

Lesson 5 Reviewing a Summary

1. Review the qualities of a good summary: a topic sentence that names the writing being summarized, detail sentences that retell important information, and an ending. Remind students that a summary only retells ideas and does not include new details.
2. Have students work independently to read and mark up "A Sport for Everyone" on p. 45, using the mark-up they did on p. 42 as a model.
3. Read aloud the summary on p. 46. Then guide students through revising the draft. Ask: **Does the first sentence tell what the article is about?** (yes) **Does it give the title of the article?** (no) **Does the summary leave out any important information?** (yes, that table tennis is good for you) **Are the details in order?** (no) Help students sequence the details. Ask: **Is there a concluding sentence?** (no)
4. Have students write their revisions on a separate sheet of paper. Invite volunteers to read aloud their revised summaries.

Page 44 / Student Book Page 29

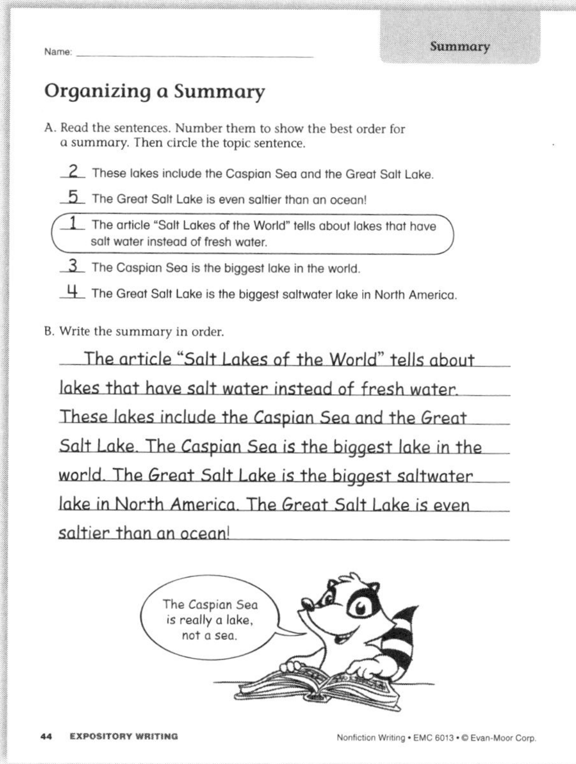

Name: ______ Summary

Organizing a Summary

A. Read the sentences. Number them to show the best order for a summary. Then circle the topic sentence.

2 These lakes include the Caspian Sea and the Great Salt Lake.
5 The Great Salt Lake is even saltier than an ocean!
1 The article "Salt Lakes of the World" tells about lakes that have salt water instead of fresh water.
3 The Caspian Sea is the biggest lake in the world.
4 The Great Salt Lake is the biggest saltwater lake in North America.

B. Write the summary in order.

The article "Salt Lakes of the World" tells about lakes that have salt water instead of fresh water. These lakes include the Caspian Sea and the Great Salt Lake. The Caspian Sea is the biggest lake in the world. The Great Salt Lake is the biggest saltwater lake in North America. The Great Salt Lake is even saltier than an ocean!

44 EXPOSITORY WRITING Nonfiction Writing • EMC 6013 • © Evan-Moor Corp.

Pp. 45–46 and Sample Revision / Student Book pp. 30–31

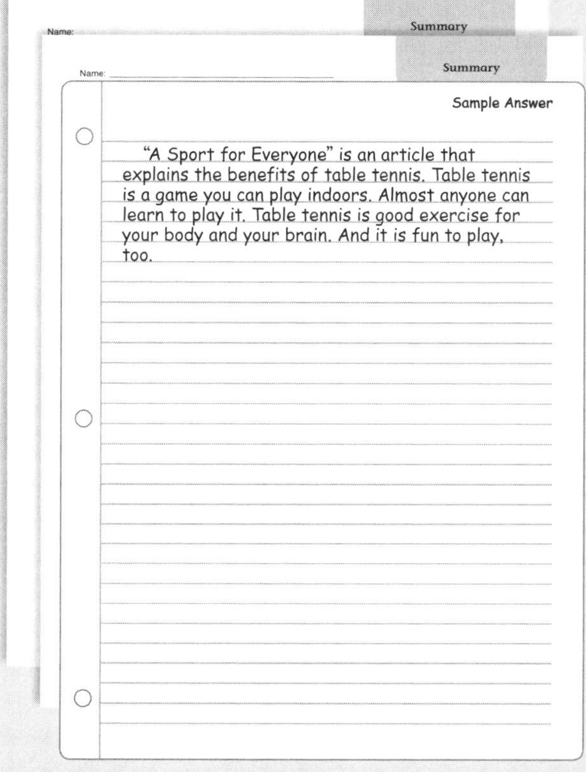

Name: Summary

Name: ______ Summary

Sample Answer

"A Sport for Everyone" is an article that explains the benefits of table tennis. Table tennis is a game you can play indoors. Almost anyone can learn to play it. Table tennis is good exercise for your body and your brain. And it is fun to play, too.

Name: ______________________________

Introducing a Summary

Read this article about George Washington.

Reading Selection

Legends of the First President

What do you know about George Washington, the first president of the United States? If you are like most people, you know a few popular stories about him. It may surprise you to learn that some tales about Washington are not true.

Most people think that Washington had wooden teeth. In fact, he did lose his teeth as a young man, so he wore false teeth. But the teeth were not made of wood. Washington's false teeth were made from ivory, gold, and even human teeth.

One legend about young George Washington is that he chopped down a cherry tree when he was not supposed to. When his father asked him if he had done such a thing, he told the truth. Most likely, this is just a good story that teaches children not to tell lies.

Another popular story is that Washington threw a silver dollar across the Potomac River in Virginia. That would be amazing, because the Potomac is a mile wide. Parts of the story are true, though. Washington once threw a rock across a river, but the river was much narrower than the Potomac.

George Washington really was a great leader. And he is famous for many things, including bravely leading the country. But some of the things that he is famous for did not really happen.

Name: ____________________________________

Introducing a Summary

Read this example of a summary.

Writing Model

The article "Legends of the First President" is about popular stories of George Washington. Some famous tales about George Washington are not true. George Washington had false teeth, but they were not made of wood. He probably did not chop down a cherry tree. And he did not throw a silver dollar across the Potomac River. Washington was a great leader, even if some stories about him are not true.

Writer's Purpose: ____________________________________

____

Name: ___________________________________

Summary

Marking Up an Article

Read this article about cave art. Do the following:

- ➤ Draw a box around the title.
- ➤ Draw a wavy line under the sentence that tells the main idea of the article.
- ➤ Draw a straight line under the topic sentence of each paragraph.

Maria's Discovery

In 1879, an eight-year-old girl named Maria made an important discovery. She wandered into a cave near her home in northern Spain. Maria found paintings of animals on the walls and ceiling of the cave. She shouted for her father, who was nearby. She wanted him to see the cave art.

Maria's father knew right away that the paintings were special. The artists who made them had lived thousands of years ago. That was long before people could write. In a way, cave art is like writing.

Cave art can tell us how people lived long ago. These paintings show herds of large wild animals with horns. They also show deer and wild pigs. These were the kinds of animals that people hunted long ago. The animals were important to the cave artists.

Name: ______________________________

Retelling in Your Own Words

A. Read each paragraph. Check the box next to the sentence that retells the paragraph best.

1. Someone who is afraid of high places has acrophobia. The word part *acro* means "top." The word part *phobia* means "fear."

   - ☐ Acrophobia is the fear of heights.
   - ☐ The word *acrophobia* comes from two Greek words.

2. The Great Lakes include five main lakes and many smaller ones. Together, they form the largest cluster of freshwater lakes in the world.

   - ☐ The Great Lakes make up the world's largest group of freshwater lakes.
   - ☐ Some of the Great Lakes are larger than others.

3. Diwali is a national holiday throughout the country of India. During the five days of Diwali, people light lamps or candles.

   - ☐ People light candles to celebrate Diwali, a five-day holiday in India.
   - ☐ Diwali is a holiday that takes place in India in autumn.

B. Read each paragraph. Then retell the paragraph's ideas in your own words.

1. Mix, color, and shine. Those are a few of the steps it takes to make candy corn, a colorful candy that looks like kernels of corn. Huge machines do all the work to make this autumn treat.

   ____

   ____

2. Granny Smith and Red Delicious are two types of apples. A ripe Granny Smith apple is green even when it is ripe. It is crunchy and tart. A Red Delicious apple is soft, sweet, and red.

   ____

   ____

Name: ______________________________

Organizing a Summary

A. Read the sentences. Number them to show the best order for a summary. Then circle the topic sentence.

____ These lakes include the Caspian Sea and the Great Salt Lake.

____ The Great Salt Lake is even saltier than an ocean!

____ The article "Salt Lakes of the World" tells about lakes that have salt water instead of fresh water.

____ The Caspian Sea is the biggest lake in the world.

____ The Great Salt Lake is the biggest saltwater lake in North America.

B. Write the summary in order.

____

____

____

____

____

____

____

Name: ____________________

Reviewing a Summary

Read this article about table tennis.

Reading Selection

A Sport for Everyone

Table tennis, or Ping-Pong, is probably not a sport that you watch on TV. Unlike football and soccer, it is not played in big stadiums. You probably cannot think of any famous table tennis players. But this sport has many benefits for people who play it.

Table tennis is a game you can play all year round. In fact, it was invented as an indoor version of tennis. You can play the game even when the weather is bad.

Table tennis is also a game that almost anyone can play. Players young and old can compete in table tennis. If you can swing a table tennis paddle, you can play the game!

Like most sports, table tennis is good exercise. It gets you moving, and it brings your heart rate up. Studies show that table tennis gives your brain a good workout, too. Best of all, table tennis is a lot of fun. And you do not have to be an expert to enjoy this fast-paced game.

Name: ______________________________

Reviewing a Summary

Revise this summary of the article "A Sport for Everyone." Use what you have learned to make it stronger. Rewrite the summary on a separate sheet of paper.

Focus on:

✓ writing a topic sentence that names the article and tells what it is about
✓ retelling the article's ideas in your own words
✓ putting the details in order
✓ writing a concluding sentence

Draft

This article explains the benefits of playing table tennis. For one thing, it is fun to play. Almost anyone can play it. Table tennis is a game you can play all year round. The game began as an indoor version of tennis.

Writing a Descriptive Paragraph

Lesson 1 Introducing a Descriptive Paragraph

A descriptive paragraph describes a person, place, thing, or event, using vivid details so readers can easily imagine it.

1. Ask students to think about how they might describe a natural event, such as a thunderstorm or a rainbow, to someone who has never experienced it. Explain that specific details help readers experience what the writer is describing.
2. Read aloud "Nature's Light Show" on p. 50. Then ask: **What is the purpose of this descriptive paragraph?** (to describe the northern lights) Have students write the purpose on the lines provided.
3. Invite students to offer opinions about what makes this a good descriptive paragraph. Prompt students by asking: **Does the writer tell you at the beginning what the paragraph will describe? Can you imagine what it would be like to watch the northern lights?**
4. Explain that students will use the model as they practice the skills needed to write a good descriptive paragraph.

➤ **Extend the Lesson:** Have students choose topics for descriptive paragraphs. You may want to display photographs of faces, animals, and places as prompts.

Lesson 2 Writing a Topic Sentence

1. Say: **A descriptive paragraph should include a *topic sentence*—a sentence that tells what the paragraph is going to describe.** Read aloud this sentence from the model on p. 50: *The colorful northern lights often appear on chilly March nights in Alaska.* Ask: **Based on this sentence, what does the paragraph describe?** (the northern lights)
2. Read aloud the directions for Activity A on p. 51. Have students complete the activity in pairs.
3. Use the example to model Activity B. Say: **This paragraph is mostly about a summer storm. The words *thick clouds, warm air,* and *wind* tell me so. The underlined sentence only names the season, so it is not a good topic sentence.** Guide students through rewriting the topic sentences in items 1 and 2.

➤ **Extend the Lesson:** Prompt students to recall an interesting natural event they have experienced or heard about, such as an eclipse or a winter storm. Have them write a topic sentence that names the event.

Page 50 / Student Book Page 33

Name: ____________________

Descriptive Paragraph

Introducing a Descriptive Paragraph

Read this example of a descriptive paragraph.

Writing Model

Nature's Light Show

The colorful northern lights often appear on chilly March nights in Alaska. The northern lights are bands of light that fold and wave in the coal-black sky. At times, the lights shimmer in brilliant reds, yellows, and greens. At other times, they glow in shadowy blues and purples. The northern lights do not crackle or sizzle like lightning. They do not make any sound at all. But they are amazing to watch.

Writer's Purpose: to describe the northern lights

50 EXPOSITORY WRITING — Nonfiction Writing • EMC 6013 • © Evan-Moor Corp.

Page 51 / Student Book Page 34

Name: ____________________

Descriptive Paragraph

Writing a Topic Sentence

A. Each paragraph has a missing topic sentence. Read the paragraph. Then check the box next to the best topic sentence to begin the paragraph.

1. ________ Every snowflake forms a six-sided shape. The pattern on some turtle shells has six-sided shapes. Also, each cell in a bee's honeycomb has six sides.
   - ☑ Many objects in nature have six sides.
   - ☐ Each white part of a black and white soccer ball has six sides.
2. ________ The stars can be red, yellow, or blue. The sun is a yellow star. Blue stars are the hottest. Stars also come in different sizes, from dwarf to giant. But even dwarf stars are much bigger than Earth.
   - ☐ Earth travels around the sun.
   - ☑ Stars are grouped by size and color.
3. ________ Silver fog surrounds the trunks of the giant trees. The air is cool and still. The forest is quiet.
   - ☑ Redwood forests are peaceful.
   - ☐ Redwood trees should be protected.

B. Rewrite each underlined sentence so it tells what the paragraph is about.

Example: It is summer. Thick clouds cover the sky. They are gray and black. The warm air feels heavy and moist. Wind whips the trees back and forth.
A summer storm is coming.

1. Firefighters have a dangerous job. They wash their trucks. They check safety gear. But they stop what they are doing when the fire alarm rings.
   Firefighters do many things besides fight fires.
2. The Great Pyramid is old. Sand drifts and piles up against the base of the pyramid. The hot desert sun bakes the stone blocks. Dry winds whistle past.
   The Great Pyramid is in the desert.

© Evan-Moor Corp. • EMC 6013 • Nonfiction Writing — EXPOSITORY WRITING 51

Page 52 / Student Book Page 35

Name: ______________________ Descriptive Paragraph

Adding Sensory Details

A. Fill in the chart with sensory details that describe a bus ride on a rainy morning.

I see...	I hear...	I smell...	I taste...	I feel...
a street with cars and trucks raindrops rolling down the window	windshield wipers swishing the roar of the bus engine	rubber floor mats gasoline	crumbs of cinnamon toast from my breakfast	water droplets on my face cold water soaking through my wet shoes

B. Follow the directions. Include sensory details in each sentence you write.

1. Describe what you can see from a window at home.
   I see huge trees in my neighbor's shady backyard.
2. Describe what you can hear on a summer day.
   I hear kids laughing and screaming on the playground.
3. Describe what you can smell at a picnic.
   I smell juicy hamburgers cooking on the grill.
4. Describe what you can taste on a Saturday morning.
   I taste pancakes with sweet maple syrup.
5. Describe what you can feel if you wade into a stream.
   I feel thick mud between my toes.

52 EXPOSITORY WRITING Nonfiction Writing • EMC 6013 • © Evan-Moor Corp.

Page 53 / Student Book Page 36

Name: ______________________ Descriptive Paragraph

Showing, Not Telling

A. Read each pair of sentences. Circle the one that **shows** instead of **tells**.

1. The cat wanted to eat the mouse.
   (The cat stared at the mouse and licked its lips.)
2. (His heart pounded as he clawed his way up the rocks.)
   The man felt scared as he climbed up the rocks.
3. (Sheets flapped wildly on the clothesline.)
   It was really windy that day.
4. The basketball player scored a point.
   (The ball swished through the net.)

B. Rewrite each sentence so it shows the action instead of telling about it.

1. The bike was going too fast.
   The bike was flying down the hill too fast to stop.
2. Juice spilled onto the floor.
   Juice dripped over the edge of the table, onto the floor.
3. The diver went into the water.
   The diver disappeared into the water with a splash.
4. The rocket took off.
   The ground shook as the rocket shot toward the sky.

© Evan-Moor Corp. • EMC 6013 • Nonfiction Writing EXPOSITORY WRITING 53

Lesson 3 Adding Sensory Details

1. Explain that writers often use sensory details, or details that appeal to the five senses, in descriptive paragraphs. Say: **Sensory details help readers imagine that they can see, hear, smell, taste, or touch what the writer is describing.**
2. Revisit the model on p. 50 and ask: **If you were outdoors viewing the northern lights, what do you think the air would feel like?** (chilly) **What would you hear?** (silence) Then guide students to find details in the paragraph that tell what the northern lights look like. *(bands of light that fold and wave; brilliant reds, yellows, and greens; shadowy blues and purples)*
3. Read aloud the directions for Activity A on p. 52. Have students work in small groups to fill in the chart.
4. Model composing the first sentence for Activity B. Then have students complete the activity independently. Remind students to write complete sentences. Invite volunteers to share their responses.

➤ **Extend the Lesson:** Have students draft descriptive sentences about a bus ride, using the sensory details in the chart they completed for Activity A on p. 52.

Lesson 4 Showing, Not Telling

1. Say: **Writing is stronger when it *shows* the action instead of telling about it.** Write this sentence on the board: *The northern lights move.* Then read aloud this sentence from p. 50: *The northern lights are bands of light that fold and wave in the coal-black sky.* Ask: **Which sentence shows the action better?** (the one on p. 50)
2. Read the directions for Activity A on p. 53. Then read the first pair of sentences and ask: **Which sentence shows what the cat did?** (the second one) **Why did the cat lick its lips?** (because it wanted to eat the mouse) Have students complete the activity independently. Then review the answers together.
3. Read the directions for Activity B. Then read the first sentence and prompt students to tell what the action would look like or feel like. Guide them in rewriting the sentence two or three different ways. Then have students complete the activity independently. Invite volunteers to share and explain their sentences.

➤ **Extend the Lesson:** Have students write "showing" sentences to describe ordinary scenes on the playground or elsewhere at school.

Lesson 5 Expanding Sentences

1. Say: **Longer sentences can give more details for readers to imagine.** Write this sentence on the board: *The northern lights appear at night in Alaska.* Say: **From this sentence, it's hard to tell what the northern lights look like.** Ask: **How can we expand this sentence to better describe the lights?** (add *colorful* before *northern* and change *appear* to *dance and glow*) Point out how the details in this expanded sentence make the description clearer.
2. Direct students to p. 54 and discuss the example. Say: **The expanded sentence tells more about the rustling trees.** Draw attention to the word in bold in each sentence. Say: **As you expand each sentence, focus on changing or telling more about the word in bold.** Write the first sentence as a class. Say: **We can make this sentence more descriptive by telling what kind of food the pigs ate.** Have students complete the activity independently or in pairs.

➤ **Extend the Lesson:** Have students add even more information to their expanded sentences.

Lesson 6 Reviewing a Descriptive Paragraph

1. Review the qualities of a good descriptive paragraph: a topic sentence that tells what is being described, sensory details, sentences that *show* rather than *tell*, and expanded sentences that add descriptive detail.
2. Read aloud "El Toro" on p. 55 as students follow along. Guide students through revising the draft. Ask: **Does the first sentence tell what the paragraph is about?** (no) Read aloud this sentence from the draft: *It is huge!* Ask: **Does the sentence *show* or *tell*?** (tell) **How could you show that the roller coaster is huge?** (e.g., tell how tall it is, compare it to a giant) Read aloud this sentence: *The coaster climbs slowly up.* To help students expand the sentence, ask: **What does the roller coaster climb on?** (steep metal tracks) Read this sentence: *At the highest part of El Toro, riders look out.* Ask: **What would the riders probably see if they looked out?** (the whole park) Ask volunteers who have been on a roller coaster to describe the sights, sounds, smells, etc. Record their ideas in a chart on the board. Suggest that students refer to the chart for good sensory details.
3. Have students write their revisions on a separate sheet of paper. Invite volunteers to read aloud their revised descriptive paragraphs.

Page 54 / Student Book Page 37

Name: ______________________

Descriptive Paragraph

Expanding Sentences

Expand each sentence to make it more descriptive. Change the word in bold or add words that relate to it.

Example

The **trees** rustled in the wind.

The graceful willow trees rustled in the wind.

1. The pigs ate **food**.
   The pigs ate oats, corn, and food scraps.
2. The truck stopped **there**.
   The truck stopped at the side of the road.
3. Gwen tasted the **sauce**.
   Gwen tasted the tangy red pasta sauce.
4. The girls called their **cousin**.
   The girls called their favorite cousin, Sheila.
5. The fish swam **downstream**.
   The fish swam down the winding river.
6. The boys rushed to **class**.
   The boys rushed to their swim class.
7. The musician **played** the drum.
   The musician tapped gently on the surface of the drum.

54 EXPOSITORY WRITING Nonfiction Writing • EMC 6013 • © Evan-Moor Corp.

Page 55 and Sample Revision / Student Book Page 38

Name: ______________________

Descriptive Paragraph

Reviewing a Descriptive Paragraph

Revise this descriptive paragraph about a roller coaster. Use what you have learned to make the writing stronger. Rewrite the paragraph on a separate sheet of paper.

Focus on:

✓ writing a topic sentence that tells what you are describing

Sample Answer

El Toro

"El Toro" is one of the steepest roller coasters in the world. It rises from the ground like a giant! And the people waiting to ride El Toro look scared. The coaster climbs slowly up the steep metal tracks. At the highest part of El Toro, riders look out across the whole park. Then the cars race down the track. Seconds later, there is a smell of grease on hot metal. The noisy ride is over in less than two minutes.

Name: ____________________

Introducing a Descriptive Paragraph

Read this example of a descriptive paragraph.

Writing Model

Nature's Light Show

The colorful northern lights often appear on chilly March nights in Alaska. The northern lights are bands of light that fold and wave in the coal-black sky. At times, the lights shimmer in brilliant reds, yellows, and greens. At other times, they glow in shadowy blues and purples. The northern lights do not crackle or sizzle like lightning. They do not make any sound at all. But they are amazing to watch.

Writer's Purpose: ____________________

____

Name: ______________________

Writing a Topic Sentence

A. Each paragraph has a missing topic sentence. Read the paragraph. Then check the box next to the best topic sentence to begin the paragraph.

1. __________ Every snowflake forms a six-sided shape. The pattern on some turtle shells has six-sided shapes. Also, each cell in a bee's honeycomb has six sides.
   - ☐ Many objects in nature have six sides.
   - ☐ Each white part of a black and white soccer ball has six sides.

2. __________ The stars can be red, yellow, or blue. The sun is a yellow star. Blue stars are the hottest. Stars also come in different sizes, from dwarf to giant. But even dwarf stars are much bigger than Earth.
   - ☐ Earth travels around the sun.
   - ☐ Stars are grouped by size and color.

3. __________ Silver fog surrounds the trunks of the giant trees. The air is cool and still. The forest is quiet.
   - ☐ Redwood forests are peaceful.
   - ☐ Redwood trees should be protected.

B. Rewrite each underlined sentence so it tells what the paragraph is about.

Example

<u>It is summer.</u> Thick clouds cover the sky. They are gray and black. The warm air feels heavy and moist. Wind whips the trees back and forth.

A summer storm is coming.

1. <u>Firefighters have a dangerous job.</u> They wash their trucks. They check safety gear. But they stop what they are doing when the fire alarm rings.

   ____

2. <u>The Great Pyramid is old.</u> Sand drifts and piles up against the base of the pyramid. The hot desert sun bakes the stone blocks. Dry winds whistle past.

   ____

Name: ____________________

Adding Sensory Details

A. Fill in the chart with sensory details that describe a bus ride on a rainy morning.

I see...	I hear...	I smell...	I taste...	I feel...

B. Follow the directions. Include sensory details in each sentence you write.

1. Describe what you can see from a window at home.

____

2. Describe what you can hear on a summer day.

____

3. Describe what you can smell at a picnic.

____

4. Describe what you can taste on a Saturday morning.

____

5. Describe what you can feel if you wade into a stream.

____

Name: ______________________________

Showing, Not Telling

A. Read each pair of sentences. Circle the one that **shows** instead of **tells**.

1. The cat wanted to eat the mouse.

   The cat stared at the mouse and licked its lips.

2. His heart pounded as he clawed his way up the rocks.

   The man felt scared as he climbed up the rocks.

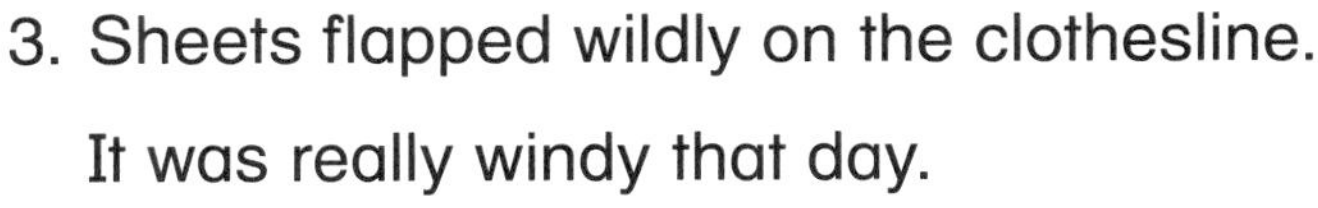

3. Sheets flapped wildly on the clothesline.

   It was really windy that day.

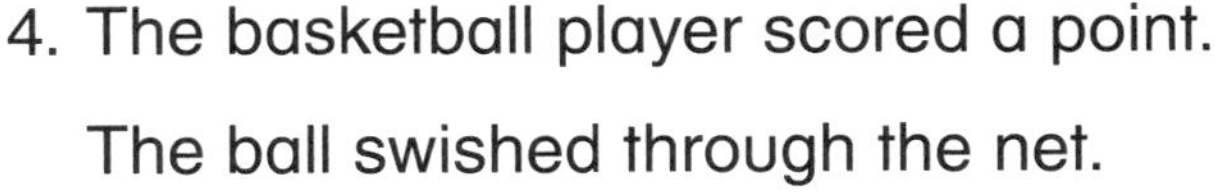

4. The basketball player scored a point.

   The ball swished through the net.

B. Rewrite each sentence so it shows the action instead of telling about it.

1. The bike was going too fast.

   ____

2. Juice spilled onto the floor.

   ____

3. The diver went into the water.

   ____

4. The rocket took off.

   ____

Name: ____________________________________

Expanding Sentences

Expand each sentence to make it more descriptive. Change the word in bold or add words that relate to it.

Example

The **trees** rustled in the wind.

The graceful willow trees rustled in the wind.

1. The pigs ate **food**.

____

2. The truck stopped **there**.

____

3. Gwen tasted the **sauce**.

____

4. The girls called their **cousin**.

____

5. The fish swam **downstream**.

____

6. The boys rushed to **class**.

____

7. The musician **played** the drum.

____

Name: ____________________

Reviewing a Descriptive Paragraph

Revise this descriptive paragraph about a roller coaster. Use what you have learned to make the writing stronger. Rewrite the paragraph on a separate sheet of paper.

Focus on:

- ✓ writing a topic sentence that tells what you are describing
- ✓ using details that tell how something looks, feels, sounds, smells, and tastes
- ✓ writing sentences that *show* rather than *tell*
- ✓ expanding sentences to give more detail

Draft

El Toro

It is one of the steepest roller coasters in the world. It is huge! And the people waiting to ride El Toro look scared. The coaster climbs slowly up. At the highest part of El Toro, riders look out. Then the cars go downhill. The noisy ride is over in less than two minutes.

Writing a Biography

Page 59 / Student Book Page 40

Name: ______________________

Biography

Introducing a Biography

Read this example of a biography.

Writing Model

Annie Oakley, Wild West Star

Annie Oakley was an amazing performer who starred in a Wild West show in the late 1800s. She was famous for her skills with a gun. She could hit targets from far away. She could even shoot a hole through a dime!

Annie had a hard childhood. She was born in Ohio in 1860. Her family was very poor. Annie learned to shoot a gun so she could hunt and help feed her family. But Annie's life changed when she was 16 years old. She entered a shooting contest against a skilled shooter named Frank Butler, and she won. Later, Annie married Frank, and they joined Buffalo Bill's Wild West Show. The show was like a circus. Annie performed tricks with a gun and became successful.

Later, Annie used her skill in other ways. She won more contests, raised money for poor families, and gave shooting lessons to women. Annie Oakley died in 1926.

Writer's Purpose: to tell about the life of Annie Oakley

© Evan-Moor Corp. • EMC 6013 • Nonfiction Writing EXPOSITORY WRITING 59

Page 60 / Student Book Page 41

Name: ______________________

Biography

Finding Important Facts

Read this encyclopedia entry. Then answer the questions.

Bell, Alexander Graham (1847–1922)

Alexander Graham Bell was one of the inventors of the telephone. Bell was born in Scotland. He was interested in sound from an early age because his mother had hearing problems. In 1870, Bell and his family moved to Canada. In 1872, he opened a school in Boston for teachers of deaf people. He was also a professor at Boston University, where he experimented with sound. At that time, he also taught deaf students how to speak.

Bell wanted to find a way to send sounds over a wire. He hired Thomas Watson to help him. Watson knew how to build machines. On March 10, 1876, Bell and Watson tested a new invention. The two men were in separate rooms when Watson heard Bell say through the device, "Mr. Watson, come here. I want to see you." The new invention was the telephone.

In 1877, Bell married Mabel Hubbard, one of his former deaf students. After he helped invent the telephone, he invented the phonograph (or record player), the metal detector, and many other things. Bell and his wife had four children. He died at age 76 in 1922.

1. Whom is this entry about? Alexander Graham Bell
2. What is this person most famous for? He helped invent the telephone.
3. Where and when was the person born? He was born in Scotland in 1847.
4. When did the person die? He died in 1922.
5. Where did the person live? He lived in Scotland, Canada, and the United States.
6. What did this person do? He was an inventor. He opened a school in Boston. He was a professor. He taught deaf students to speak.

60 EXPOSITORY WRITING Nonfiction Writing • EMC 6013 • © Evan-Moor Corp.

Lesson 1 Introducing a Biography

A biography gives important information about a person's life and describes major events in the order in which they happened.

1. Tell students that a biography is a type of writing that gives facts about someone's life, including when and where the person was born, what the person is known for, and what events were important in the person's life.
2. Read aloud "Annie Oakley, Wild West Star" on p. 59 as students follow along. Ask: **What is the purpose of this biography?** (to tell about the life of Annie Oakley) Have students write the purpose on the lines provided.
3. Invite students to offer opinions about what makes this a good biography. Prompt students by asking: **Does the first sentence tell whom the biography is about and why she is important? Does the biography tell important details and interesting facts about her life? Are the events in the order in which they happened?** Then explain that students will use the model as they practice the skills needed to write a good biography.

➤ **Extend the Lesson:** As a class, brainstorm topics for a biography. Generate a list of people that students may want to write about, including people who are familiar but not famous (e.g., parents).

Lesson 2 Finding Important Facts

1. Remind students that a biography includes when and where a person was born, important things that the person has done, and what that person is known for.
2. Say: **A good biography tells facts that are important to know about a person.** Direct students to the model on p. 59. Ask: **Whom is this biography about?** (Annie Oakley) **When and where was she born?** (1860, Ohio) **What is she best known for?** (her skills with a gun) Guide students to identify other facts in the model.
3. Say: **To write a biography of someone, you must first gather information about that person.** Point out the encyclopedia entry on p. 60. Ask: **Whom is this entry about?** (Alexander Graham Bell) **What do the dates after his name represent?** (when he was born and when he died) Tell students that they will use information from the entry to complete the activity. Then read the entry aloud and have students complete the activity in small groups. Encourage students to write their answers as complete sentences. Ask volunteers to share their answers.

Lesson 3 Choosing Good Details

1. Review the purpose of a biography. Then say: **A biography should only contain important details about your subject's life.**
2. Revisit "Annie Oakley, Wild West Star" on p. 59. Say: **All of the details in this biography are important for understanding Annie and her life.** Then point out: **Annie and Frank joined Buffalo Bill's Wild West Show. When the writer gathered facts for this biography, she probably found a lot of information about Buffalo Bill.** Write this sentence on the board: *Buffalo Bill's real name was William Cody.* **Ask: Would this be a good detail to add to the biography about Annie Oakley?** (no) **Why not?** (It isn't important to understanding Annie's life.)
3. Have students read the biography on p. 61 and complete Activity A. Invite students to share the details they underlined.
4. Read aloud the instructions for Activity B. If necessary, complete the first item as a class. Explain that the detail about Aaron's nickname is better because it relates to baseball. Have students complete the activity in pairs. Invite volunteers to share their answers.

Lesson 4 Writing a Good Beginning

1. Direct students to the model on p. 59 and say: **The first sentence of a biography should tell whom the biography is about and why he or she is important.** Read aloud the first sentence of "Annie Oakley, Wild West Star" and say: **This sentence tells us that the biography is about a woman who was the star of a Wild West show in the 1800s.**
2. Direct students to Activity A on p. 62. Read aloud the instructions, the first paragraph, and its answer choices. Ask: **Which sentence tells whom the biography is about and why he is important?** (the second one) Repeat the process for item 2.
3. Have students complete Activity B in pairs. Ask volunteers to share their sentences and have other students confirm that the sentences tell whom the biography is about and why he or she is important.

➤ **Extend the Lesson:** Have students write beginning sentences for a few of the people they listed in the Lesson 1 extension activity.

Page 61 / Student Book Page 42

Name: ______________________

Biography

Choosing Good Details

A. Read this biography about a famous baseball player. Underline three details about him that you find most interesting.

Hank Aaron, A Baseball Legend

Henry "Hank" Aaron is considered one of the best baseball players of all time. He was born in 1934 in Mobile, Alabama. Aaron showed talent for baseball at a young age. He was a star player in high school. But he could not play in the Major Leagues because he was African American.

In 1954, African American players were finally able to play on Major League teams. Aaron joined the Atlanta Braves. He hit 13 home runs in his first season with the Braves. Over time, Aaron hit more and more home runs. In 1974, he broke Babe Ruth's record for the most home runs.

Hank Aaron retired from baseball in 1976. He was voted into the National Baseball Hall of Fame in 1982. He will always remain a baseball legend.

B. Read each pair of sentences. Underline the sentence that belongs in the biography.

1. Aaron also played football in high school.
   Aaron was called "Hammerin' Hank" because he hit the baseball very hard.
2. Babe Ruth died before Aaron broke Ruth's record.
   Hank Aaron hit 755 home runs.
3. Aaron now works for a baseball team and helps kids achieve their dreams.
   The National Baseball Hall of Fame was created in 1936.
4. Aaron played on a professional team in the Negro Leagues when he was only 17 years old.
   Satchel Paige played in the Negro Leagues, too.

Page 62 / Student Book Page 43

Name: ______________________

Biography

Writing a Good Beginning

A. Each paragraph has a missing first sentence. Read the paragraph. Then choose the sentence that is better for the beginning of a biography.

1. __________ He wrote more than 45 books for children. Dr. Seuss was also an artist and drew the pictures for his books. His books have been made into TV shows, movies, and plays.
   - ☐ Theodor Geisel, called Dr. Seuss, was born in 1904 in Bavaria.
   - ☑ Theodor Geisel, called Dr. Seuss, was a famous author of picture books.
2. __________ Her first CD came out when she was only 16 years old. She writes her own songs, which are mostly about her experiences in life. Swift has already won many awards for her music.
   - ☐ She is a popular singer who also plays the guitar.
   - ☑ Taylor Swift is a popular country music singer.

B. Write a beginning sentence for each paragraph. Make sure it names the subject and tells why that person is important.

1. __________ He started drawing when he was very young. Then he learned to paint. Pablo Picasso helped create a new style of art called *cubism*. The people and objects in many of his paintings are represented by flat shapes.
   Pablo Picasso was an important artist.
2. __________ His brother gave him a skateboard when he was 9 years old. Tony Hawk loved it, and he practiced a lot. Soon he was winning contests. Tony Hawk is currently considered the best skateboarder of all time.
   Tony Hawk is a champion skateboarder.
3. __________ She was the first Hispanic American woman to go into space. Her first mission was in 1993. Ochoa is a scientist and an inventor. From space, she studied the way the sun's energy helps and hurts Earth. Ellen Ochoa now helps other astronauts train to go into space.
   Ellen Ochoa is a famous astronaut.

Page 63 / Student Book Page 44

Name: ______________________ Biography

Organizing a Biography

A. Read the details about author J. K. Rowling's life. Number them to show the order that they happened.

3 gets idea for Harry Potter book while riding on a train in 1990
2 writes first story at age six
4 1997: first Harry Potter book is published
1 born in England on July 31, 1965
5 1998–2007: six more Harry Potter novels are published

B. Use the numbered details to write a short biography of J. K. Rowling. Put the events in the order that they happened. The first sentence is written for you.

J. K. Rowling is the author of the famous Harry Potter books. Rowling was born in England on July 31, 1965. She wrote her first story at age six. She got the idea for the first Harry Potter book while on a train in 1990. The book was published in 1997. She wrote six more Harry Potter novels, which were published between 1998 and 2007.

© Evan-Moor Corp. • EMC 6013 • Nonfiction Writing EXPOSITORY WRITING 63

Page 64 and Sample Revision / Student Book Page 45

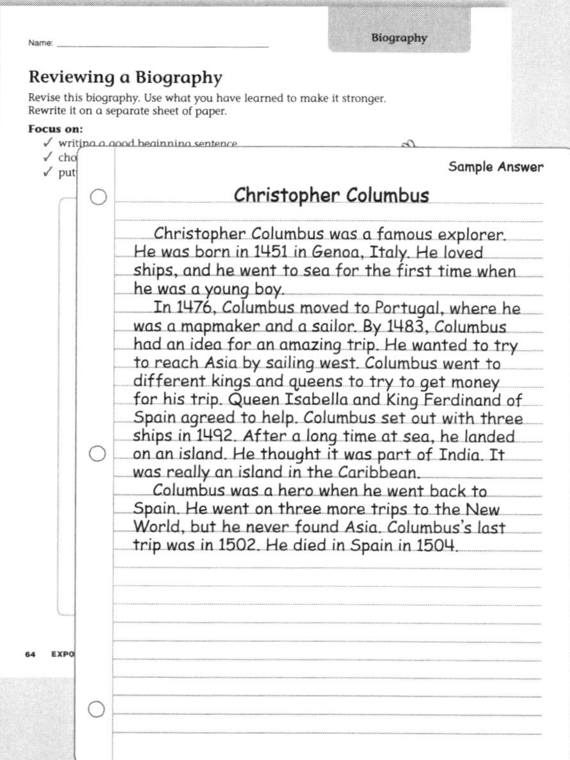
Name: ______________________ Biography

Reviewing a Biography

Revise this biography. Use what you have learned to make it stronger. Rewrite it on a separate sheet of paper.

Focus on:
✓ writing a good beginning sentence
✓ cho
✓ put

Sample Answer

Christopher Columbus

Christopher Columbus was a famous explorer. He was born in 1451 in Genoa, Italy. He loved ships, and he went to sea for the first time when he was a young boy.

In 1476, Columbus moved to Portugal, where he was a mapmaker and a sailor. By 1483, Columbus had an idea for an amazing trip. He wanted to try to reach Asia by sailing west. Columbus went to different kings and queens to try to get money for his trip. Queen Isabella and King Ferdinand of Spain agreed to help. Columbus set out with three ships in 1492. After a long time at sea, he landed on an island. He thought it was part of India. It was really an island in the Caribbean.

Columbus was a hero when he went back to Spain. He went on three more trips to the New World, but he never found Asia. Columbus's last trip was in 1502. He died in Spain in 1504.

64 EXPO

Lesson 5 Organizing a Biography

1. Review the purpose of a biography.
2. Say: **Because a biography tells about a person's life, the facts are usually organized in time order, or the order in which events happened.**
3. Have students identify the events from "Annie Oakley, Wild West Star." List them in order on the board. Point out that the biography follows time order. Ask: **What clues tell us the order of the events?** (dates, age, time words such as *later*)
4. Have students complete Activity A on p. 63 in pairs or small groups. Review the answers together.
5. Have students complete Activity B independently. You may want to point out that the details are in present tense but that students should use past tense in their writing. Ask volunteers to share their paragraphs.

➤ **Extend the Lesson:** Have each student create a list of five important events and dates from his or her own life. Have students exchange their lists with a partner and write short biographies of each other. Remind students to write about the events in the order that they happened.

Lesson 6 Reviewing a Biography

1. Review the qualities a good biography: a good beginning sentence, important facts, good details, and chronological organization.
2. Build background by discussing Columbus's voyage to the New World. Challenge students to locate Italy, Portugal, Spain, India, and the Caribbean on a map or globe. Then read aloud "Christopher Columbus" on p. 64 as students follow along. Guide students through revising the draft. Ask: **Whom is this biography about?** (Christopher Columbus) **Why is Columbus important?** (e.g., He was a famous explorer.) **Does the first sentence tell us who Columbus was and why he was important?** (no) **Are the details in the order that they happened?** (no) Have students list the details in order on the board. Then ask: **Which detail in the biography is not important to understanding Columbus's life?** *(The weather was very nice there.)* **Cross out that detail.** Encourage students to gather facts about Columbus and add important details to the biography.
3. Have students write their revisions on a separate sheet of paper. Invite volunteers to share them with the class.

Name: ______________________________

Introducing a Biography

Read this example of a biography.

Writing Model

Annie Oakley, Wild West Star

Annie Oakley was an amazing performer who starred in a Wild West show in the late 1800s. She was famous for her skills with a gun. She could hit targets from far away. She could even shoot a hole through a dime!

Annie had a hard childhood. She was born in Ohio in 1860. Her family was very poor. Annie learned to shoot a gun so she could hunt and help feed her family. But Annie's life changed when she was 16 years old. She entered a shooting contest against a skilled shooter named Frank Butler, and she won. Later, Annie married Frank, and they joined Buffalo Bill's Wild West Show. The show was like a circus. Annie performed tricks with a gun and became successful.

Later, Annie used her skill in other ways. She won more contests, raised money for poor families, and gave shooting lessons to women. Annie Oakley died in 1926.

Writer's Purpose: ______________________________

____

Name: ____________________

Finding Important Facts

Read this encyclopedia entry. Then answer the questions.

Bell, Alexander Graham (1847–1922)

Alexander Graham Bell was one of the inventors of the telephone. Bell was born in Scotland. He was interested in sound from an early age because his mother had hearing problems. In 1870, Bell and his family moved to Canada. In 1872, he opened a school in Boston for teachers of deaf people. He was also a professor at Boston University, where he experimented with sound. At that time, he also taught deaf students how to speak.

Bell wanted to find a way to send sounds over a wire. He hired Thomas Watson to help him. Watson knew how to build machines. On March 10, 1876, Bell and Watson tested a new invention. The two men were in separate rooms when Watson heard Bell say through the device, "Mr. Watson, come here. I want to see you." The new invention was the telephone.

In 1877, Bell married Mabel Hubbard, one of his former deaf students. After he helped invent the telephone, he invented the phonograph (or record player), the metal detector, and many other things. Bell and his wife had four children. He died at age 76 in 1922.

1. Whom is this entry about? ____________________

2. What is this person most famous for? ____________________

3. Where and when was the person born? ____________________

4. When did the person die? ____________________

5. Where did the person live? ____________________

____

6. What did this person do? ____________________

____

____

Name: ______________________________

Choosing Good Details

A. Read this biography about a famous baseball player. Underline three details about him that you find most interesting.

Hank Aaron, A Baseball Legend

Henry "Hank" Aaron is considered one of the best baseball players of all time. He was born in 1934 in Mobile, Alabama. Aaron showed talent for baseball at a young age. He was a star player in high school. But he could not play in the Major Leagues because he was African American.

In 1954, African American players were finally able to play on Major League teams. Aaron joined the Atlanta Braves. He hit 13 home runs in his first season with the Braves. Over time, Aaron hit more and more home runs. In 1974, he broke Babe Ruth's record for the most home runs.

Hank Aaron retired from baseball in 1976. He was voted into the National Baseball Hall of Fame in 1982. He will always remain a baseball legend.

B. Read each pair of sentences. Underline the sentence that belongs in the biography.

1. Aaron also played football in high school.

   Aaron was called "Hammerin' Hank" because he hit the baseball very hard.

2. Babe Ruth died before Aaron broke Ruth's record.

   Hank Aaron hit 755 home runs.

3. Aaron now works for a baseball team and helps kids achieve their dreams.

   The National Baseball Hall of Fame was created in 1936.

4. Aaron played on a professional team in the Negro Leagues when he was only 17 years old.

   Satchel Paige played in the Negro Leagues, too.

Name: ________________________________

Writing a Good Beginning

A. Each paragraph has a missing first sentence. Read the paragraph. Then choose the sentence that is better for the beginning of a biography.

1. __________ He wrote more than 45 books for children. Dr. Seuss was also an artist and drew the pictures for his books. His books have been made into TV shows, movies, and plays.

   - ☐ Theodor Geisel, called Dr. Seuss, was born in 1904 in Bavaria.
   - ☐ Theodor Geisel, called Dr. Seuss, was a famous author of picture books.

2. __________ Her first CD came out when she was only 16 years old. She writes her own songs, which are mostly about her experiences in life. Swift has already won many awards for her music.

   - ☐ She is a popular singer who also plays the guitar.
   - ☐ Taylor Swift is a popular country music singer.

B. Write a beginning sentence for each paragraph. Make sure it names the subject and tells why that person is important.

1. __________ He started drawing when he was very young. Then he learned to paint. Pablo Picasso helped create a new style of art called *cubism*. The people and objects in many of his paintings are represented by flat shapes.

   ____

2. __________ His brother gave him a skateboard when he was 9 years old. Tony Hawk loved it, and he practiced a lot. Soon he was winning contests. Tony Hawk is currently considered the best skateboarder of all time.

   ____

3. __________ She was the first Hispanic American woman to go into space. Her first mission was in 1993. Ochoa is a scientist and an inventor. From space, she studied the way the sun's energy helps and hurts Earth. Ellen Ochoa now helps other astronauts train to go into space.

   ____

Name: ____________________________________

Organizing a Biography

A. Read the details about author J. K. Rowling's life. Number them to show the order that they happened.

____ gets idea for Harry Potter book while riding on a train in 1990

____ writes first story at age six

____ 1997: first Harry Potter book is published

____ born in England on July 31, 1965

____ 1998–2007: six more Harry Potter novels are published

B. Use the numbered details to write a short biography of J. K. Rowling. Put the events in the order that they happened. The first sentence is written for you.

J. K. Rowling is the author of the famous Harry Potter books. ________________

____

____

____

____

____

____

____

____

Name: ______________________________

Reviewing a Biography

Revise this biography. Use what you have learned to make it stronger. Rewrite it on a separate sheet of paper.

Focus on:

✓ writing a good beginning sentence
✓ choosing good details
✓ putting the details in the order that they happened

Draft

Christopher Columbus

He was born in 1451 in Genoa, Italy. In 1476, Columbus moved to Portugal, where he was a mapmaker and a sailor. He loved ships, and he went to sea for the first time when he was a young boy. Columbus's last trip was in 1502. He died in Spain in 1504.

By 1483, Columbus had an idea for an amazing trip. He wanted to try to reach Asia by sailing west. Columbus went to different kings and queens to try to get money for his trip. Queen Isabella and King Ferdinand of Spain agreed to help. Columbus set out with three ships in 1492. After a long time at sea, Columbus landed on an island. He thought it was part of India. It was really an island in the Caribbean. The weather was very nice there.

Columbus was a hero when he went back to Spain. He went on three more trips to the New World, but he never found Asia.

Writing How-to Instructions

Lesson 1 Introducing How-to Instructions

How-to instructions tell the reader how to make or do something.

1. Tell students that when they want to explain in writing how to make something, such as a paper airplane, or how to do something, such as wash a pet, they can write how-to instructions.
2. Read aloud "Edible Bugs" on p. 68 as students follow along. Explain that something that is *edible* can be eaten. Check comprehension by having two or three students retell how to make "bugs on a log."
3. Ask: **What is the purpose of these instructions?** (to tell how to make a snack called "bugs on a log") Have students write the purpose on the lines provided.
4. Invite students to offer opinions about what makes these good how-to instructions. Prompt students by asking: **Does the first sentence tell what the instructions are for? Do the instructions tell you what you need before you get started? Are the steps clear and easy to follow? Are they in order from first to last?**
5. Explain that students will use the model as they practice the skills needed to write how-to instructions.

➤ **Extend the Lesson:** Point out that how-to instructions often use bulleted or numbered lists, pictures, or diagrams to make information clearer. Help students find examples of how-to texts that use these elements (e.g., recipes, manuals for putting together toys, or craft instructions).

Lesson 2 Writing an Introduction

1. Review the purpose of how-to instructions. Say: **It's important when writing instructions that you first tell readers what they will be making or doing, and what materials they will need. The introduction is the best place for this information.**
2. Say: **A good introduction has a topic sentence that tells readers what they will make or do.** Have students find and underline the topic sentence in "Edible Bugs." *(Here is how you can make a tasty snack …)*
3. Say: **A good introduction also tells readers what materials they will need in order to follow the instructions.** Have students name the materials needed to make "bugs on a log." (celery, peanut butter, raisins, and a knife)

Page 68 / Student Book Page 47

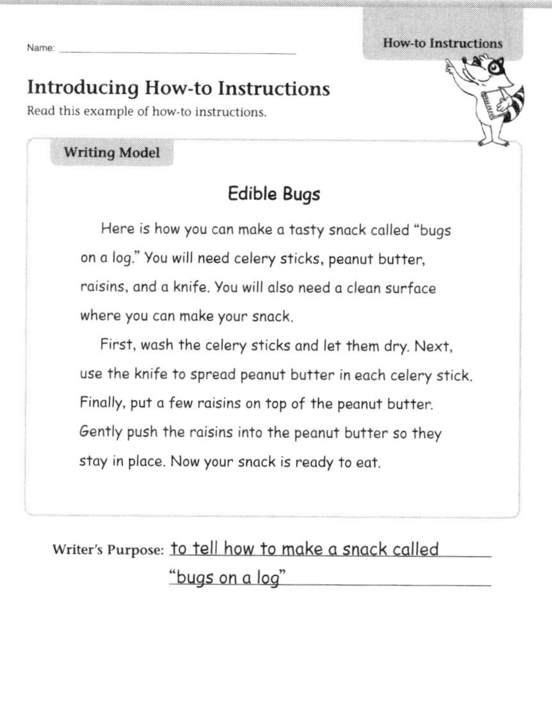

Name: ______________________

How-to Instructions

Introducing How-to Instructions

Read this example of how-to instructions.

Writing Model

Edible Bugs

Here is how you can make a tasty snack called "bugs on a log." You will need celery sticks, peanut butter, raisins, and a knife. You will also need a clean surface where you can make your snack.

First, wash the celery sticks and let them dry. Next, use the knife to spread peanut butter in each celery stick. Finally, put a few raisins on top of the peanut butter. Gently push the raisins into the peanut butter so they stay in place. Now your snack is ready to eat.

Writer's Purpose: to tell how to make a snack called "bugs on a log"

68 EXPOSITORY WRITING Nonfiction Writing • EMC 6013 • © Evan-Moor Corp.

Page 69 / Student Book Page 48

Name: ______________________ How-to Instructions

Writing an Introduction

Read each topic for making or doing something. Then write an introduction for the instructions.

1. **Topic:** how to make invisible ink

   It is fun to make and use invisible ink. To make it, you will need baking soda, water, a cup, and a spoon.

   First, put about two spoonfuls of baking soda into a cup. Add two spoonfuls of water. Then stir the mixture until it is smooth. Now the ink is ready to use.

2. **Topic:** how to make a beaded bracelet

   A beaded bracelet is a nice gift. To make one, you will need stretchy cord, scissors, and beads.

   First, loosely wrap some stretchy cord around your wrist. Cut the cord and tie a knot at one end. String beads onto the cord. Finally, tie the cord in a loop. Your bracelet is ready to wear or give to a friend.

3. **Topic:** how to put batteries in a remote control

   Putting new batteries in your remote control is easy. You need two AA batteries.

   First, open the battery cover on the back of the remote control. Notice which way the batteries face. Then remove the batteries. Put two new AA batteries in place. Make sure they face the right way. Now put the cover back on the remote control.

© Evan-Moor Corp. • EMC 6013 • Nonfiction Writing EXPOSITORY WRITING 69

Page 70 / Student Book Page 49

Name: ______________________ How-to Instructions

Giving Clear Directions

A. Read these directions for teaching a dog how to sit. For each step, choose the sentence that gives the clearer direction.

1. ☑ Get some treats, such as dog cookies.
   ☐ Get some treats.
2. ☐ Be near the dog.
   ☑ Stand facing the dog.
3. ☑ Hold a treat over the dog's head, near enough so the dog can smell it.
   ☐ Hold a treat in one of your hands, near the dog but not too near it.
4. ☐ Say "sit" and gently touch the dog.
   ☑ Say "sit" and gently press down on the dog's back.
5. ☑ As soon as the dog sits, say "good."
   ☐ If the dog happens to sit, say something.
6. ☑ When the dog sits, give the dog the treat.
   ☐ Give the dog the treat.
7. ☑ Practice the command with the dog.
   ☐ Practice sitting with the dog.

B. Revise these directions for playing tag. Make them clearer.

One person is "it." He or she chases the others. Whoever gets caught is "it."

One person is "it." He or she gives the other players a head start before chasing them. Everyone else tries to run away. The player who gets tagged is the next "it."

70 EXPOSITORY WRITING Nonfiction Writing • EMC 6013 • © Evan-Moor Corp.

4. Read aloud the directions on p. 69. Then read the first topic and set of instructions. Help students form a topic sentence that tells what the instructions are for and another sentence that names the materials needed for making invisible ink, based on the instructions. Point out that there is more than one way to write a good introduction, and lead the class in brainstorming other ways to begin the instructions.
5. Have students complete the activity in pairs. Provide vocabulary support as needed. For the third topic, you may want to demonstrate, using an actual remote control.

➤ **Extend the Lesson:** Have students practice writing introductions for other how-to topics (e.g., simple recipes, crafts, or instructions for simple games).

Lesson 3 Giving Clear Directions

1. Say: **Good instructions are clear, specific, and easy to follow.** Write this sentence on the board: *Clean the celery.* Then write the following sentence from "Edible Bugs": *First, wash the celery sticks and let them dry.* Ask: **How does this sentence make the directions clearer?** (It tells what to do to prepare the celery.)
2. Read aloud the directions for Activity A on p. 70. Say: **People can train dogs to follow certain commands such as how to stay or sit.** Tap into prior knowledge by asking if students have ever trained a dog to sit. Then use the first item to model the activity. After reading each choice, say: **The second choice is unclear because it does not tell what kind of treats to get. The first choice gives an example, so it is more specific.** Have students complete the activity in pairs or small groups. Review the answers as a class and invite students to explain their thinking.
3. Read Activity B aloud, pausing between the steps. Ask: **Do these instructions for playing tag clearly tell who "it" chases?** (no) **What else is unclear?** (e.g., The directions don't say that "it" gives the other players a head start before chasing them; they don't say that the other players try to run away from "it." Guide students through rewriting the instructions.

➤ **Extend the Lesson:** Have students continue the Lesson 2 extension activity to draft a complete set of instructions for doing or making something. Then have them exchange papers and note where the instructions could be clearer.

Lesson 4 Organizing Instructions

1. Review the purpose of how-to instructions. Say: **It's important to write the steps in the correct order. Otherwise, people can make a mistake when they follow the instructions.** Have students recall "Edible Bugs." Ask: **What's the first step in making "bugs on a log"?** (washing the celery and letting it dry) **What's the last step?** (pushing the raisins into the peanut butter) **What would happen if the steps were out of order?** (Your snack would turn out different than it should.)
2. Say: **Using signal words such as *first*, *second*, *next*, *then*, and *finally* also helps readers follow along.** Have students circle the signal words in the model.
3. Read aloud the directions for Activity A on p. 71. Guide students to identify the first and second sentences. Then have them complete the activity in pairs or small groups. Check the answers together.
4. Have students complete Activity B in small groups. Prompt them to read all of the signal words in the chart and act out the steps before filling in the directions. Then invite volunteers to share their sentences.

Page 71 / Student Book Page 50

Name: ____________________ How-to Instructions

Organizing Instructions

A. Number the sentences to show the best order for these instructions.

Banana-Berry Shake

1 A cool banana-berry shake is easy to make.
5 Then add the yogurt and juice.
3 First, peel the banana and break it into a few pieces.
6 Next, blend the mixture until it is smooth.
4 Put the banana pieces and the berries into the blender.
7 Pour the mixture into a glass and take a sip!
2 You need a banana, some frozen berries, yogurt, juice, a blender, and a glass.

B. Complete the instructions to tell how to brush your teeth.

Topic sentence: Brushing your teeth helps keep them healthy.

Step 1: First, put some toothpaste on your toothbrush.

Step 2: Next, brush all surfaces of your teeth.

Step 3: After that, spit out the toothpaste.

Step 4: Finally, rinse your mouth with water. Rinse your toothbrush, too.

 EXPOSITORY WRITING 71

Lesson 5 Reviewing How-to Instructions

1. Review the qualities of good how-to instructions: an introduction that states the topic and what is needed for the task or the activity, clear directions, steps organized in the order they occur, and words that signal sequence.
2. Read aloud "Hide-and-Seek" on p. 72 as students follow along. Then guide students through revising the draft. Ask: **Does the introduction tell what the game is?** (no) **Does it tell what you need in order to play?** (no) **What is the first step in playing hide-and-seek?** (choosing "it") **Do the instructions give this step first?** (no) **Which step happens at the same time that "it" counts to 100?** (The other players hide.) **What time order word could we use to signal that two things happen at the same time?** (e.g., *meanwhile*) **Are any steps missing?** (Yes. After yelling "Ready or not, here I come," the player called "it" looks for the players who are hiding.)
3. Have students write their how-to instructions on a separate sheet of paper. Invite volunteers to share their revisions with the class.

Page 72 and Sample Revision / Student Book Page 51

Name: ____________________ How-to Instructions

Sample Answer

Hide-and-Seek

Hide-and-seek is a fun game that you can play indoors or outdoors. To play this game, you need a big space with lots of places to hide.

First, the players pick someone to be "it." That player covers his or her eyes and counts to 100. Meanwhile, the other players run off and find a place to hide. When "it" is finished counting, he or she yells, "Ready or not, here I come!" Then "it" looks for the players who are hiding. When "it" finally finds someone, that person becomes "it."

72

Name: ______________________________

Introducing How-to Instructions

Read this example of how-to instructions.

Writing Model

Edible Bugs

Here is how you can make a tasty snack called "bugs on a log." You will need celery sticks, peanut butter, raisins, and a knife. You will also need a clean surface where you can make your snack.

First, wash the celery sticks and let them dry. Next, use the knife to spread peanut butter in each celery stick. Finally, put a few raisins on top of the peanut butter. Gently push the raisins into the peanut butter so they stay in place. Now your snack is ready to eat.

Writer's Purpose: ______________________________

____

Name: ____________________________________

Writing an Introduction

Read each topic for making or doing something. Then write an introduction for the instructions.

1. **Topic:** how to make invisible ink

____

____

First, put about two spoonfuls of baking soda into a cup. Add two spoonfuls of water. Then stir the mixture until it is smooth. Now the ink is ready to use.

2. **Topic:** how to make a beaded bracelet

____

____

First, loosely wrap some stretchy cord around your wrist. Cut the cord and tie a knot at one end. String beads onto the cord. Finally, tie the cord in a loop. Your bracelet is ready to wear or give to a friend.

3. **Topic:** how to put batteries in a remote control

____

____

First, open the battery cover on the back of the remote control. Notice which way the batteries face. Then remove the batteries. Put two new AA batteries in place. Make sure they face the right way. Now put the cover back on the remote control.

Name: ____________________

Giving Clear Directions

A. Read these directions for teaching a dog how to sit. For each step, choose the sentence that gives the clearer direction.

1. ☐ Get some treats, such as dog cookies.
   ☐ Get some treats.

2. ☐ Be near the dog.
   ☐ Stand facing the dog.

3. ☐ Hold a treat over the dog's head, near enough so the dog can smell it.
   ☐ Hold a treat in one of your hands, near the dog but not too near it.

4. ☐ Say "sit" and gently touch the dog.
   ☐ Say "sit" and gently press down on the dog's back.

5. ☐ As soon as the dog sits, say "good."
   ☐ If the dog happens to sit, say something.

6. ☐ When the dog sits, give the dog the treat.
   ☐ Give the dog the treat.

7. ☐ Practice the command with the dog.
   ☐ Practice sitting with the dog.

B. Revise these directions for playing tag. Make them clearer.

One person is "it." He or she chases the others. Whoever gets caught is "it."

____

____

____

____

Name: ______________________________

Organizing Instructions

A. Number the sentences to show the best order for these instructions.

Banana-Berry Shake

____ A cool banana-berry shake is easy to make.

____ Then add the yogurt and juice.

____ First, peel the banana and break it into a few pieces.

____ Next, blend the mixture until it is smooth.

____ Put the banana pieces and the berries into the blender.

____ Pour the mixture into a glass and take a sip!

____ You need a banana, some frozen berries, yogurt, juice, a blender, and a glass.

B. Complete the instructions to tell how to brush your teeth.

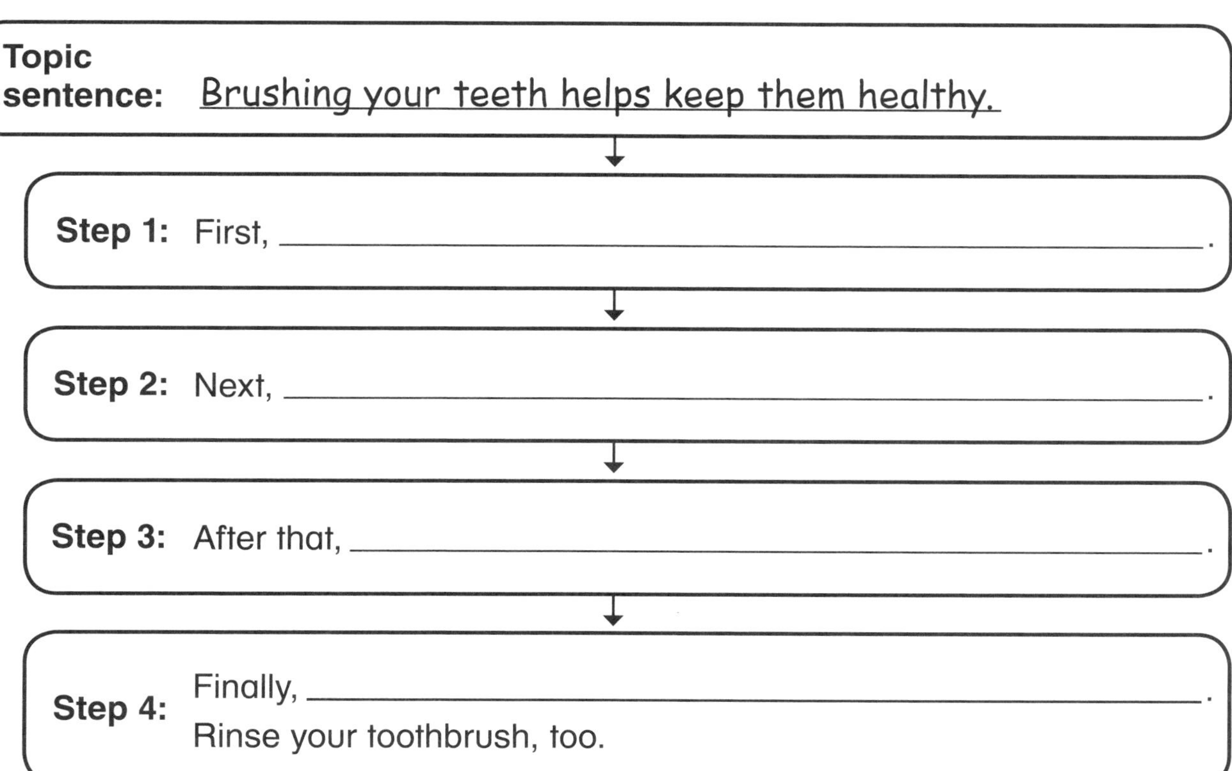

Topic sentence: Brushing your teeth helps keep them healthy.

Step 1: First, ______________________________.

Step 2: Next, ______________________________.

Step 3: After that, ______________________________.

Step 4: Finally, ______________________________. Rinse your toothbrush, too.

Name: ______________________________

Reviewing How-to Instructions

Revise these how-to instructions for playing hide-and-seek. Use what you have learned to make them stronger. Rewrite the instructions on a separate sheet of paper.

Focus on:

- ✓ telling what the topic is and what you need for playing the game
- ✓ making the directions clear
- ✓ putting the steps in order
- ✓ using signal words to make the sequence clear

Draft

Hide-and-Seek

You can play this game indoors or outdoors.

Everyone runs off and finds a place to hide. But first the players need to pick someone to be "it." That player covers his or her eyes and counts to 100. "It" yells, "Ready or not, here I come!" When "it" finally finds someone, that person becomes "it."

Writing a News Article

Lesson 1 Introducing a News Article

A news article is a type of writing that reports facts and information about an event that has just happened. It answers who, what, where, when, why, *and* how *about the event.*

1. Display a newspaper article and say: **News articles tell about something that actually happened. The writer is usually called a *reporter*.** Point out elements of the article, such as the headline, byline, lead, and body paragraphs.
2. Read aloud "Local School Hosts Circus Night" on p. 76 as students follow along. Encourage them to listen for the facts in the article.
3. Ask: **What is the purpose of this news article?** (to tell about a special event at Spring Green School) Have students write the purpose on the lines provided.
4. Invite students to offer opinions about what makes this a good news article. Prompt students by asking: **Does the reporter tell right away what the event was? Does the article tell when, where, and why the event happened and who was involved?**
5. Explain that students will use the model as they practice the skills needed to write a good news article.

➤ **Extend the Lesson:** Bring a variety of news articles from local sources to share. As a class, compile a list of article topics and note those that occur with frequency, such as sports, election news, or weather.

Lesson 2 Answering the 5Ws and H

1. Review the purpose of a news article. Say: **A reporter gives readers all of the information about an event by answering a few basic questions: *Who? What? Where? When? Why?* and *How?* We call these questions the "5Ws and H."** Point out that sometimes a reporter can answer only some of these questions.
2. Help students identify the 5Ws and H in "Local School Hosts Circus Night" on p. 76. Ask: ***What* happened?** (A local school had a Circus Night event.) ***Where* did the show occur?** (Spring Green School gym) ***When* did it take place?** (Saturday, October 15, at 7 p.m.) ***Why* did the school have the show?** (to earn money to fix the playground) ***Who* planned the show?** (Ms. Monroe, the P.E. teacher) ***Who* performed?** (the students)

Page 76 / Student Book Page 53

Name: ____________________ News Article

Introducing a News Article

Read this example of a news article.

Writing Model

Local School Hosts Circus Night

On Saturday, October 15, students at Spring Green School held an event called Circus Night. The show began at 7:00 p.m. and took place in the new gym.

Students performed a variety of circus tricks, such as juggling and clown acts. The purpose of the event was to raise money to fix the school playground. About $1,500 was raised.

The school's P.E. teacher, Ms. Monroe, planned the event. More than 50 students helped out. "Everyone worked hard to get ready for this show," Ms. Monroe said. "As a result, Circus Night was spectacular!"

Writer's Purpose: to tell about a special event at Spring Green School

76 EXPOSITORY WRITING Nonfiction Writing • EMC 6013 • © Evan-Moor Corp.

Page 77 / Student Book Page 54

Name: ______________ News Article

Answering the 5Ws and H

Complete this chart for a recent event that happened in your town. Write questions that would be important for a news article to answer about that event. Then answer the questions.

Event: The tallest tree in Lakeside Park fell over.

Questions	Answers
Who first discovered it?	an early-morning jogger named Jasmine Zarin
What did the tree damage when it fell over?	flowers and shrubs
Where did it happen?	at the south end of the park, near the carousel
When did it happen?	late Tuesday night, April 12
Why did the tree fall?	lightning struck it during a bad storm
How old was the tree?	75 years old

© Evan-Moor Corp. • EMC 6013 • Nonfiction Writing EXPOSITORY WRITING 77

Page 78 / Student Book Page 55

Name: ______________ News Article

Writing Good Leads

A. Read each pair of sentences. Check the box next to the sentence that makes a better lead for a news article.

1. ☐ It was fun to ride the new trolley when it finally began running downtown.
   ☑ The new trolley at Bond City Center began to run on March 7.
2. ☑ The Blue Note Singers won the Pine Bluffs singing competition last week.
   ☐ The Blue Note Singers won a trophy last week.
3. ☐ A black bear does not belong on Sherman School grounds.
   ☑ A bear was seen on the Sherman School grounds last Friday.
4. ☐ Bike owners of all ages came to the bike safety fair.
   ☑ Gray Lake police held a bike safety fair at City Hall on Saturday.

B. Read the facts for each event. Write a lead sentence using at least two facts.

1. **EVENT:** a volcano erupts suddenly
   What: Mount Etna, an active volcano
   Where: Sicily, Italy
   When: last Tuesday at 5:48 a.m.
   Who: no one was hurt

   Italy's Mount Etna suddenly erupted last Tuesday at 5:48 a.m.

2. **EVENT:** crossing guard saves dog's life
   Where: corner of Lowell Avenue and Tenth Street
   When: October 1
   Who: Lateesha Michaels
   How: stopped traffic so dog could reach sidewalk

   While working on October 1, crossing guard Lateesha Michaels saved a dog's life.

78 EXPOSITORY WRITING Nonfiction Writing • EMC 6013 • © Evan-Moor Corp.

3. Draw attention to p. 77 and read aloud the directions. Help students brainstorm current events. (e.g., a bad storm, a festival or parade, a new teacher at school, a new store opening) Take a vote to choose one event to write about. Help students word the questions for the left column of the chart. Then have them work in small groups to answer the questions.

➤ **Extend the Lesson:** Have students play the role of reporter, each one interviewing a partner about an event, such as a birthday party or a sports competition.

Lesson 3 Writing Good Leads

1. Tell students that a good news article includes a *lead*—a sentence that introduces the news article, grabs the reader's attention, and answers at least one of the 5Ws and H. Say: **A lead should identify the topic of the news article.**
2. Have students underline the lead in "Local School Hosts Circus Night." *(On Saturday, October 15, students at Spring Green School held an event called Circus Night.)* Ask: **Does this sentence answer the question *What happened*?** (yes) **What other questions does it answer?** (*who, where,* and *when*)
3. Direct students to Activity A on p. 78. Then ask a volunteer to read aloud the two sentences in item 1. Ask: **What facts does the first choice give?** (that a new trolley began to run downtown) **What facts does the second choice give?** (where and when the new trolley began to run) Say: **The second choice is a better lead because it tells more about the topic.** Have students complete the activity in pairs. Discuss the answers.
4. Read aloud the directions for Activity B. Encourage students to be creative while also using the facts. Have them complete the activity in pairs.

➤ **Extend the Lesson:** Have students practice writing leads for articles, based on the interviews they conducted during the Lesson 2 extension activity.

Lesson 4 Organizing a News Article

1. Review the purpose of a news article. Then say: **A news article has three main parts. The first part is the introduction, which includes the *lead*. Next is the *body*, which gives more details about the topic. The last part is the *conclusion*, or ending, which wraps up the article or tells what may happen next.**

2. Revisit the writing model on p. 76 and help students identify the details that make up the body of the article. (who performed, what they performed, the purpose of the event, and how much money was raised) Say: **The reporter closes with a quote from Ms. Monroe.** Tell students to double-underline the last sentence. *("As a result, Circus Night was spectacular!")* Ask: **How does this sentence wrap up the article?** (It tells what the show was like.)
3. Invite volunteers to read aloud the reporter's notes on p. 79. Check comprehension by asking questions such as: **What event did the reporter attend?** (an annual hole-digging contest) Then have students work in small groups to complete the activity. Invite volunteers to read aloud their articles and explain the organization. Point out that the lead tells what happened, the body gives additional details, and the ending wraps up the event.

➤ **Extend the Lesson:** Cut apart several short news articles into three distinct parts (lead, body, and conclusion) and have students work in small groups to reassemble the articles.

Lesson 5 Reviewing a News Article

1. Review the qualities of a good news article: a lead sentence that tells the topic and answers some of the 5Ws and H, interesting details that answer more questions, and a concluding sentence that wraps up the article.
2. Read aloud "Skate Park Opens in Silver City" on p. 80 as students follow along. Then guide students through revising the draft. Ask: **What news does this article report?** (the opening of a new skate park) Reread the first sentence and ask: **Does the lead identify the topic?** (yes) **What other information could it include?** (some of the 5Ws and H—e.g., where the park is and when it opened) Read aloud the last sentence of the article: *This new outdoor skate park is near the public swimming pool in Silver City.* Ask: **Is this the best place for this information?** (no) **Why not?** (e.g., It belongs at the beginning because it's important to know.) **How might you conclude the article?** (e.g., repeat that skateboarders are happy about the park, say that the park will be busy, or tell people to go there)
3. Have students write their news articles on a separate sheet of paper. Invite volunteers to share their revisions.

Page 79 / Student Book Page 56

Name: ______________________ News Article

Organizing a News Article

Read these notes from a reporter's notebook. Follow the directions to write sentences for a news article about the National Hole-Digging Competition.

EVENT: National Hole-Digging Competition, held every year
When: Sunday, February 6
Where: a field near Tokyo, Japan
Who: more than 200 teams in the competition
What happened: teams tried to dig the deepest hole in 30 minutes
How: using hand shovels
Why: to win prize money and the Golden Shovel award
What happened after: machines filled in the holes with dirt

1. Write a lead that names the event, tells when it took place, and identifies the city and country.

The yearly National Hole-Digging Competition took place on Sunday, February 6, near Tokyo, Japan.

2. Write the body of the article.
   - Write a sentence that tells who took part in the event.
   - Write a sentence that tells what the competitors did.
   - Then write a sentence that explains why people competed in the event.

More than 200 teams competed in the event. Each team tried to dig the deepest hole in 30 minutes using hand shovels. The teams competed for prize money and an award.

3. Write an ending that tells what happened after the competition.

Afterward, machines filled in the holes with dirt.

© Evan-Moor Corp. • EMC 6013 • Nonfiction Writing EXPOSITORY WRITING 79

Page 80 and Sample Revision / Student Book Page 57

Name: ______________________ News Article

Sample Answer

Skate Park Opens in Silver City

Silver City skaters love the new skate park that opened last week near the public pool. The park gives skaters a safe place to practice. It has curved walls and ramps for tricks. The park is open only to skateboarders and in-line skaters. BMX bikes are not allowed. The park is always full of happy skaters.

80

Name: ______________________________

Introducing a News Article

Read this example of a news article.

Writing Model

Local School Hosts Circus Night

On Saturday, October 15, students at Spring Green School held an event called Circus Night. The show began at 7:00 p.m. and took place in the new gym.

Students performed a variety of circus tricks, such as juggling and clown acts. The purpose of the event was to raise money to fix the school playground. About $1,500 was raised.

The school's P.E. teacher, Ms. Monroe, planned the event. More than 50 students helped out. "Everyone worked hard to get ready for this show," Ms. Monroe said. "As a result, Circus Night was spectacular!"

Writer's Purpose: ______________________________

____

Name: ______________________________

Answering the 5Ws and H

Complete this chart for a recent event that happened in your town. Write questions that would be important for a news article to answer about that event. Then answer the questions.

Event: ______________________________

Questions	Answers
Who ______________________________ ______________________________?	______________________________ ______________________________
What ______________________________ ______________________________?	______________________________ ______________________________
Where ______________________________ ______________________________?	______________________________ ______________________________
When ______________________________ ______________________________?	______________________________ ______________________________
Why ______________________________ ______________________________?	______________________________ ______________________________
How ______________________________ ______________________________?	______________________________ ______________________________

Name: ______________________________

Writing Good Leads

A. Read each pair of sentences. Check the box next to the sentence that makes a better lead for a news article.

1. ☐ It was fun to ride the new trolley when it finally began running downtown.
   ☐ The new trolley at Bond City Center began to run on March 7.

2. ☐ The Blue Note Singers won the Pine Bluffs singing competition last week.
   ☐ The Blue Note Singers won a trophy last week.

3. ☐ A black bear does not belong on Sherman School grounds.
   ☐ A bear was seen on the Sherman School grounds last Friday.

4. ☐ Bike owners of all ages came to the bike safety fair.
   ☐ Gray Lake police held a bike safety fair at City Hall on Saturday.

B. Read the facts for each event. Write a lead sentence using at least two facts.

1.

EVENT: a volcano erupts suddenly
What: Mount Etna, an active volcano
Where: Sicily, Italy
When: last Tuesday at 5:48 a.m.
Who: no one was hurt

____

____

2.

EVENT: crossing guard saves dog's life
Where: corner of Lowell Avenue and Tenth Street
When: October 1
Who: Lateesha Michaels
How: stopped traffic so dog could reach sidewalk

____

____

Name: ______________________________

Organizing a News Article

Read these notes from a reporter's notebook. Follow the directions to write sentences for a news article about the National Hole-Digging Competition.

EVENT: National Hole-Digging Competition, held every year
When: Sunday, February 6
Where: a field near Tokyo, Japan
Who: more than 200 teams in the competition
What happened: teams tried to dig the deepest hole in 30 minutes
How: using hand shovels
Why: to win prize money and the Golden Shovel award
What happened after: machines filled in the holes with dirt

1. Write a lead that names the event, tells when it took place, and identifies the city and country.

____

____

2. Write the body of the article.
   - Write a sentence that tells who took part in the event.
   - Write a sentence that tells what the competitors did.
   - Then write a sentence that explains why people competed in the event.

____

____

____

3. Write an ending that tells what happened after the competition.

____

Name: ______________________________

Reviewing a News Article

Revise this news article. Use what you have learned to make it stronger. Rewrite your news article on a separate sheet of paper.

Focus on:

- ✓ writing a lead sentence that gives important information
- ✓ answering as many of the 5W-and-H questions as possible
- ✓ writing an ending that wraps up the article

Draft

Skate Park Opens in Silver City

Silver City skaters love the new skate park that opened. The park gives skaters a safe place to practice. It has curved walls and ramps for tricks. The park is open only to skateboarders and in-line skaters. BMX bikes are not allowed. This new outdoor skate park is near the public swimming pool in Silver City.

Writing a Response to Literature

Lesson 1 Introducing a Response to Literature

A response to literature is writing that responds to a prompt about a reading selection.

1. Explain that students may be asked to respond to a story, a passage, or a poem on a test or for homework. Say: **Writing about something that you have read is called a *response to literature*. You may be asked specific questions, or you may be asked just to write your thoughts or ideas about the story. These questions are called *prompts*.**
2. Explain to students that they will read a West African fable about a spider named Anansi. Read aloud the prompt at the bottom of p. 84. Say: **Think about this question as you read the story.** Then read the story as students follow along.
3. Say: **Let's read how one writer responded to the prompt.** Have a volunteer read aloud the writing model on p. 85. Ask: **What is the purpose of this response to literature?** (to describe Anansi's personality using one word and explain why that word suits him) Have students write the purpose on the lines provided.
4. Invite students to offer opinions about what makes this a good response to literature. Prompt students by asking: **Does the first sentence include the title of the story? Does the writer answer the prompt? Does the writer give details from the story?** Then explain that students will use the reading selection and the writing model as they practice the skills needed to write a good response to literature.

Lesson 2 Understanding the Prompt

1. Review the purpose of a response to literature. Say: **The first step is to make sure you understand what the prompt is asking.** Write the prompt from p. 84 on the board. Say: **This prompt asks the writer to do two things: think of a word that describes Anansi and explain why that word describes him.**
2. Read aloud the directions to the activity on p. 86. Guide students through the example, modeling how to decide what the prompt is asking for. Clarify that students do not need to answer the prompt itself. If necessary, suggest that students begin each answer with "I will look for ..."
3. Have students complete the activity in pairs. Invite volunteers to share their responses.

Pages 84–85 / Student Book Pages 59–60

Name: ____________________ Response to Literature

Name: ____________________ Response to Literature

Introducing a Response to Literature

Read this example of a response to literature.

Writing Model

Selfish is the word that best describes Anansi in "Anansi and the Pot of Wisdom." Nyame gives away the wisdom so everyone can have some. He tells Anansi to share it. But Anansi wants to keep it all for himself. He even tries to hide the wisdom at the top of a tree. That is a very selfish thing to do. Anansi does give the wisdom away at the end of the story, but he does not mean to. He just does it accidentally when he gets angry and throws the pot down. All Anansi cares about is himself.

Writer's Purpose: to describe Anansi's personality using one word and explain why that word suits him

 EXPOSITORY WRITING 85

Page 86 / Student Book Page 61

Name: ____________________ Response to Literature

Understanding the Prompt

Read each prompt. Think about what it is asking. Then write what you will look for in the story to show that you understand the prompt.

Example

Prompt: Why does Anansi throw the pot of wisdom from the tree?

I will look for the reason that Anansi throws the pot of wisdom from the tree.

1. **Prompt:** Why does Anansi break his promise to Nyame?
   I will look for the reason that Anansi breaks his promise about sharing the wisdom.
2. **Prompt:** What is one thing Anansi does that shows he is not wise?
   I will look for an example of something that Anansi does that is not very smart.
3. **Prompt:** Why do you think Nyame wants Anansi to share the wisdom?
   I will look for clues that tell me what Nyame thinks about wisdom.
4. **Prompt:** What lesson about wisdom does the author want you to learn?
   I will look for the author's ideas about how Anansi's actions affect the whole world.
5. **Prompt:** Why does Anansi think that his son is wiser than he is?
   I will look for reasons why Anansi thinks that his son is wiser than he is.

86 EXPOSITORY WRITING

Page 87 / Student Book Page 62

Name: ______________________ Response to Literature

Writing a Topic Sentence

A. Read each prompt. Make a check next to the best topic sentence.

1. **Prompt:** What lesson do you think Anansi was supposed to learn?
   - ☑ In "Anansi and the Pot of Wisdom," Anansi was supposed to learn to share.
   - ☐ In the story, Anansi should have learned that wisdom is not for just one person.
2. **Prompt:** If you were Anansi, what would you have done with the wisdom?
   - ☑ If I were Anansi in "Anansi and the Pot of Wisdom," I would have shared the wisdom.
   - ☐ In "Anansi and the Pot of Wisdom," Anansi should not have gotten angry.

B. Read each story summary and prompt. Then write a topic sentence to answer the prompt.

1. "The Boy Who Cried Wolf" is about a boy who lies and tells everyone he has seen a wolf, just as a joke. When he really sees a wolf, no one believes him.
   Prompt: What lesson does the boy learn in "The Boy Who Cried Wolf"?
   In "The Boy Who Cried Wolf," the boy learns he should not lie or play jokes on people.
2. "The Three Little Pigs" is about three pig brothers. One builds his house out of straw. One builds his house out of sticks. One builds his house out of bricks. A wolf blows down the houses made from straw and sticks.
   Prompt: Which pig is the wisest in "The Three Little Pigs"?
   The wisest pig in "The Three Little Pigs" is the one that builds his house out of bricks.
3. "The Ugly Duckling" is about a baby swan that is raised by ducks. The baby ducks think he is ugly because he looks different from them. But when he grows up, he becomes a beautiful swan.
   Prompt: Is the ugly duckling in the story actually ugly? Explain.
   The ugly duckling in "The Ugly Duckling" is not ugly, but he looks different because he is really a swan.

© Evan-Moor Corp. • EMC 6013 • Nonfiction Writing EXPOSITORY WRITING 87

Page 88 / Student Book Page 63

Name: ______________________ Response to Literature

Marking Up the Story

Read the prompt and the story. Do the following to mark up the story:
- ➤ Draw a box around the title.
- ➤ Underline each sentence that tells what the North Wind does to win.
- ➤ Circle each sentence that tells what the Sun does to win.

The North Wind and the Sun

The North Wind was very proud of his great strength.

"I'm much stronger than you are," the North Wind boasted to the Sun.

"Is that so?" replied the Sun with a sly smile. "Perhaps we should have a little contest to see which of us truly is more powerful."

"What sort of contest do you propose?" asked the North Wind.

"A traveler is coming down the road," said the Sun. "He is wearing a long wool cape. Let's see which of us can take it from him. Whoever has the strength to remove that cape wins the contest."

"OK," agreed the North Wind. "I'll go first." The North Wind turned his face to the traveler and began to blast cold wind at him. The traveler clutched his cape and pulled it tightly around his shivering body. The North Wind continued to blow fiercely, but the traveler's cape did not come off.

"I give up," sighed the North Wind finally.

"Then it's my turn," said the Sun. "You tried to use force to get the cape off, and that did not work. I shall try another way."

The Sun turned her face to the traveler and began to shine pleasant rays down on him. At first the traveler just glanced upward and smiled. But after some time in the bright sunshine, sweat began to run down his forehead. A few minutes later, the traveler took off his wool cape, folded it, and sat down in the shade of a tree.

"I win," said the Sun. And the North Wind was forced to agree.

Prompt: Compare and contrast what the Sun and the North Wind did to win the contest.

88 EXPOSITORY WRITING Nonfiction Writing • EMC 6013 • © Evan-Moor Corp.

Lesson 3 Writing a Topic Sentence

1. Say: **When you write a response to literature, begin with a topic sentence that names the story and clearly answers the prompt.**
2. Read aloud the first sentence in the model on p. 85. Ask: **Does this sentence give the title of the story that the writer is responding to?** (yes) Point out that the title is in quotation marks. Have students underline the part of the sentence that answers the prompt. (Selfish *is the word that best describes Anansi.*)
3. Read aloud the directions for Activity A on p. 87. Have students complete the activity independently. Review the answers with the class.
4. Read the directions for Activity B. Point out that each item is based on a familiar fairy tale, and review the stories ("The Boy Who Cried Wolf," "The Three Little Pigs," and "The Ugly Duckling") as needed. Use item 1 to model writing a good topic sentence. Then have students complete the activity in pairs or small groups. Invite volunteers to share their topic sentences.

➤ **Extend the Lesson:** Have students write topic sentences for the prompts on p. 86.

Lesson 4 Marking Up the Story

1. Say: **Once you decide how to answer a prompt, you can look for details in the story that support your answer. Marking up the story will help you find it details. To mark up a story, you can underline or circle words or sentences.**
2. Display p. 84 and review the prompt. Say: **I'll draw a box around the title to remind me to include it in my topic sentence. As I read, I'll look for details that show Anansi's personality.** Read aloud this sentence: *Anansi the Spider wanted to have all the wisdom in the world.* Say: **This detail shows that Anansi is concerned only about himself. I'll underline the sentence so I can easily find it later.** Continue guiding students through marking up the story.
3. Draw attention to p. 88. Read aloud the directions and the story as students follow along. Have students complete the activity independently. Then have students work in small groups to compare and discuss what they marked up.

➤ **Extend the Lesson:** Have students mark up a reading selection (one that has a prompt) from a reading textbook or a released state test.

Lesson 5 Using Details from the Story

1. Have students recall how they marked up the story in Lesson 4. Say: **You can use the details that you marked to support your response to the literature.**
2. Read a few of the details that you underlined in "Anansi and the Pot of Wisdom" on p. 84. Have students give a thumbs-up if the detail shows that Anansi is selfish and a thumbs-down if it does not. Say: **In her response, the writer used certain details to show that Anansi is selfish.** Help students find these detail sentences in the model response on p. 85.
3. Direct students to p. 89. Have volunteers read aloud the story, paragraph by paragraph. Use item 1 to model finding details to complete the sentence. Say: **I can look back at the story to find out why Mrs. Wolski took Cocoa to a school for dogs. The story tells us that Cocoa "ran when he was told to sit" and "dashed when he was told to stay." In other words, Cocoa did not do as he was told.** Have students complete the activity in pairs. Invite them to share their sentences with the class.

Lesson 6 Reviewing a Response to Literature

1. Review the qualities of a good response to literature: a topic sentence that names the story and answers the prompt, and details that support the answer.
2. Read aloud the prompt on p. 90. Then read "The Wise Old Woman" as students follow along. Ask: **What do we have to do to answer this prompt?** (explain how we know that the story is make-believe) Have students mark up the story. Say: **Draw a box around the title. Then underline the parts of the story that tell you it is make-believe.** Review what students have marked. (animals talking, woman in giant pumpkin, etc.)
3. Ask a volunteer to read aloud the response to literature on p. 91. Then ask: **Does the topic sentence state the title of the story?** (no) **Does it answer the prompt?** (no) **Does the response give some details from the story to show that it is make-believe?** (Yes. It says that a person could not get inside a pumpkin.) Guide students to use other details to explain how they know that the story is make-believe.
4. Have students revise the response independently, using a separate sheet of paper. Remind them that there may be different ways to revise the response. Invite volunteers to share their revisions with the class.

Page 89 / Student Book Page 64

Name: ______________________ Response to Literature

Using Details from the Story

Read the story. Then complete each sentence below, using details from the story.

Come! Sit! Stay!

Cocoa was a frisky puppy. He had more energy than a schoolyard full of kids. And Cocoa always did whatever he wanted to do. He ran when he was told to sit, and he dashed when he was told to stay. Mrs. Wolski, his owner, decided to take Cocoa to a school for dogs.

The school was in a big pet store. Mrs. Wolski placed Cocoa on the floor next to a large sheepdog named Princess. Cocoa nudged the sheepdog with his elbow and winked. "Want to go scare some cats?" he asked.

Princess shook her head and replied, "No, thank you."

"How about some treats?" Cocoa pointed to a shelf full of small bags. "I can rip open a bag with one bite," he boasted.

"N-O spells *no*," replied Princess. "I want to be the very best student in the class."

Cocoa didn't care about being a good student, but he did care what Princess thought of him. So he sat still and listened to the teacher. He hoped Princess would notice!

1. Mrs. Wolski takes Cocoa to school because Cocoa does whatever he wants to do instead of what she tells him to do.
2. "Princess" is a good name for the sheepdog because she acts as if she is perfect.
3. Princess does not want to scare cats or eat treats because she wants to be the best student in the class.
4. Cocoa sits and listens to the teacher because he wants to please Princess.

© Evan-Moor Corp. • EMC 6013 • Nonfiction Writing EXPOSITORY WRITING 89

Pp. 90–91 and Sample Revision / Student Book pp. 65–66

Name: Response to Literature

Name: ______________________ Response to Literature

Reviewing a Response to Literature

Revise this response to "The Wise Old Woman." Use what you have learned to make the response stronger. Rewrite it on a separate sheet of paper.

Focus on:

✓ understanding the prompt that appears at the end of the story
✓ writing a topic sentence that includes the title and answers the prompt
✓ using details from the story to support the topic sentence

Draft

This is a make-believe story because

Sample Answer

"The Wise Old Woman" is a make-believe story because the events could not happen in real life. In the story, the wolf and the bear tell the wise old woman that they want to eat her. Animals do not talk in real life. Then the woman gets inside a giant pumpkin and rolls around. I do not think a person could do that because most pumpkins do not grow that big. Finally, if a real wolf and a real bear were hungry, they would probably eat the woman instead of fighting each other. That is how I know that the story is make-believe.

Name: ______________________________

Introducing a Response to Literature

Read this West African fable about a spider.

Reading Selection

Anansi and the Pot of Wisdom

Anansi the Spider wanted to have all the wisdom in the world. So he went to Nyame the Sun to ask for more wisdom.

"You know everything, Nyame," Anansi said. "You see everything. Will you give me your wisdom?"

"I am happy to give you my wisdom," said Nyame. "But you must promise to share it with everyone in the world."

"I promise," said Anansi.

And so Nyame gave Anansi the wisdom. Anansi put it into a big pot so he could carry it.

People saw Anansi carrying his heavy pot.

"What's in the pot?" they asked. "Can we have some?"

Anansi had promised to share the wisdom. But now he didn't want to. He thought about how powerful he could be if he kept all the wisdom for himself.

"Never mind what's in the pot," Anansi said to everyone. "It's mine."

Anansi decided to hide the wisdom at the top of a tall tree. He tied the pot to his belly and began to climb the tree. But he could only climb slowly because the huge pot banged against him.

Anansi's son came to see what his father was doing.

"Father," the boy called up from the bottom of the tree. "That pot looks heavy. Why don't you tie it onto your back? Then you can climb more easily."

Anansi untied the pot and put it on his back. He could indeed climb more easily. Anansi grew angry.

"I've got this big pot of wisdom," he fumed, "but my son still has more wisdom than I do. I'll never have all the wisdom in the world!"

In anger, Anansi threw down the heavy pot. As it fell, the wisdom scattered everywhere.

And from that day on, no one has ever had all the wisdom in the world. Instead, each of us has just a little bit of it.

Prompt: What word would you use to describe Anansi's personality? Why?

Name: ______________________________

Introducing a Response to Literature

Read this example of a response to literature.

Writing Model

Selfish is the word that best describes Anansi in "Anansi and the Pot of Wisdom." Nyame gives away the wisdom so everyone can have some. He tells Anansi to share it. But Anansi wants to keep it all for himself. He even tries to hide the wisdom at the top of a tree. That is a very selfish thing to do. Anansi does give the wisdom away at the end of the story, but he does not mean to. He just does it accidentally when he gets angry and throws the pot down. All Anansi cares about is himself.

Writer's Purpose: ______________________________

____

____

Name: ______________________

Understanding the Prompt

Read each prompt. Think about what it is asking. Then write what you will look for in the story to show that you understand the prompt.

Example

Prompt: Why does Anansi throw the pot of wisdom from the tree?

I will look for the reason that Anansi throws the pot of wisdom from the tree.

1. **Prompt:** Why does Anansi break his promise to Nyame?

____

____

2. **Prompt:** What is one thing Anansi does that shows he is not wise?

____

____

3. **Prompt:** Why do you think Nyame wants Anansi to share the wisdom?

____

____

4. **Prompt:** What lesson about wisdom does the author want you to learn?

____

____

5. **Prompt:** Why does Anansi think that his son is wiser than he is?

____

____

Name: ___________________________

Writing a Topic Sentence

A. Read each prompt. Make a check next to the best topic sentence.

1. **Prompt:** What lesson do you think Anansi was supposed to learn?
   - ☐ In "Anansi and the Pot of Wisdom," Anansi was supposed to learn to share.
   - ☐ In the story, Anansi should have learned that wisdom is not for just one person.

2. **Prompt:** If you were Anansi, what would you have done with the wisdom?
   - ☐ If I were Anansi in "Anansi and the Pot of Wisdom," I would have shared the wisdom.
   - ☐ In "Anansi and the Pot of Wisdom," Anansi should not have gotten angry.

B. Read each story summary and prompt. Then write a topic sentence to answer the prompt.

1. "The Boy Who Cried Wolf" is about a boy who lies and tells everyone he has seen a wolf, just as a joke. When he really sees a wolf, no one believes him.

   Prompt: What lesson does the boy learn in "The Boy Who Cried Wolf"?

   ____

   ____

2. "The Three Little Pigs" is about three pig brothers. One builds his house out of straw. One builds his house out of sticks. One builds his house out of bricks. A wolf blows down the houses made from straw and sticks.

   Prompt: Which pig is the wisest in "The Three Little Pigs"?

   ____

   ____

3. "The Ugly Duckling" is about a baby swan that is raised by ducks. The baby ducks think he is ugly because he looks different from them. But when he grows up, he becomes a beautiful swan.

   Prompt: Is the ugly duckling in the story actually ugly? Explain.

   ____

   ____

Name: ____

Marking Up the Story

Read the prompt and the story. Do the following to mark up the story:

- ➤ Draw a box around the title.
- ➤ Underline each sentence that tells what the North Wind does to win.
- ➤ Circle each sentence that tells what the Sun does to win.

The North Wind and the Sun

The North Wind was very proud of his great strength.

"I'm much stronger than you are," the North Wind boasted to the Sun.

"Is that so?" replied the Sun with a sly smile. "Perhaps we should have a little contest to see which of us truly is more powerful."

"What sort of contest do you propose?" asked the North Wind.

"A traveler is coming down the road," said the Sun. "He is wearing a long wool cape. Let's see which of us can take it from him. Whoever has the strength to remove that cape wins the contest."

"OK," agreed the North Wind. "I'll go first." The North Wind turned his face to the traveler and began to blast cold wind at him. The traveler clutched his cape and pulled it tightly around his shivering body. The North Wind continued to blow fiercely, but the traveler's cape did not come off.

"I give up," sighed the North Wind finally.

"Then it's my turn," said the Sun. "You tried to use force to get the cape off, and that did not work. I shall try another way."

The Sun turned her face to the traveler and began to shine pleasant rays down on him. At first the traveler just glanced upward and smiled. But after some time in the bright sunshine, sweat began to run down his forehead. A few minutes later, the traveler took off his wool cape, folded it, and sat down in the shade of a tree.

"I win," said the Sun. And the North Wind was forced to agree.

Prompt: Compare and contrast what the Sun and the North Wind did to win the contest.

Name: ______________________________

Using Details from the Story

Read the story. Then complete each sentence below, using details from the story.

Come! Sit! Stay!

Cocoa was a frisky puppy. He had more energy than a schoolyard full of kids. And Cocoa always did whatever he wanted to do. He ran when he was told to sit, and he dashed when he was told to stay. Mrs. Wolski, his owner, decided to take Cocoa to a school for dogs.

The school was in a big pet store. Mrs. Wolski placed Cocoa on the floor next to a large sheepdog named Princess. Cocoa nudged the sheepdog with his elbow and winked. "Want to go scare some cats?" he asked.

Princess shook her head and replied, "No, thank you."

"How about some treats?" Cocoa pointed to a shelf full of small bags. "I can rip open a bag with one bite," he boasted.

"N-O spells *no,*" replied Princess. "I want to be the very best student in the class."

Cocoa didn't care about being a good student, but he did care what Princess thought of him. So he sat still and listened to the teacher. He hoped Princess would notice!

1. Mrs. Wolski takes Cocoa to school because ______________________________

   ______________________________.

2. "Princess" is a good name for the sheepdog because ______________________________

   ______________________________.

3. Princess does not want to scare cats or eat treats because ______________________________

   ______________________________.

4. Cocoa sits and listens to the teacher because ______________________________

   ______________________________.

Name: ______________________________

Reviewing a Response to Literature

Read this story about a wise old woman.

Reading Selection

The Wise Old Woman

A wise old woman lived at the edge of the woods. One day, she filled a basket with muffins to take to her son, who lived on the other side of the woods. On the way, she met a bushy-tailed gray wolf.

"I am hungry. I'm going to eat you," barked the wolf.

"Don't eat me now," said the old woman. I am just skin and bones. When I come back from my son's house, I'll be fatter."

"OK, I will wait for you," barked the wolf.

The old woman continued down the path until she saw a large black bear.

"I am hungry. I'm going to eat you," growled the bear.

"Don't eat me now," warned the old woman. "I am just skin and bones. When I come back from my son's house, I will be fatter."

The wise old woman reached her son's house just in time for lunch. She and her son ate and ate. Then she took a nap. When she woke up, she said to her son, "Now I must go home. But may I have that giant pumpkin in your garden?"

The wise woman cut a hole in the pumpkin and took out all the seeds. Then she crawled inside the pumpkin and rolled into the woods.

The bear and the wolf saw the pumpkin rolling through the woods, but they were waiting for the old woman. Suddenly, the pumpkin rolled into a tree and broke open with a loud "Crack!"

"It's the old woman!" barked the wolf. "I'm going to eat her now!"

"No!" growled the bear. "She's going to be *my* dinner."

The wise old woman announced, "The stronger of you can eat me." Then, as the two animals began to fight, the wise old woman ran all the way home.

Prompt: How do you know this story is make-believe?

Name: ____

Reviewing a Response to Literature

Revise this response to "The Wise Old Woman." Use what you have learned to make the response stronger. Rewrite it on a separate sheet of paper.

Focus on:

- ✓ understanding the prompt that appears at the end of the story
- ✓ writing a topic sentence that includes the title and answers the prompt
- ✓ using details from the story to support the topic sentence

Draft

This is a make-believe story because the events are funny. In the story, the wise old woman tricks the wolf and the bear. She talks them out of eating her. Then the woman gets inside a giant pumpkin and rolls around. I don't think a person could do that. Finally, the bear and the wolf end up fighting each other instead of eating the wise old woman. I liked this story even if it is make-believe.

Writing a Research Report

Page 98 / Student Book Page 68

Name: ______________________

Research Report

Introducing a Research Report

Read this example of a research report.

Writing Model

The Peculiar Platypus

What lays eggs like a reptile but has a bill like a duck's and fur like a beaver's? A platypus! According to SuperScientificKids.org, "The first British scientist to study the platypus thought that someone was playing a joke on him!" The scientist thought the animal was a fake. It is easy to see why. The platypus, which is an Australian mammal, has some unusual features.

A platypus is a small water mammal with brown fur. It is about 18 inches long and weighs about 3 pounds. Its fur protects it in cold water. The animal uses its paddle-shaped tail and webbed feet to swim. It uses its flat bill to dig for food.

A platypus gets its food by hunting in rivers and streams. It scoops up insects, shellfish, and worms. Then it stores food in its cheek pouches as it swims back to the surface to eat.

The platypus is one of only two mammals that lay eggs. A mother platypus digs special holes called burrows for her eggs. A baby platypus that hatches from its egg is called a *puggle*.

Although a platypus may look cuddly, people should not touch it! It is not friendly. A male platypus has sharp spurs on its back legs that contain venom. Being stung by a platypus hurts!

This odd animal may be funny-looking, but its unusual features help it stay alive. A platypus can live for about 13 years in the wild. So maybe being strange is not such a bad idea!

Writer's Purpose: to tell readers about the unusual features of the platypus

98 EXPOSITORY WRITING — Nonfiction Writing • EMC 6013 • © Evan-Moor Corp.

Page 99 / Student Book Page 69

Name: ______________________

Research Report

Introducing a Research Report

Read these examples of a bibliography and an outline.

Bibliography Model

"Duck-Billed Platypus." SuperScientificKids.org. <http://superscientifickids.org/animaltales/platypus>

Estevez, Avi. "The Life of a Puggle." Puggle. 1 Feb. 2009: 19–22.

Roberts, Quin. Amazing Australian Animals. Sydney: Science Press, 2006.

Outline Model

I. The platypus is a strange-looking animal.
  A. It is about 18 inches long and weighs about 3 pounds.
  B. Its fur, which is brown, protects it in cold water.
  C. It uses its tail and webbed feet to swim.
  D. It uses its flat bill to dig.

II. The platypus hunts in rivers and streams.
  A. It uses its bill to scoop up insects, shellfish, and worms to eat.
  B. It stores food in its cheeks.

III. The platypus is one of only two mammals that lay eggs.
  A. Mothers dig burrows for eggs.
  B. Babies are called "puggles."

IV. People should not try to touch a platypus.
  A. It is not a friendly animal.
  B. Males have sharp spurs on their back legs.
  C. The spurs contain venom that stings.

© Evan-Moor Corp. • EMC 6013 • Nonfiction Writing — EXPOSITORY WRITING 99

Lesson 1 Introducing a Research Report

A research report is a report that gives details and facts about a topic, using information gathered from different sources.

1. Tell students that the purpose of a research report is to give interesting facts about a topic. Say: **When you want to find out about a topic, you can research by looking in books, magazines, or encyclopedias; looking on the Internet; or asking an expert. You can report on what you find by writing a research report.**
2. Display "The Peculiar Platypus" on p. 98. If possible, build background by showing a photo of a platypus. Read aloud the first paragraph and have students look for details that they think the writer found by doing research. Then say: **The writer mentions SuperScientificKids.org. He must have looked at that Web site to find some of these details.**
3. Finish reading the report as students follow along. Ask: **What is the purpose of this research report?** (to tell readers about the unusual features of the platypus) Have students write the purpose on the lines provided.
4. Invite students to offer opinions about what makes this a good research report. Prompt them by asking: **Is there one sentence that tells the topic of the report? Does each paragraph tell you something new? Do all of the details seem like they belong in the report?** Then explain that students will use the writing model, along with the bibliography and outline models on p. 99, as they practice the skills needed to write a good research report.

➤ **Extend the Lesson:** Have students brainstorm topics for their own research reports. Encourage them to think of topics that would be easy to research.

Lesson 2 Thinking of Questions

1. Review the purpose of a research report. Then say: **Before you begin researching, you should figure out the most important things you need to learn about the topic. One way to do this is to write questions that you think your report should answer.**
2. Direct students to p. 100. Point out the example and say: **To get started with the report, the writer first wrote a few important questions about platypuses. Then he answered those questions in his report.** Read each question in the example and have students find the answer in "The Peculiar Platypus."

3. Help students complete item 1 on p. 100 by brainstorming questions about penguins and recording students' responses on the board. Ask: **Which are the most important questions to answer about penguins?** (e.g., where they live, how they act, what they look like)
4. Have students complete items 2 and 3 in pairs or small groups. If necessary, build background about the topics before students begin.

➤ **Extend the Lesson:** Have students choose an animal that interests them and write three questions that they could find the answers to by doing research.

Lesson 3 Finding Information

1. Say: **After you write your questions, you're ready to begin researching. You can get information from different *sources*, which can be books, articles, or people.** Use the model bibliography on p. 99 to discuss the sources used for "The Peculiar Platypus." (Web site, magazine, book) Provide examples of other research resources, such as textbooks, an encyclopedia, or an almanac. Explain that some sources may be better than others for certain topics. Ask: **Which would be better for learning about trees—a magazine about outdoor activities or an encyclopedia of plants?** (an encyclopedia of plants)
2. Direct students to Activity A on p. 101. Say: **Each source gives information in a different way.** Point out the address bar on the sample Web page. Say: **The address bar tells us the Web page address, or what to type in to find the page.** Ask: **What are some other parts of this Web page?** (title, links, scroll bar) Read aloud the main text as students follow along. Complete the three questions as a class.
3. Direct students to Activity B. Remind students that an encyclopedia is a set of books that contains information about many topics. Explain that the entries are in alphabetical order. Then read aloud the entry on platypuses. Have students complete the activity independently, and review the answers.

➤ **Extend the Lesson:** Have students locate at least two resources they might use to research the animal they chose in the Lesson 2 extension activity.

Page 100 / Student Book Page 70

Name: ______________________ Research Report

Thinking of Questions

Read each topic. Write three important questions to answer in a report about the topic.

Example
Topic: the platypus
Questions:
What does a platypus look like?
Where does a platypus live?
How does a platypus eat?

Do you quack like a duck?

1. Topic: penguins
Questions:
Where do penguins live?
How do they act?
What do penguins look like?

2. Topic: Abraham Lincoln
Questions:
Why was he important?
Where did he grow up?
When was he president?

3. Topic: the sun
Questions:
How hot is the sun?
How far away is it from Earth?
How big is it?

100 EXPOSITORY WRITING Nonfiction Writing • EMC 6013 • © Evan-Moor Corp.

Page 101 / Student Book Page 71

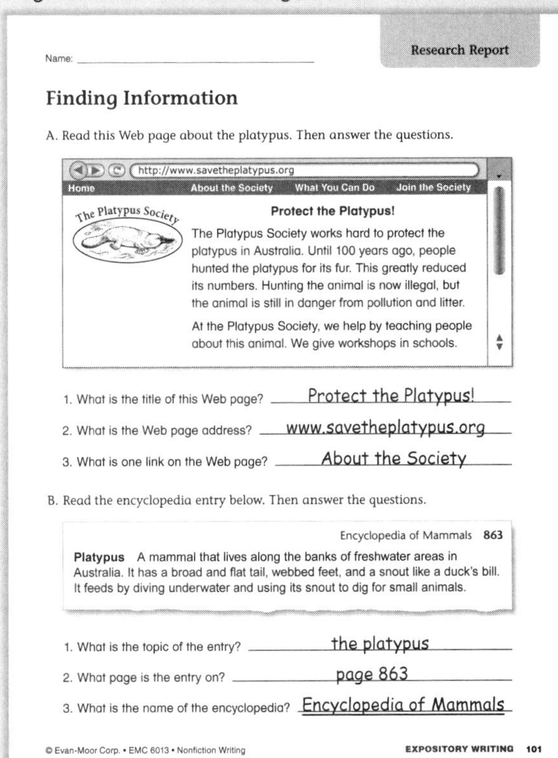
Name: ______________________ Research Report

Finding Information

A. Read this Web page about the platypus. Then answer the questions.

http://www.savetheplatypus.org
Home | About the Society | What You Can Do | Join the Society
The Platypus Society
Protect the Platypus!
The Platypus Society works hard to protect the platypus in Australia. Until 100 years ago, people hunted the platypus for its fur. This greatly reduced its numbers. Hunting the animal is now illegal, but the animal is still in danger from pollution and litter.
At the Platypus Society, we help by teaching people about this animal. We give workshops in schools.

1. What is the title of this Web page? Protect the Platypus!
2. What is the Web page address? www.savetheplatypus.org
3. What is one link on the Web page? About the Society

B. Read the encyclopedia entry below. Then answer the questions.

Encyclopedia of Mammals 863
Platypus A mammal that lives along the banks of freshwater areas in Australia. It has a broad and flat tail, webbed feet, and a snout like a duck's bill. It feeds by diving underwater and using its snout to dig for small animals.

1. What is the topic of the entry? the platypus
2. What page is the entry on? page 863
3. What is the name of the encyclopedia? Encyclopedia of Mammals

© Evan-Moor Corp. • EMC 6013 • Nonfiction Writing EXPOSITORY WRITING 101

Page 102 / Student Book Page 72

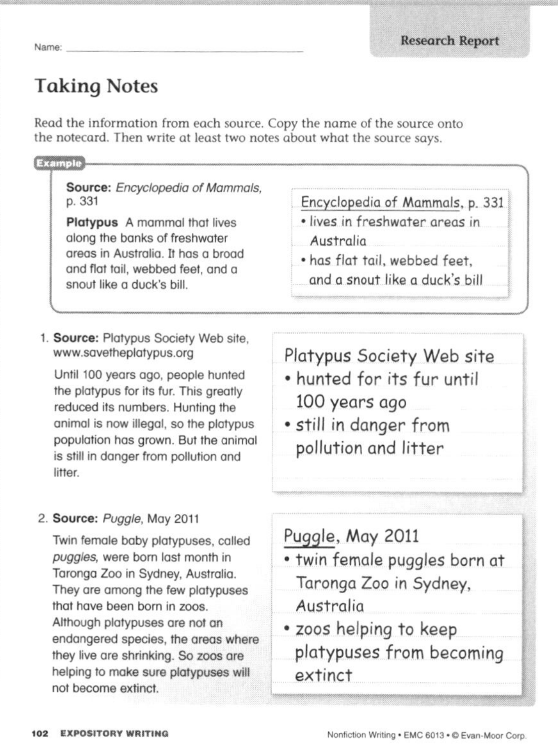

Name: ______________

Research Report

Taking Notes

Read the information from each source. Copy the name of the source onto the notecard. Then write at least two notes about what the source says.

Example

Source: *Encyclopedia of Mammals*, p. 331

Platypus A mammal that lives along the banks of freshwater areas in Australia. It has a broad and flat tail, webbed feet, and a snout like a duck's bill.

Encyclopedia of Mammals, p. 331
- lives in freshwater areas in Australia
- has flat tail, webbed feet, and a snout like a duck's bill

1. **Source:** Platypus Society Web site, www.savetheplatypus.org

Until 100 years ago, people hunted the platypus for its fur. This greatly reduced its numbers. Hunting the animal is now illegal, so the platypus population has grown. But the animal is still in danger from pollution and litter.

Platypus Society Web site
- hunted for its fur until 100 years ago
- still in danger from pollution and litter

2. **Source:** *Puggle*, May 2011

Twin female baby platypuses, called *puggles*, were born last month in Taronga Zoo in Sydney, Australia. They are among the few platypuses that have been born in zoos. Although platypuses are not an endangered species, the areas where they live are shrinking. So zoos are helping to make sure platypuses will not become extinct.

Puggle, May 2011
- twin female puggles born at Taronga Zoo in Sydney, Australia
- zoos helping to keep platypuses from becoming extinct

102 EXPOSITORY WRITING   Nonfiction Writing • EMC 6013 • © Evan-Moor Corp.

Page 103 / Student Book Page 73

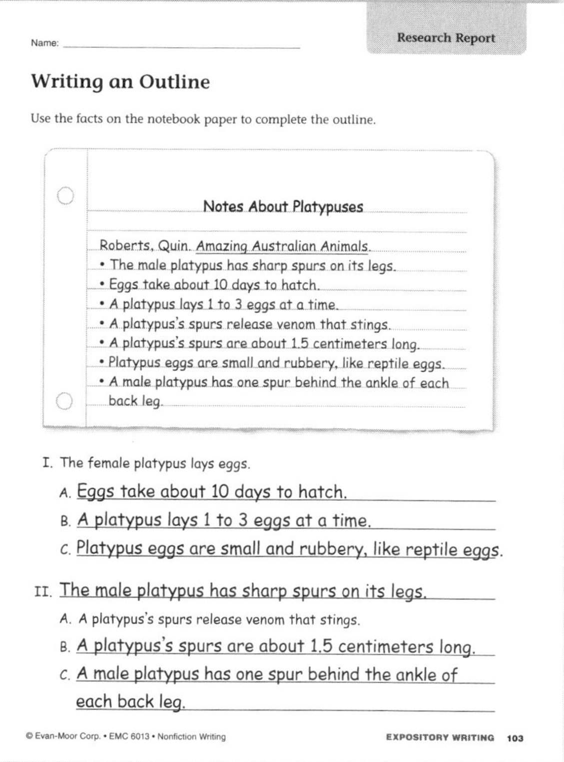

Name: ______________

Research Report

Writing an Outline

Use the facts on the notebook paper to complete the outline.

Notes About Platypuses

Roberts, Quin. Amazing Australian Animals.
- The male platypus has sharp spurs on its legs.
- Eggs take about 10 days to hatch.
- A platypus lays 1 to 3 eggs at a time.
- A platypus's spurs release venom that stings.
- A platypus's spurs are about 1.5 centimeters long.
- Platypus eggs are small and rubbery, like reptile eggs.
- A male platypus has one spur behind the ankle of each back leg.

I. The female platypus lays eggs.
   A. Eggs take about 10 days to hatch.
   B. A platypus lays 1 to 3 eggs at a time.
   C. Platypus eggs are small and rubbery, like reptile eggs.

II. The male platypus has sharp spurs on its legs.
   A. A platypus's spurs release venom that stings.
   B. A platypus's spurs are about 1.5 centimeters long.
   C. A male platypus has one spur behind the ankle of each back leg.

© Evan-Moor Corp. • EMC 6013 • Nonfiction Writing   EXPOSITORY WRITING 103

Lesson 4 Taking Notes

1. Remind students that a *source* is the material in which they will find answers to their research questions.
2. Explain what it means to take notes. Say: **When you take notes, you write down the good information that you want to use. You also need to write the name of the source and the page number so you can find more facts later or reread the facts noted.**
3. Direct students to p. 102 and discuss the example. Point out that the notecard includes the source, the page number, and two facts. Before having students complete the activity in pairs, read through the sources as a class. To make sure students understand the concepts and vocabulary, ask questions such as: **Why are platypuses still in danger?** (because of pollution and litter) **What is a puggle?** (a baby platypus)

➤ **Extend the Lesson:** Point out that writers usually take notes by writing key words and phrases rather than complete sentences. Have students practice taking notes from a section in one of their textbooks.

Lesson 5 Writing an Outline

1. Direct students to the model outline on p. 99. Explain that the purpose of writing an outline is to organize notes into what will later become paragraphs. Remind students that the *main idea* is what a paragraph is mostly about.
2. Point out the parts of an outline. Say: **The sentence after each Roman numeral gives a main idea. The sentence after each capital letter gives a detail that supports the main idea.** Help students identify the main ideas and detail sentences in the outline on p. 99.
3. Direct students to p. 103 and ask a volunteer to read the sentence for Roman numeral I. Ask: **What is this sentence about?** (platypus eggs) Tell students to look for notes about platypus eggs as you read aloud the sentences on the notebook paper. *(Eggs take about …, A platypus lays 1 to 3 eggs …, Platypus eggs are small …)* Have students write the details in the outline.
4. Ask: **What are the other notes about?** (a male platypus's spurs) **Which note sounds like a main idea?** *(The male platypus has sharp spurs …)* **Where should this sentence go in the outline?** (as Roman numeral II) Then have students work independently to write the remaining details in the outline.

Lesson 6 Using an Outline to Write

1. Review the purpose of an outline. (to organize ideas)
2. Have students compare the model outline on p. 99 to the model report on p. 98. Say: **The outline helped the writer stay organized. Each main idea and its supporting details became a paragraph in the research report.** Read Roman numeral II from the outline: *The platypus hunts in rivers and streams.* Ask: **Which paragraph on p. 98 is mostly about this main idea?** (paragraph 3) Have students identify detail sentences in paragraph 3 that correspond with sentences A and B of Roman numeral II in the outline. Repeat for other main ideas and details.
3. Direct students to p. 104. Point out that each section of the outline could lead to a separate paragraph. Say: **Write the main idea and all of the details about the camping burrow in one paragraph. Then write the main idea and all of the details about the nesting burrow in another paragraph.**
4. Encourage students to write the ideas in their own words without changing the meaning of the notes. Have students write their paragraphs independently. Invite volunteers to share their paragraphs with the class.

Lesson 7 Writing a Topic Sentence

1. Say: **Each paragraph in a research report should have a topic sentence. The topic sentence states the main idea of the paragraph. Topic sentences are supported by details in the paragraph.**
2. Have students underline the topic sentences in paragraphs 2 through 5 of "The Peculiar Platypus" (the first sentence in each paragraph). Discuss how the detail sentences tell more about the main ideas.
3. Read the directions for Activity A on p. 105. Then conduct the activity with the class.
4. Read aloud the directions for Activity B and have students complete the activity in pairs or small groups. Invite volunteers to share their topic sentences and explain how they decided what to write.

➤ **Extend the Lesson:** Have students choose one of the topics on p. 100 and then work in small groups to write topic sentences that answer the questions, drawing from textbooks or other sources.

Page 104 / Student Book Page 74

Name: ____________ Research Report

Using an Outline to Write

Use the notes from the outline to complete two paragraphs about platypuses.

I. The adult platypus lives in a camping burrow.
  A. Burrows are holes dug underground.
  B. A tunnel leads to the burrow.
  C. The tunnel's opening is hidden by grass and bushes.

II. The female platypus digs a nesting burrow.
  A. She puts folded wet leaves in it.
  B. She covers the opening.
  C. She lays her eggs in it.

An adult platypus lives in a camping burrow. A burrow is a hole dug underground. There is a tunnel leading to the burrow. The opening of the tunnel is hidden by grass and bushes.

A female platypus digs a nesting burrow. First, she puts folded wet leaves in the burrow. Then she covers the opening. Finally, she lays her eggs in the nest.

104 EXPOSITORY WRITING — Nonfiction Writing • EMC 6013 • © Evan-Moor Corp.

Page 105 / Student Book Page 75

Name: ____________ Research Report

Writing a Topic Sentence

A. Each paragraph has a missing topic sentence. Read each paragraph. Then check the box next to the best topic sentence to begin the paragraph.

1. ________ As glaciers slowly move across land, they push everything in their way. They drag rocks and trees. They carve out valleys. Glaciers even grind down mountains.
   - ☑ Glaciers are very powerful.
   - ☐ Glaciers are easy to spot.

2. ________ Some Native Americans who lived in woodlands built homes from birch trees. Those who lived in the desert often made houses from clay and sand. Plains tribes lived in teepees, which could be moved.
   - ☐ The houses that people live in have changed over time.
   - ☑ Native Americans have lived in different kinds of homes.

B. Read each paragraph. Write a topic sentence that tells the main idea of the paragraph.

1. Hurricanes can cause a lot of damage.
Hurricane winds often lift roofs from buildings. They send cars sailing through the air. Hurricanes can also cause flooding. They bring a lot of rain, which causes the water level to rise quickly in lakes and rivers. The water can flood homes and stores.

2. English and Hawaiian are both spoken in Hawaii.
People in Hawaii speak English at school and at work. Some people also speak Hawaiian, especially at home. Because both languages are important, they are both official languages of the state.

3. Old tires are used to make many things.
Sometimes old tires are cut up into small pieces. The rubber bits are used to make the floor of children's playgrounds softer. Many old tires are used to make shoes. Tires can also be used to make a new kind of sidewalk.

© Evan-Moor Corp. • EMC 6013 • Nonfiction Writing — EXPOSITORY WRITING 105

Page 106 / Student Book Page 76

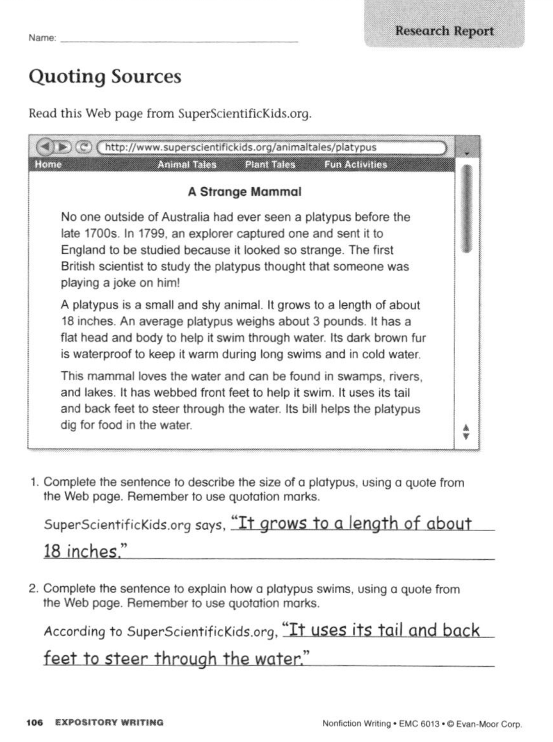
Name: ______________________ Research Report

Quoting Sources

Read this Web page from SuperScientificKids.org.

http://www.superscientifickids.org/animaltales/platypus

Home Animal Tales Plant Tales Fun Activities

A Strange Mammal

No one outside of Australia had ever seen a platypus before the late 1700s. In 1799, an explorer captured one and sent it to England to be studied because it looked so strange. The first British scientist to study the platypus thought that someone was playing a joke on him!

A platypus is a small and shy animal. It grows to a length of about 18 inches. An average platypus weighs about 3 pounds. It has a flat head and body to help it swim through water. Its dark brown fur is waterproof to keep it warm during long swims and in cold water.

This mammal loves the water and can be found in swamps, rivers, and lakes. It has webbed front feet to help it swim. It uses its tail and back feet to steer through the water. Its bill helps the platypus dig for food in the water.

1. Complete the sentence to describe the size of a platypus, using a quote from the Web page. Remember to use quotation marks.

   SuperScientificKids.org says, "It grows to a length of about 18 inches."

2. Complete the sentence to explain how a platypus swims, using a quote from the Web page. Remember to use quotation marks.

   According to SuperScientificKids.org, "It uses its tail and back feet to steer through the water."

106 EXPOSITORY WRITING Nonfiction Writing • EMC 6013 • © Evan-Moor Corp.

Lesson 8 Quoting Sources

1. Have students underline the quotation in the first paragraph of "The Peculiar Platypus." *("The first British scientist to study the platypus ...")* Explain that a quotation is someone's exact words.
2. Say: **When you want to use the exact words from a source, you must write the words inside quotation marks and tell who said them or which source they came from.** Point out that in "The Peculiar Platypus," the author tells us that the quotation comes from SuperScientificKids.org.
3. Direct students to p. 106 and explain that the Web page is from SuperScientificKids.org. Read it aloud and have students underline the sentence that was quoted in "The Peculiar Platypus."
4. Say: **The writer of "The Peculiar Platypus" could have used other quotations from this source. Which sentence from the Web page on p. 106 could the writer have used to describe where a platypus lives?** (e.g., *This mammal loves the water ...*)
5. Read aloud the first item on p. 106 and complete it with the class. Then have students complete item 2 independently.

Page 107 / Student Book Page 77

Name: ______________________ Research Report

Removing Unimportant Details

Read each paragraph. Underline the sentence that tells the main idea. Then cross out the sentence that does not belong.

1. The Chumash were Native Americans who once lived along the coast of Central and Southern California. They were very good at fishing. ~~The Yokuts and Ohlone were other tribes in the area.~~ The Chumash were one of the few tribes that traveled in boats on the ocean. They used boats for trading, fishing, and whaling.
2. Some animals use poison to protect themselves. For example, the fire salamander squirts poison at its enemies from glands on its back. A few types of octopus release poisonous ink when they are threatened. ~~And some lizards are the same color as the plants and rocks where they live.~~
3. Art has been popping up on sidewalks everywhere. Chalk artists create amazing drawings on the ground. ~~I wish I could draw well.~~ Some of the drawings look like paintings. Others are 3-D. One artist made it look like he was falling into a hole in the ground!
4. The ice-cream cone was invented at the 1904 World's Fair. The person selling ice cream ran out of dishes. ~~Vanilla was the most popular flavor.~~ The person in the booth next door was selling a thin kind of waffle. That person had the idea of rolling the waffles into cones and putting the ice cream on top.
5. Mercury is the closest planet to the sun, which gives the planet some unique features. Mercury has a temperature of 800°F during the day. ~~It is the smallest planet.~~ And if someone stood on Mercury, the sun would look three times bigger than it does on Earth.
6. Experts now think that blue jeans were invented in Italy in the 1650s. Paintings from that time show people sewing and wearing denim. Denim is the material that jeans are made from. ~~Blue jeans are very comfortable.~~ At one time, people thought that denim was first made in France.

© Evan-Moor Corp. • EMC 6013 • Nonfiction Writing EXPOSITORY WRITING 107

Lesson 9 Removing Unimportant Details

1. Say: **As you research, you will find a lot of information. But you may not need all of it in your report.** Point out how all of the information in "The Peculiar Platypus" is about the platypus, and that the details in each paragraph support the topic sentence.
2. Direct students to p. 107. Read item 1 aloud. Ask: **What is the topic sentence?** *(The Chumash were ...)* **Do all of the detail sentences tell about the Chumash?** (no) **Which one tells something different?** *(The Yokuts and Ohlone ...)* Say: **That sentence may be a fact, but it does not tell about the Chumash. It should not be in the paragraph.** Have students cross out the sentence.
3. Have students complete the activity independently or in pairs. Review the answers as a class.

➤ **Extend the Lesson:** Challenge students to research one of the topics on p. 107 and write a new sentence to replace the one they crossed out.

Lesson 10 Listing Sources

1. Display the bibliography model on p. 99 and say: **A research report always includes a *bibliography*, or list of sources that the writer used to research the topic and write about it. A bibliography tells where the information came from. It is important to list your sources so your audience knows where you found the information.**
2. Point out the first entry in the model and say: **If your source is a Web page, like this one, you should list the title of the Web page, the organization or person who created the Web page, and the Web page address.** Point out that the other sources listed in the bibliography are a magazine and a book. Discuss the features of each entry.
3. Read aloud the directions on p. 108 and guide students through item 1. Have students complete items 2 and 3 in pairs. Review the answers as a class.

➤ **Extend the Lesson:** Have students locate the bibliographies in various nonfiction texts.

Lesson 11 Reviewing a Research Report

1. Review some of the qualities of a good research report: paragraphs with topic sentences and supporting details, facts that answer questions about the topic, and quotations from different sources.
2. Read aloud the Web page, the notecard, and the draft on p. 109. Ask: **What source did the writer use?** (AustralianAnimals.com) **What question was the writer trying to answer?** (What makes dingoes special?) Then guide students through revising the draft. Ask: **Is there one sentence that tells the main idea of the paragraph?** (no) Encourage students to suggest a suitable topic sentence that states the main idea—that dingoes are special animals. Then ask: **Does the paragraph include all of the facts from the notes?** (No. It doesn't say that dingoes hardly ever bark.) Read aloud this sentence from the paragraph: *Dingoes are brown.* Ask: **Is this detail important to the topic?** (no) Suggest that students omit this detail from their revised paragraphs. Read the final sentence: *A Web site says that dingoes can open doors.* Ask: **How can we change this sentence to make it stronger?** (add a quotation from the source)
3. Have students write their revisions on a separate sheet of paper. Invite volunteers to share their reports.

Page 108 / Student Book Page 78

Name: ______________________ Research Report

Listing Sources

Read each bibliography entry. Then answer the questions to identify information about the source.

1. **Book**

   Taylor, Frank. *The Life of a Platypus.* New York: Yancey Press, 2005.

   What is the title of the book? The Life of a Platypus

   Who is the author? Frank Taylor

   When was the book published? 2005

2. **Internet source**

   "Secrets of the Platypus." *Amazing Mammals.* <http://amazingmammals.org/secrets.>

   What is the name of the Internet source? Amazing Mammals

   What is the name of the Web page? "Secrets of the Platypus"

3. **Magazine article**

   Leisner, Tamika. "Very Special Puggles." *Wildlife.* 21 Feb. 2009: 8–10.

   What is the name of the article? "Very Special Puggles"

   What is the name of the magazine? Wildlife

   Who wrote the article? Tamika Leisner

   Which pages is the article on? pages 8–10

108 EXPOSITORY WRITING Nonfiction Writing • EMC 6013 • © Evan-Moor Corp.

Page 109 and Sample Revision / Student Book Page 79

Name: ______________________ Research Report

Sample Answer

Dingoes

Dingoes are special animals that live in Australia. They look like dogs, but they are wild animals. Dingoes howl, huff, and whine, but they hardly ever bark. Dingoes have wrists that are not like a dog's wrists. A dingo can bend and turn its wrists. "This means that a dingo can learn how to turn a doorknob," says the Web site AustralianAnimals.com.

Name: ______________________________

Introducing a Research Report

Read this example of a research report.

Writing Model

The Peculiar Platypus

What lays eggs like a reptile but has a bill like a duck's and fur like a beaver's? A platypus! According to SuperScientificKids.org, "The first British scientist to study the platypus thought that someone was playing a joke on him!" The scientist thought the animal was a fake. It is easy to see why. The platypus, which is an Australian mammal, has some unusual features.

A platypus is a small water mammal with brown fur. It is about 18 inches long and weighs about 3 pounds. Its fur protects it in cold water. The animal uses its paddle-shaped tail and webbed feet to swim. It uses its flat bill to dig for food.

A platypus gets its food by hunting in rivers and streams. It scoops up insects, shellfish, and worms. Then it stores food in its cheek pouches as it swims back to the surface to eat.

The platypus is one of only two mammals that lay eggs. A mother platypus digs special holes called burrows for her eggs. A baby platypus that hatches from its egg is called a *puggle*.

Although a platypus may look cuddly, people should not touch it! It is not friendly. A male platypus has sharp spurs on its back legs that contain venom. Being stung by a platypus hurts!

This odd animal may be funny-looking, but its unusual features help it stay alive. A platypus can live for about 13 years in the wild. So maybe being strange is not such a bad idea!

Writer's Purpose: ______________________________

____

Name: ____________________________________

Introducing a Research Report

Read these examples of a bibliography and an outline.

Bibliography Model

"Duck-Billed Platypus." SuperScientificKids.org. <http://superscientifickids.org/animaltales/platypus>

Estevez, Avi. "The Life of a Puggle." Puggle. 1 Feb. 2009: 19–22.

Roberts, Quin. Amazing Australian Animals. Sydney: Science Press, 2006.

Outline Model

I. The platypus is a strange-looking animal.
   A. It is about 18 inches long and weighs about 3 pounds.
   B. Its fur, which is brown, protects it in cold water.
   C. It uses its tail and webbed feet to swim.
   D. It uses its flat bill to dig.

II. The platypus hunts in rivers and streams.
   A. It uses its bill to scoop up insects, shellfish, and worms to eat.
   B. It stores food in its cheeks.

III. The platypus is one of only two mammals that lay eggs.
   A. Mothers dig burrows for eggs.
   B. Babies are called "puggles."

IV. People should not try to touch a platypus.
   A. It is not a friendly animal.
   B. Males have sharp spurs on their back legs.
   C. The spurs contain venom that stings.

Name: ______________________

Thinking of Questions

Read each topic. Write three important questions to answer in a report about the topic.

Example

Topic: the platypus

Questions:

What does a platypus look like?

Where does a platypus live?

How does a platypus eat?

1. **Topic:** penguins

   Questions:

   ____

   ____

   ____

2. **Topic:** Abraham Lincoln

   Questions:

   ____

   ____

   ____

3. **Topic:** the sun

   Questions:

   ____

   ____

   ____

Name: ______________________________

Finding Information

A. Read this Web page about the platypus. Then answer the questions.

1. What is the title of this Web page? ______________________________
2. What is the Web page address? ______________________________
3. What is one link on the Web page? ______________________________

B. Read the encyclopedia entry below. Then answer the questions.

Encyclopedia of Mammals **863**

Platypus A mammal that lives along the banks of freshwater areas in Australia. It has a broad and flat tail, webbed feet, and a snout like a duck's bill. It feeds by diving underwater and using its snout to dig for small animals.

1. What is the topic of the entry? ______________________________
2. What page is the entry on? ______________________________
3. What is the name of the encyclopedia? ______________________________

Name: ____

Taking Notes

Read the information from each source. Copy the name of the source onto the notecard. Then write at least two notes about what the source says.

Example

Source: *Encyclopedia of Mammals,* p. 331

Platypus A mammal that lives along the banks of freshwater areas in Australia. It has a broad and flat tail, webbed feet, and a snout like a duck's bill.

Encyclopedia of Mammals, p. 331
- lives in freshwater areas in Australia
- has flat tail, webbed feet, and a snout like a duck's bill

1. **Source:** Platypus Society Web site, www.savetheplatypus.org

   Until 100 years ago, people hunted the platypus for its fur. This greatly reduced its numbers. Hunting the animal is now illegal, so the platypus population has grown. But the animal is still in danger from pollution and litter.

2. **Source:** *Puggle*, May 2011

   Twin female baby platypuses, called *puggles,* were born last month in Taronga Zoo in Sydney, Australia. They are among the few platypuses that have been born in zoos. Although platypuses are not an endangered species, the areas where they live are shrinking. So zoos are helping to make sure platypuses will not become extinct.

Name: ______________________________

Writing an Outline

Use the facts on the notebook paper to complete the outline.

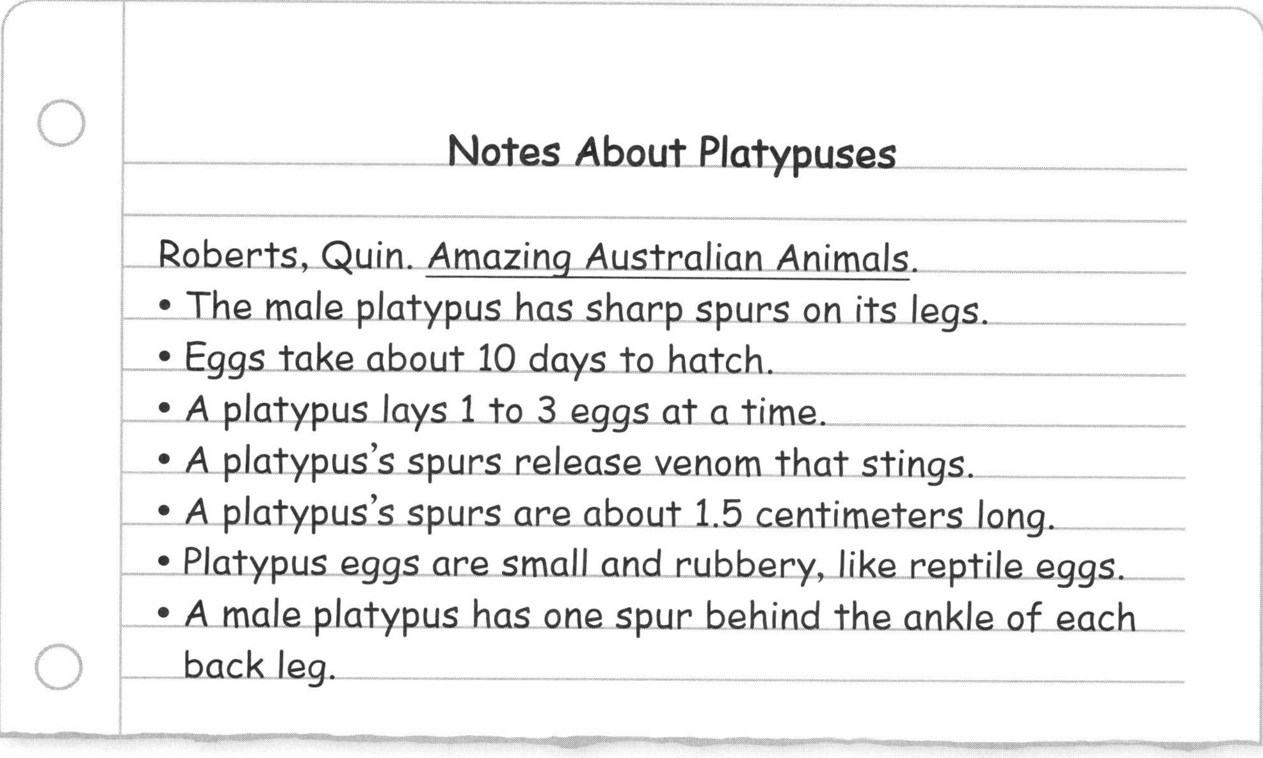

Notes About Platypuses

Roberts, Quin. Amazing Australian Animals.

- The male platypus has sharp spurs on its legs.
- Eggs take about 10 days to hatch.
- A platypus lays 1 to 3 eggs at a time.
- A platypus's spurs release venom that stings.
- A platypus's spurs are about 1.5 centimeters long.
- Platypus eggs are small and rubbery, like reptile eggs.
- A male platypus has one spur behind the ankle of each back leg.

I. The female platypus lays eggs.

A. ______________________________

B. ______________________________

C. ______________________________

II. ______________________________

A. A platypus's spurs release venom that stings.

B. ______________________________

C. ______________________________

____

Name: ____

Using an Outline to Write

Use the notes from the outline to complete two paragraphs about platypuses.

I. The adult platypus lives in a camping burrow.
   A. Burrows are holes dug underground.
   B. A tunnel leads to the burrow.
   C. The tunnel's opening is hidden by grass and bushes.

II. The female platypus digs a nesting burrow.
   A. She puts folded wet leaves in it.
   B. She covers the opening.
   C. She lays her eggs in it.

An adult platypus lives in a camping burrow. ____________________

____

____

____

____

A female platypus digs a nesting burrow. ____________________

____

____

____

____

Name: ______________________________

Writing a Topic Sentence

A. Each paragraph has a missing topic sentence. Read each paragraph. Then check the box next to the best topic sentence to begin the paragraph.

1. __________ As glaciers slowly move across land, they push everything in their way. They drag rocks and trees. They carve out valleys. Glaciers even grind down mountains.

   ☐ Glaciers are very powerful.

   ☐ Glaciers are easy to spot.

2. __________ Some Native Americans who lived in woodlands built homes from birch trees. Those who lived in the desert often made houses from clay and sand. Plains tribes lived in teepees, which could be moved.

   ☐ The houses that people live in have changed over time.

   ☐ Native Americans have lived in different kinds of homes.

B. Read each paragraph. Write a topic sentence that tells the main idea of the paragraph.

1. ____

   Hurricane winds often lift roofs from buildings. They send cars sailing through the air. Hurricanes can also cause flooding. They bring a lot of rain, which causes the water level to rise quickly in lakes and rivers. The water can flood homes and stores.

2. ____

   People in Hawaii speak English at school and at work. Some people also speak Hawaiian, especially at home. Because both languages are important, they are both official languages of the state.

3. ____

   Sometimes old tires are cut up into small pieces. The rubber bits are used to make the floor of children's playgrounds softer. Many old tires are used to make shoes. Tires can also be used to make a new kind of sidewalk.

Name: ______________________________

Quoting Sources

Read this Web page from SuperScientificKids.org.

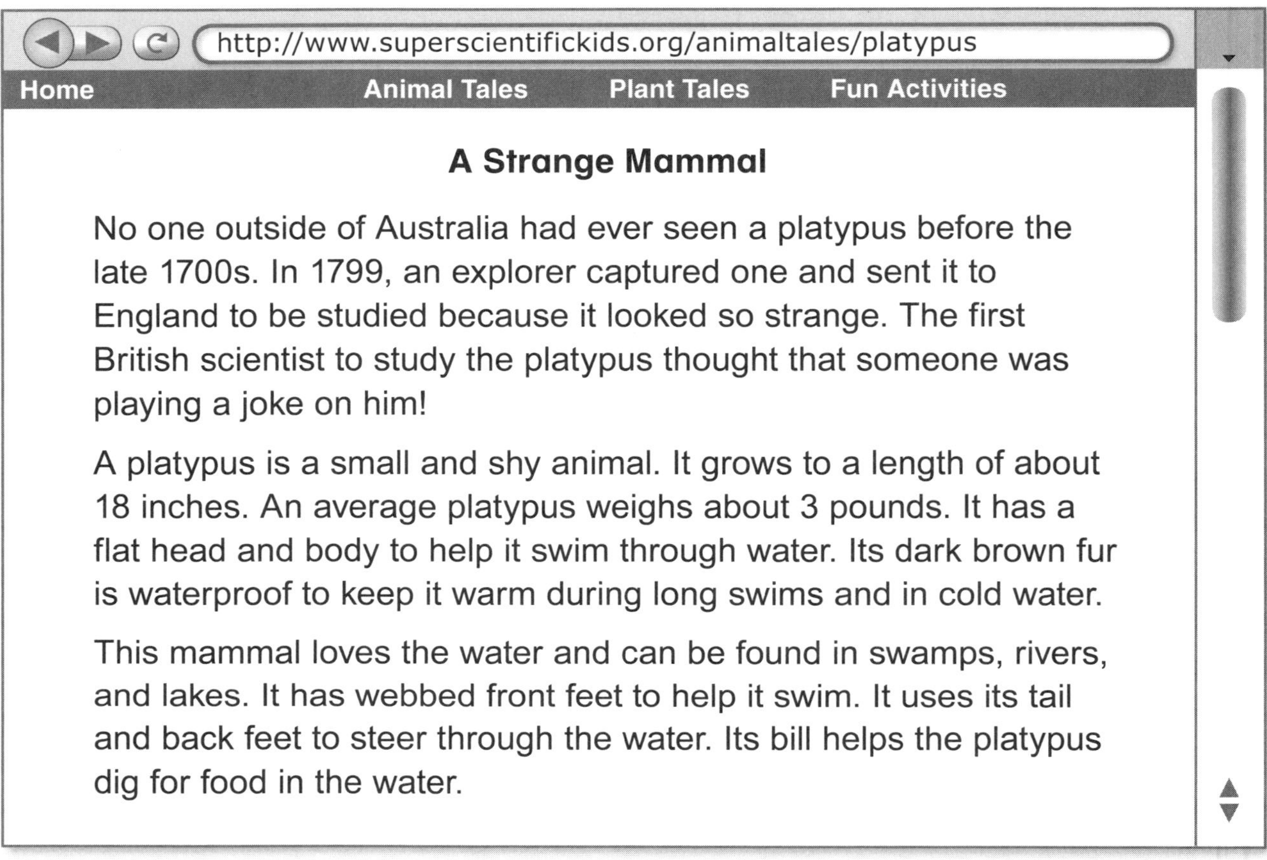

http://www.superscientifickids.org/animaltales/platypus

Home Animal Tales Plant Tales Fun Activities

A Strange Mammal

No one outside of Australia had ever seen a platypus before the late 1700s. In 1799, an explorer captured one and sent it to England to be studied because it looked so strange. The first British scientist to study the platypus thought that someone was playing a joke on him!

A platypus is a small and shy animal. It grows to a length of about 18 inches. An average platypus weighs about 3 pounds. It has a flat head and body to help it swim through water. Its dark brown fur is waterproof to keep it warm during long swims and in cold water.

This mammal loves the water and can be found in swamps, rivers, and lakes. It has webbed front feet to help it swim. It uses its tail and back feet to steer through the water. Its bill helps the platypus dig for food in the water.

1. Complete the sentence to describe the size of a platypus, using a quote from the Web page. Remember to use quotation marks.

   SuperScientificKids.org says, ______________________________

   ____

2. Complete the sentence to explain how a platypus swims, using a quote from the Web page. Remember to use quotation marks.

   According to SuperScientificKids.org, ______________________________

   ____

Name: ______________________________

Removing Unimportant Details

Read each paragraph. Underline the sentence that tells the main idea. Then cross out the sentence that does not belong.

1. The Chumash were Native Americans who once lived along the coast of Central and Southern California. They were very good at fishing. The Yokuts and Ohlone were other tribes in the area. The Chumash were one of the few tribes that traveled in boats on the ocean. They used boats for trading, fishing, and whaling.

2. Some animals use poison to protect themselves. For example, the fire salamander squirts poison at its enemies from glands on its back. A few types of octopus release poisonous ink when they are threatened. And some lizards are the same color as the plants and rocks where they live.

3. Art has been popping up on sidewalks everywhere. Chalk artists create amazing drawings on the ground. I wish I could draw well. Some of the drawings look like paintings. Others are 3-D. One artist made it look like he was falling into a hole in the ground!

4. The ice-cream cone was invented at the 1904 World's Fair. The person selling ice cream ran out of dishes. Vanilla was the most popular flavor. The person in the booth next door was selling a thin kind of waffle. That person had the idea of rolling the waffles into cones and putting the ice cream on top.

5. Mercury is the closest planet to the sun, which gives the planet some unique features. Mercury has a temperature of 800°F during the day. It is the smallest planet. And if someone stood on Mercury, the sun would look three times bigger than it does on Earth.

6. Experts now think that blue jeans were invented in Italy in the 1650s. Paintings from that time show people sewing and wearing denim. Denim is the material that jeans are made from. Blue jeans are very comfortable. At one time, people thought that denim was first made in France.

Name: ______________________________

Listing Sources

Read each bibliography entry. Then answer the questions to identify information about the source.

1. **Book**

   Taylor, Frank. *The Life of a Platypus.*
   New York: Yancey Press, 2005.

   What is the title of the book? ______________________________

   Who is the author? ______________________________

   When was the book published? ______________________________

2. **Internet source**

   "Secrets of the Platypus." *Amazing Mammals.*
   <http://amazingmammals.org/secrets.>

   What is the name of the Internet source? ______________________________

   What is the name of the Web page? ______________________________

3. **Magazine article**

   Leisner, Tamika. "Very Special Puggles."
   Wildlife. 21 Feb. 2009: 8–10.

   What is the name of the article? ______________________________

   What is the name of the magazine? ______________________________

   Who wrote the article? ______________________________

   Which pages is the article on? ______________________________

Name: ____

Reviewing a Research Report

Read the Web page and the notes. Use them to revise the first paragraph of a research report about dingoes. Write your paragraph on a separate sheet of paper.

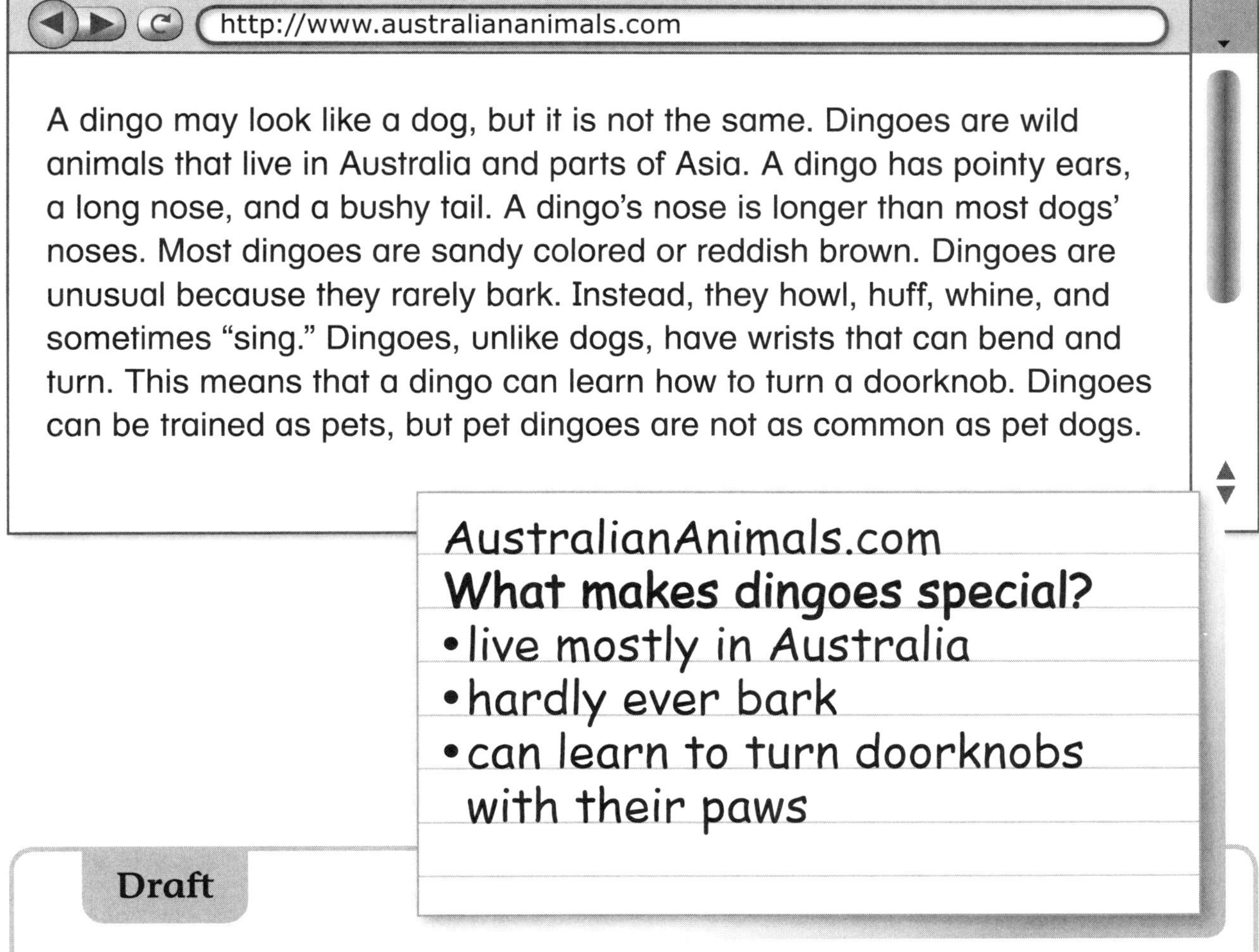

Draft

Dingoes

A dingo looks like a dog, but it is not a dog. Dingoes live in Australia. They make many different kinds of noises. Dingoes are brown. Dingoes can move their wrists. A Web site says that dingoes can open doors.

Writing a Persuasive Paragraph

Page 113 / Student Book Page 81

Name: ______________________

Persuasive Paragraph

Introducing a Persuasive Paragraph

Read this example of a persuasive paragraph.

Writing Model

Let's Keep Our Field

I know that our school is getting a new playground where the field is, but half of the field should be kept as it is. That would give students space to run around and play sports. The area could also be used for gym classes. And the school would save money because it would not have to buy as much playground equipment. That is why I think it is important to change the playground plans immediately and leave half of the area as a grassy field.

Writer's Purpose: to persuade readers that only half of a field at school should become a playground

© Evan-Moor Corp. • EMC 6013 • Nonfiction Writing   PERSUASIVE WRITING 113

Page 114 / Student Book Page 82

Name: ______________________

Persuasive Paragraph

Writing a Topic Sentence

A. Read each paragraph. Then check the box next to the best topic sentence for the paragraph.

1. __________ Sometimes it gets very hot at school. Recess is not fun when we have to wear long pants. Shorts would keep us cooler.
   - ☐ We get too hot when we ride the bus after school.
   - ☑ Students should be able to wear shorts to school.

2. __________ A class pet would teach us how to care for an animal. We would feed it and give it water. We would learn what it needs to live. We could also take turns playing with it.
   - ☑ We should have a class pet.
   - ☐ Some kids would like to get a hamster.

B. Write a topic sentence for each paragraph.

1. Students should have more computer time at school. Now we use computers only 30 minutes a week. That is not very long. If we had more time on the computer, we could read science and social studies articles on the Internet. We could use computers for class projects. We could even talk with other students from around the world.

2. The city streets should have more bike lanes. More people than ever ride their bikes to school and to work. Riding on roads that do not have bike lanes is not safe. Bike lanes would help protect riders. And if there were bike lanes on more roads, even more people would ride bikes.

114 PERSUASIVE WRITING   Nonfiction Writing • EMC 6013 • © Evan-Moor Corp.

Lesson 1 Introducing a Persuasive Paragraph

A persuasive paragraph is written to persuade others to agree with the writer or to take a specific action.

1. Invite students to tell about an experience in which they tried to persuade their parents to let them do something. Then say: **Another way to persuade people to agree with you or to take a certain action is to put your opinion in writing.**

2. Direct students to "Let's Keep Our Field" on p. 113. Read it aloud as students follow along. Then ask: **What is the purpose of this paragraph?** (to persuade readers that only half of a field at school should become a playground) Have students write the purpose on the lines provided.

3. Invite students to offer opinions about what makes this a good persuasive paragraph. Prompt students by asking: **Does the writer clearly state her opinion about the plans for the playground? Does she give good reasons why the playground should take up only half of the field? Does the conclusion of the paragraph state the writer's opinion in a new way?** Then explain that students will use the model as they practice the skills needed to write a good persuasive paragraph.

Lesson 2 Writing a Topic Sentence

1. Remind students that every paragraph should have a topic sentence, or a sentence that tells what the paragraph is about. Then say: **The topic sentence of a persuasive paragraph should also give an opinion.** Ask: **What is the topic sentence in "Let's Keep Our Field"?** (the first sentence) **What is the writer's opinion?** (that half of the field should be kept as it is)

2. Read aloud the first item in Activity A on p. 114. Ask: **What is the topic of the paragraph?** (school clothes in hot weather) **Which sentence choice states an opinion about school clothes?** (the second one) Have students answer item 2 in pairs.

3. Read aloud the directions for Activity B. Have students complete the activity in pairs. Invite volunteers to share their answers and explain why they are good topic sentences.

➤ **Extend the Lesson:** Make copies of persuasive paragraphs that have had their topic sentences removed. Have students write topic sentences for those paragraphs.

Lesson 3 Using Persuasive Language

1. Remind students that a persuasive paragraph needs to be convincing. Have a volunteer read aloud the first sentence in "Let's Keep Our Field." Then have students find and circle the word *should* in the sentence. Say: **When you want to be persuasive, use words such as *should* and *must* to make your point stronger.**
2. Have a student read aloud the last sentence of the model. Say: **This sentence also contains powerful words.** Ask: **Which words tell you how strongly the writer feels?** *(important, immediately)* Have students circle those words. Point out that words such as *always, never, definitely, now,* and *necessary* may also be used in persuasive writing.
3. Have students complete Activity A on p. 115 in pairs. Review the answers as a class, and discuss how the circled words make the sentences persuasive.
4. Read the directions for Activity B. Discuss the first item and invite students to brainstorm other possible sentences. Then have students complete the activity in pairs. Invite volunteers to share their answers.

➤ **Extend the Lesson:** Have students write additional persuasive sentences using the words in the box on p. 115.

Lesson 4 Giving Reasons

1. Say: **When you want to be persuasive, you must give good reasons for your opinion.** Direct students to "Let's Keep Our Field." Ask: **What reasons does this writer give for keeping half of the field as an open space?** (so students have a place to run around and play sports; so they have an area for gym classes; to save money)
2. Read the directions for Activity A on p. 116. Then read aloud the first item and ask: **Which sentence gives a better reason why the school should have an art teacher?** (the second one) Have students complete item 2 independently.
3. Read aloud the directions for Activity B. Then read aloud the first opinion. Ask: **Why might it be a good idea to know how to swim?** Guide students to record two reasons. Then have students complete the second item in pairs. Invite volunteers to share their answers.

➤ **Extend the Lesson:** Have students choose one of the topics on p. 115 and complete a graphic organizer like the ones on p. 116 for that topic.

Page 115 / Student Book Page 83

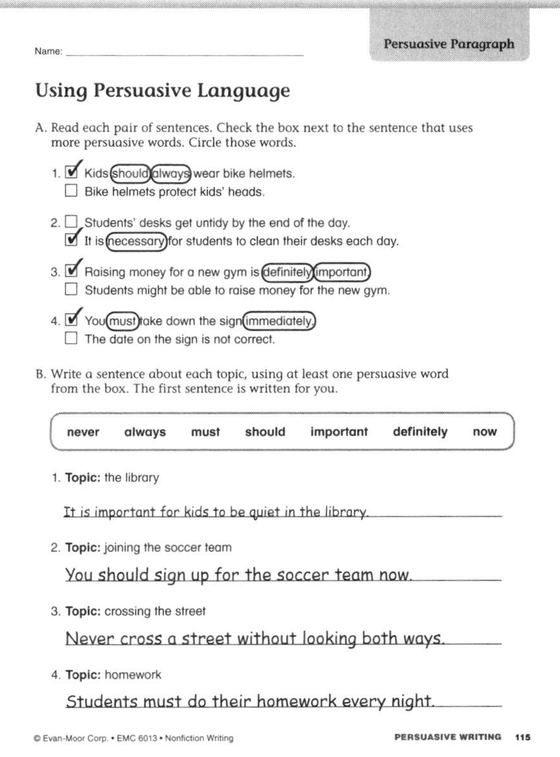

Name: ______________________ Persuasive Paragraph

Using Persuasive Language

A. Read each pair of sentences. Check the box next to the sentence that uses more persuasive words. Circle those words.

1. ☑ Kids (should) (always) wear bike helmets.
   ☐ Bike helmets protect kids' heads.
2. ☐ Students' desks get untidy by the end of the day.
   ☑ It is (necessary) for students to clean their desks each day.
3. ☑ Raising money for a new gym is (definitely) (important).
   ☐ Students might be able to raise money for the new gym.
4. ☑ You (must) take down the sign (immediately).
   ☐ The date on the sign is not correct.

B. Write a sentence about each topic, using at least one persuasive word from the box. The first sentence is written for you.

never	always	must	should	important	definitely	now

1. **Topic:** the library
   It is important for kids to be quiet in the library.
2. **Topic:** joining the soccer team
   You should sign up for the soccer team now.
3. **Topic:** crossing the street
   Never cross a street without looking both ways.
4. **Topic:** homework
   Students must do their homework every night.

© Evan-Moor Corp. • EMC 6013 • Nonfiction Writing PERSUASIVE WRITING 115

Page 116 / Student Book Page 84

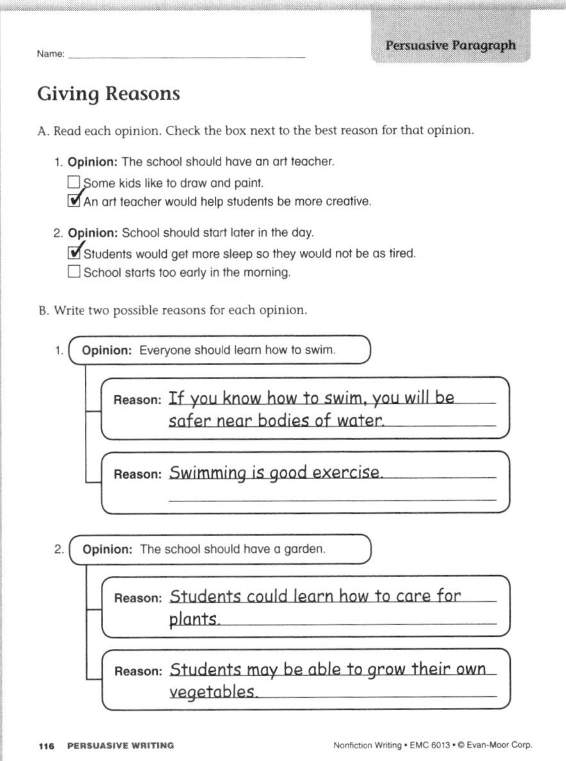

Name: ______________________ Persuasive Paragraph

Giving Reasons

A. Read each opinion. Check the box next to the best reason for that opinion.

1. **Opinion:** The school should have an art teacher.
   ☐ Some kids like to draw and paint.
   ☑ An art teacher would help students be more creative.
2. **Opinion:** School should start later in the day.
   ☑ Students would get more sleep so they would not be as tired.
   ☐ School starts too early in the morning.

B. Write two possible reasons for each opinion.

1. **Opinion:** Everyone should learn how to swim.
   Reason: If you know how to swim, you will be safer near bodies of water.
   Reason: Swimming is good exercise.
2. **Opinion:** The school should have a garden.
   Reason: Students could learn how to care for plants.
   Reason: Students may be able to grow their own vegetables.

116 PERSUASIVE WRITING Nonfiction Writing • EMC 6013 • © Evan-Moor Corp.

Page 117 / Student Book Page 85

Name: ______________________ Persuasive Paragraph

Writing a Conclusion

Read each paragraph. Underline the topic sentence. Then write a concluding sentence that retells the topic sentence in a different way.

1. Kids should walk to school if they can. Walking is good exercise. It helps people stay fit. It helps get kids going in the morning so they are ready to learn. Walking even gives kids more energy to play after school.

   The more often kids walk to school, the better they will feel.

2. Kids should eat more fruit. Fruits such as apples and oranges give us important vitamins. They also give us energy to learn and play. Fruits are tasty and easy to eat, and they make good snacks.

   Kids should eat fruit every day.

3. Parents should not let their kids ride a bike without a helmet. Children can easily fall off their bikes or get hit by a car. They need bike helmets for protection. Without a helmet, a bike rider can be hurt badly.

   Parents need to make sure their kids always wear a helmet.

4. Kids should try to keep their rooms clean. It is easier to find things in a neat and tidy room than it is in a messy room. It is also easier to do your homework in a space where everything is in order. Keeping your room clean will help your toys and clothes stay nice. A clean room will even help you feel happier.

   Be sure to clean your room today.

5. It is important to wash your hands often. You should always wash your hands after using the bathroom and before eating. Dirty hands spread germs, which can make people ill. Washing your hands will help you and others stay healthy.

   Wash your hands whenever you can.

© Evan-Moor Corp. • EMC 6013 • Nonfiction Writing PERSUASIVE WRITING 117

Page 118 and Sample Revision / Student Book Page 86

Name: ______________________ Persuasive Paragraph

Sample Answer

Snacks in Class

Teachers should allow students to eat snacks during class. Some kids get really hungry before lunch. Some kids have had to miss breakfast. If kids could eat snacks in class, then they would be able to pay attention better. They would have more energy to work and learn. Teachers need to let students have snacks in the classroom so they do not get hungry.

Lesson 5 Writing a Conclusion

1. Say: **The final sentence in a persuasive paragraph is your last chance to persuade your readers to agree with you about the topic.** Ask a volunteer to read the last sentence in "Let's Keep Our Field." Then review the topic sentence and explain: **The conclusion states the topic again and gives the writer's opinion in a fresh way.**

2. Direct students to p. 117. Use the first item to model the activity. Ask: **What is this paragraph mostly about?** (the benefits of walking to school) **What is the writer's opinion on this topic?** (that kids should walk to school) **What is the topic sentence of this paragraph?** *(Kids should walk to school if they can.)* **To write a good conclusion, we need to make the same strong, persuasive point.** Ask students for suggestions. Then have them complete the activity independently or in pairs.

➤ **Extend the Lesson:** Have students write a conclusion for each paragraph in Activity B on p. 114.

Lesson 6 Reviewing a Persuasive Paragraph

1. Review the qualities of a good persuasive paragraph: a topic sentence that states an opinion and tells the topic; powerful, persuasive language; convincing reasons; and a strong conclusion that restates the topic and the opinion.

2. Read aloud "Snacks in Class" on p. 118 as students follow along. Then ask: **What is the topic of the paragraph?** (eating snacks during classtime) **Does the topic sentence state an opinion about snacks in class?** (no) As a class, brainstorm topic sentences that clearly state an opinion. Then invite students to suggest other ways in which the paragraph could be improved. Prompt by asking: **Does the paragraph contain strong persuasive words?** (no) **What are some reasons that students should be allowed to eat snacks in class?** (Some kids get hungry and can't pay attention.) **Can you think of other reasons?** (e.g., Some kids have to skip breakfast.) **Does the paragraph have a concluding sentence that tells the opinion in a new way?** (no)

3. Have students revise the paragraph independently on a separate sheet of paper. Remind them that there may be different ways to revise it.

4. Invite students to share their revisions with the class.

Name: ____________________________________

Introducing a Persuasive Paragraph

Read this example of a persuasive paragraph.

Writing Model

Let's Keep Our Field

I know that our school is getting a new playground where the field is, but half of the field should be kept as it is. That would give students space to run around and play sports. The area could also be used for gym classes. And the school would save money because it would not have to buy as much playground equipment. That is why I think it is important to change the playground plans immediately and leave half of the area as a grassy field.

Writer's Purpose: ____________________________________

____

Name: ______________________________

Writing a Topic Sentence

A. Read each paragraph. Then check the box next to the best topic sentence for the paragraph.

1. ____________ Sometimes it gets very hot at school. Recess is not fun when we have to wear long pants. Shorts would keep us cooler.

   - ☐ We get too hot when we ride the bus after school.
   - ☐ Students should be able to wear shorts to school.

2. ____________ A class pet would teach us how to care for an animal. We would feed it and give it water. We would learn what it needs to live. We could also take turns playing with it.

   - ☐ We should have a class pet.
   - ☐ Some kids would like to get a hamster.

B. Write a topic sentence for each paragraph.

1. ____

   Now we use computers only 30 minutes a week. That is not very long. If we had more time on the computer, we could read science and social studies articles on the Internet. We could use computers for class projects. We could even talk with other students from around the world.

2. ____

   More people than ever ride their bikes to school and to work. Riding on roads that do not have bike lanes is not safe. Bike lanes would help protect riders. And if there were bike lanes on more roads, even more people would ride bikes.

Name: ______________________________

Using Persuasive Language

A. Read each pair of sentences. Check the box next to the sentence that uses more persuasive words. Circle those words.

1. ☐ Kids should always wear bike helmets.
   ☐ Bike helmets protect kids' heads.

2. ☐ Students' desks get untidy by the end of the day.
   ☐ It is necessary for students to clean their desks each day.

3. ☐ Raising money for a new gym is definitely important.
   ☐ Students might be able to raise money for the new gym.

4. ☐ You must take down the sign immediately.
   ☐ The date on the sign is not correct.

B. Write a sentence about each topic, using at least one persuasive word from the box. The first sentence is written for you.

never	always	must	should	important	definitely	now

1. **Topic:** the library

   It is important for kids to be quiet in the library.

2. **Topic:** joining the soccer team

   ____

3. **Topic:** crossing the street

   ____

4. **Topic:** homework

   ____

Name: ____________________

Giving Reasons

A. Read each opinion. Check the box next to the best reason for that opinion.

1. **Opinion:** The school should have an art teacher.
   - ☐ Some kids like to draw and paint.
   - ☐ An art teacher would help students be more creative.

2. **Opinion:** School should start later in the day.
   - ☐ Students would get more sleep so they would not be as tired.
   - ☐ School starts too early in the morning.

B. Write two possible reasons for each opinion.

1. **Opinion:** Everyone should learn how to swim.

   Reason: ____________________

   ____

   Reason: ____________________

   ____

2. **Opinion:** The school should have a garden.

   Reason: ____________________

   ____

   Reason: ____________________

   ____

Name: ________________________________

Writing a Conclusion

Read each paragraph. Underline the topic sentence. Then write a concluding sentence that retells the topic sentence in a different way.

1. Kids should walk to school if they can. Walking is good exercise. It helps people stay fit. It helps get kids going in the morning so they are ready to learn. Walking even gives kids more energy to play after school.

____

2. Kids should eat more fruit. Fruits such as apples and oranges give us important vitamins. They also give us energy to learn and play. Fruits are tasty and easy to eat, and they make good snacks.

____

3. Parents should not let their kids ride a bike without a helmet. Children can easily fall off their bikes or get hit by a car. They need bike helmets for protection. Without a helmet, a bike rider can be hurt badly.

____

4. Kids should try to keep their rooms clean. It is easier to find things in a neat and tidy room than it is in a messy room. It is also easier to do your homework in a space where everything is in order. Keeping your room clean will help your toys and clothes stay nice. A clean room will even help you feel happier.

____

5. It is important to wash your hands often. You should always wash your hands after using the bathroom and before eating. Dirty hands spread germs, which can make people ill. Washing your hands will help you and others stay healthy.

____

Name: ____________________________________

Reviewing a Persuasive Paragraph

Revise this persuasive paragraph. Use what you have learned to make it stronger. Rewrite it on a separate sheet of paper.

Focus on:

- ✓ writing a topic sentence that gives an opinion
- ✓ using powerful, persuasive words
- ✓ giving reasons for the writer's opinion
- ✓ writing a conclusion that tells the writer's opinion in a different way

Draft

Snacks in Class

Kids like to eat snacks. Some kids get really hungry before lunch. If kids could eat snacks in class, then they would be able to pay attention better. They would have more energy to work and learn.

Writing a Persuasive Letter

Lesson 1 Introducing a Persuasive Letter

A persuasive letter is a letter written to persuade someone to agree with the writer or to take a specific action.

1. Say: **If you want to convince someone to do something, you can write a persuasive letter to that person.**
2. Direct students to p. 122 and explain that this letter is from a child to the president of a toy company. Ask: **Who wrote the letter?** (Anita Rangan) **To whom did she write it?** (Ivan Tahaffun) Say: **The person you write a letter to is your *audience*.** Read aloud the letter as students follow along. Then ask: **What is the purpose of this letter?** (to persuade the president of a toy company to reduce the price of a game) Have students write the audience and purpose on the lines provided.
3. Invite students to offer opinions about what makes this a good persuasive letter. Prompt students by asking: **Does the first sentence clearly state what Anita wants or believes? Does she give strong reasons to support her opinion? Does she include all of the necessary parts of a letter, such as a date and a greeting?** Then explain that students will use the model as they practice the skills needed to write a good persuasive letter.

➤ **Extend the Lesson:** Suggest topics for a persuasive letter (e.g., adding a specific feature to a toy or game or making a product easier to use). Have students brainstorm other topics.

Lesson 2 Writing an Opinion Statement

1. Review the purpose of a persuasive letter. Then say: **It is important to tell your audience right away why you're writing. You can do that by starting your letter with an *opinion statement*, or a sentence that tells your audience what you want them to do or believe.** Direct students to the model. Read aloud the first sentence and say: **This is the opinion statement. It clearly tells what the writer wants.**
2. Read aloud the directions for Activity A on p. 123. Guide students through the first item. Read aloud the sentences and say: **The first sentence states an opinion—that the diner should put garlic fries back on the menu. The second sentence just states a fact.** Have students complete the activity in pairs.
3. Read the example for Activity B and discuss why the revision is better. Then have students complete the activity in small groups and share their answers.

Page 122 / Student Book Page 88

Name: ______________________ **Persuasive Letter**

Introducing a Persuasive Letter

Read this example of a persuasive letter.

Writing Model

March 16, 2012

Mr. Ivan Tahaffun, President
True Toy Company, Inc.
P.O. Box 98765
Orlando, FL 52761

Dear Mr. Tahaffun,

You should reduce the price of your *Super Sleuth* video game. It costs too much for a game that can only be played once. The game is fun for just a few hours. The mysteries are fun to solve, but they are too easy. My five-year-old sister even solved one! Plus, I cannot play online with my friends. That is the best part of any video game. Forty dollars is a lot for a game with these problems. If you reduce the price, then more people might buy it.

Sincerely,
Anita Rangan

Writer's Audience: Ivan Tahaffun, president of True Toy Company

Writer's Purpose: to persuade the president of a toy company to reduce the price of a game

122 PERSUASIVE WRITING Nonfiction Writing • EMC 6013 • © Evan-Moor Corp.

Page 123 / Student Book Page 89

Name: ______________________ **Persuasive Letter**

Writing an Opinion Statement

A. Read each pair of sentences. Check the box next to the sentence that makes a better opinion statement.

1. ☑ You should put those yummy garlic fries back on the menu at Cozy's Diner.
   ☐ We used to order the garlic fries when we went to Cozy's Diner.
2. ☐ The Mega-Puzzle has a lot of pieces that come in a cardboard box.
   ☑ The Mega-Puzzle should have a stronger box.
3. ☑ The library needs a room just for teenagers so they can talk and make noise.
   ☐ Teenagers make too much noise in the library when they talk.
4. ☑ The school newspaper should include an article about our class pet iguana.
   ☐ Our class just got a pet iguana named Ernie.

B. Rewrite each statement so it is clear and tells an opinion.

Example
Mini-Wheels Toy Cars come wrapped in a lot of extra plastic.
You should not wrap Mini-Wheels Toy Cars in so much plastic.

1. Two of the swings on the playground have broken seats.
   The swings on the playground need to be fixed.
2. Maybe you could coach our soccer team on the weekends if you felt like it.
   You should coach our soccer team on the weekends.
3. A lot of kids have small pets that they want to bring to school.
   Our school should allow students to bring small pets.
4. I bought the game, but I couldn't understand the directions.
   The game directions need to be written more clearly.

© Evan-Moor Corp. • EMC 6013 • Nonfiction Writing PERSUASIVE WRITING 123

Page 124 / Student Book Page 90

Name: ______________________ Persuasive Letter

Writing for Your Audience

A. Read each pair of sentences. Circle the sentence that is better for addressing the audience of a persuasive letter.

1. No way am I paying that much money for a baseball bat!
   That baseball bat costs far too much money.
2. Buyers should be aware of these problems.
   Don't you think people should be told what's going on?
3. In the future, please make these socks in other colors.
   You really need to come out with some better colors of socks.
4. We would prefer if the campground had cabins.
   It would be really awesome if the campground had cabins.
5. You should totally let us see this movie.
   This is an important movie for everyone to see.

B. Rewrite each sentence to make it sound more polite.

1. You really should knock down those prices.
   I believe that you should reduce your prices.
2. I don't know what's with all these new rules.
   I am confused about some of the new rules.
3. The directions on that game are totally impossible.
   I found the game directions too difficult to follow.
4. The popcorn at your theater is so salty that I had to spit it out.
   I could not eat the popcorn, because it was too salty.

124 PERSUASIVE WRITING Nonfiction Writing • EMC 6013 • © Evan-Moor Corp.

Page 125 / Student Book Page 91

Name: ______________________ Persuasive Letter

Giving Specific Reasons

A. Read each opinion statement. Check the box next to the reason that best supports the opinion statement.

1. **Opinion statement:** Laurel Elementary needs a school Web site.
   ☑ **Reason:** The school could use it to share important information.
   ☐ **Reason:** Web sites are fun to visit.
2. **Opinion statement:** We should go to Colorado this summer.
   ☑ **Reason:** We could canoe and hike there.
   ☐ **Reason:** The biggest city in Colorado is Denver.
3. **Opinion statement:** The library should be open on weekends.
   ☐ **Reason:** The library has many books and magazines.
   ☑ **Reason:** Hundreds of kids go to the library every weekend.
4. **Opinion statement:** Children under 10 years old should be able to visit the science museum for free.
   ☑ **Reason:** It is important for all children to learn about science.
   ☐ **Reason:** The science museum is a fun place to visit.

B. Write a specific reason in support of each opinion statement.

1. **Opinion statement:** Our family should get a dog.
   Reason: The dog could guard the house when we are gone.
2. **Opinion statement:** I need swim lessons.
   Reason: I want to feel safe when I go to the beach.
3. **Opinion statement:** The school needs new computers.
   Reason: The old ones do not always work well.

© Evan-Moor Corp. • EMC 6013 • Nonfiction Writing PERSUASIVE WRITING 125

Lesson 3 Writing for Your Audience

1. Remind students of the purpose of a persuasive letter. Say: **When you write a persuasive letter, think about who will read it.** Ask: **To whom would you write a persuasive letter asking for a longer recess at school?** (the school principal or vice principal)
2. Draw attention to the model on p. 122 and ask: **Who is the audience for Anita's letter?** (the president of True Toy Company) **Is her letter appropriate for the audience?** (yes) **Why?** (He is most likely the person who can decide whether to reduce the price of *Super Sleuth*.)
3. Point out that because you are trying to convince someone to do something when you write a persuasive letter, it is important to choose words carefully and to be polite. The reader is more likely to give a positive response. Write this sentence on the board: *Forty dollars is way, way too much to pay for a dumb game.* Challenge students to find the sentence on p. 122 that states the idea in a more polite way. *(Forty dollars is a lot for a game with these problems.)*
4. Read aloud the directions for Activity A on p. 124. Have students complete the activity in small groups. Ask volunteers to share and explain their answers.
5. Read aloud the directions for Activity B. Model rewriting one of the sentences. Then have students complete the activity in pairs.

Lesson 4 Giving Specific Reasons

1. Say: **When you write a persuasive letter, you must include specific reasons that will convince your reader to agree with you.** Direct students to the model. Ask: **What reasons does Anita give for why the game's price should be reduced?** (The game can only be played once; the mysteries are too easy; players can't play online.) **Are these good reasons?** (yes) **Why?** (They explain why the game isn't worth the price.)
2. Read aloud the directions for Activity A on p. 125. Then read aloud item 1. Ask: **Which reason is more specific?** (the first one) Have students complete the activity independently or in pairs. Discuss the answers.
3. Read aloud the directions for Activity B and complete item 1 as a class. Ask: **What are some reasons that a family might want to get a dog?** (companionship, protection, etc.) List the reasons on the board. Then choose one and write it as a sentence. Have students complete the activity independently. Invite volunteers to share their sentences.

Lesson 5 Organizing Your Letter

1. Point out the following parts of a letter, using the writing model: *date, address, greeting, body, closing,* and *signature.* Draw attention to the closing and ask: **In what other ways can you close a letter besides saying *Sincerely*?** (e.g., *Love, Yours truly, Thank you, Regards*) Ask: **Why do you think Anita chose *Sincerely*?** (It's appropriate for the audience.)
2. Read aloud the directions for Activity A on p. 126 and have students complete the activity independently. Review the answers together.
3. Discuss the sentences that make up the body of Anita's letter. Point out that the first sentence is the opinion statement; it tells what Anita wants. The next few sentences give reasons. The last sentence is a *concluding sentence.* Say: **The concluding sentence restates what the opinion statement says, but in a different way.**
4. Point out the concluding sentence in the letter in Activity A. Then have students complete Activity B in pairs. Ask volunteers to read aloud their answers.

➤ **Extend the Lesson:** Explain that persuasive letters to people you know well can be formatted like friendly letters. You may want to explain how to format business letters, with block paragraphs, for more formal persuasive letters.

Lesson 6 Reviewing a Persuasive Letter

1. Review the qualities of a good persuasive letter: the correct parts of a letter, writing that is appropriate for the audience, a clear opinion statement, specific reasons, and a concluding sentence.
2. Have students read the letter on p. 127. Discuss how it can be improved. Ask: **What does the writer want?** (a new desk) **Does the first sentence say that?** (no) **Is each reason that the writer gives a good reason?** (no) **Which reason would you take out?** *(I don't like the color.)* **Why?** (Not liking the color isn't a good reason to get a new desk.) **Do all of the sentences seem appropriate for the audience?** (no) **Which one does not?** *(It's totally annoying to the other kids.)* **Are any parts of the letter missing?** (yes; the date and the closing)
3. Have students revise the letter independently on a separate sheet of paper. Remind them that there may be different ways to revise it. Then invite students to share their revisions with the class.

Page 126 / Student Book Page 92

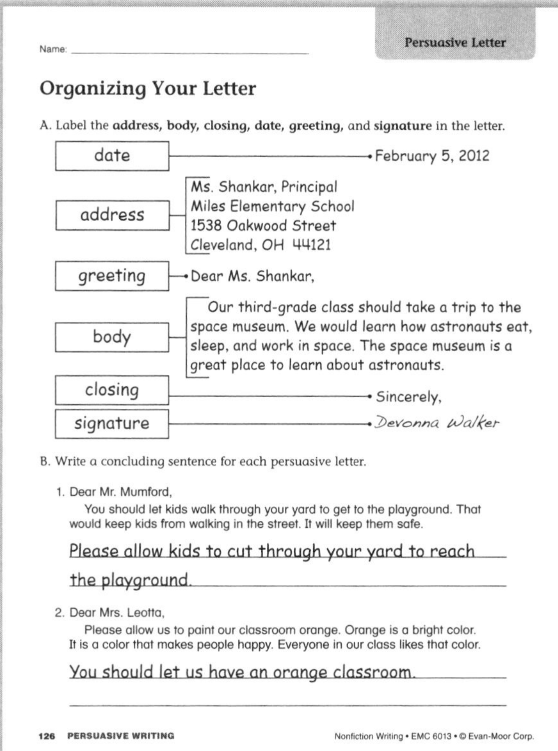

Name:

Persuasive Letter

Organizing Your Letter

A. Label the **address, body, closing, date, greeting,** and **signature** in the letter.

date → February 5, 2012

address → Ms. Shankar, Principal
Miles Elementary School
1538 Oakwood Street
Cleveland, OH 44121

greeting → Dear Ms. Shankar,

body → Our third-grade class should take a trip to the space museum. We would learn how astronauts eat, sleep, and work in space. The space museum is a great place to learn about astronauts.

closing → Sincerely,

signature → Devonna Walker

B. Write a concluding sentence for each persuasive letter.

1. Dear Mr. Mumford,
You should let kids walk through your yard to get to the playground. That would keep kids from walking in the street. It will keep them safe.
Please allow kids to cut through your yard to reach the playground.

2. Dear Mrs. Leotta,
Please allow us to paint our classroom orange. Orange is a bright color. It is a color that makes people happy. Everyone in our class likes that color.
You should let us have an orange classroom.

126 PERSUASIVE WRITING Nonfiction Writing • EMC 6013 • © Evan-Moor Corp.

Page 127 and Sample Revision / Student Book Page 93

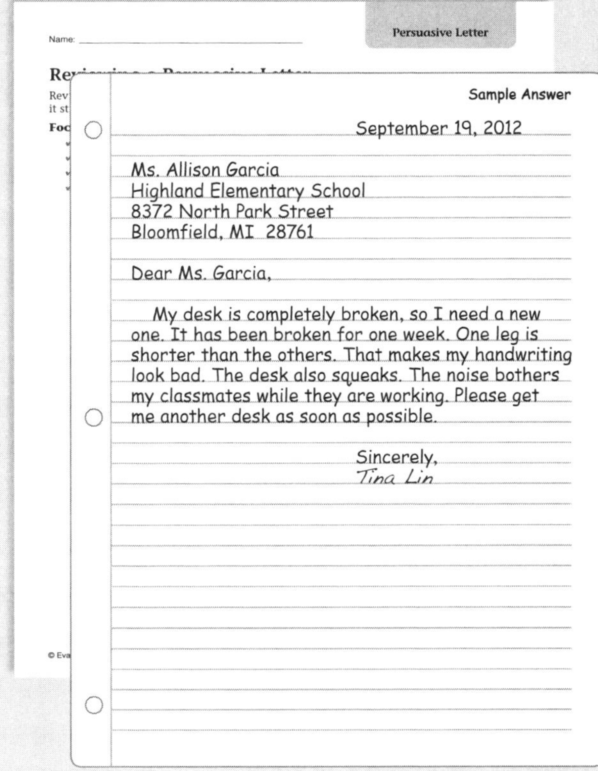

Name:

Persuasive Letter

Sample Answer

September 19, 2012

Ms. Allison Garcia
Highland Elementary School
8372 North Park Street
Bloomfield, MI 28761

Dear Ms. Garcia,

My desk is completely broken, so I need a new one. It has been broken for one week. One leg is shorter than the others. That makes my handwriting look bad. The desk also squeaks. The noise bothers my classmates while they are working. Please get me another desk as soon as possible.

Sincerely,
Tina Lin

Name: ______________________________

Introducing a Persuasive Letter

Read this example of a persuasive letter.

Writing Model

March 16, 2012

Mr. Ivan Tahaffun, President
True Toy Company, Inc.
P.O. Box 98765
Orlando, FL 52761

Dear Mr. Tahaffun,

You should reduce the price of your *Super Sleuth* video game. It costs too much for a game that can only be played once. The game is fun for just a few hours. The mysteries are fun to solve, but they are too easy. My five-year-old sister even solved one! Plus, I cannot play online with my friends. That is the best part of any video game. Forty dollars is a lot for a game with these problems. If you reduce the price, then more people might buy it.

Sincerely,
Anita Rangan

Writer's Audience: ______________________________

Writer's Purpose: ______________________________

____

Name: ______________________________

Writing an Opinion Statement

A. Read each pair of sentences. Check the box next to the sentence that makes a better opinion statement.

1. ☐ You should put those yummy garlic fries back on the menu at Cozy's Diner.
   ☐ We used to order the garlic fries when we went to Cozy's Diner.

2. ☐ The Mega-Puzzle has a lot of pieces that come in a cardboard box.
   ☐ The Mega-Puzzle should have a stronger box.

3. ☐ The library needs a room just for teenagers so they can talk and make noise.
   ☐ Teenagers make too much noise in the library when they talk.

4. ☐ The school newspaper should include an article about our class pet iguana.
   ☐ Our class just got a pet iguana named Ernie.

B. Rewrite each statement so it is clear and tells an opinion.

Example

Mini-Wheels Toy Cars come wrapped in a lot of extra plastic.

You should not wrap Mini-Wheels Toy Cars in so much plastic.

1. Two of the swings on the playground have broken seats.

   ____

2. Maybe you could coach our soccer team on the weekends if you felt like it.

   ____

3. A lot of kids have small pets that they want to bring to school.

   ____

4. I bought the game, but I couldn't understand the directions.

   ____

Name: ____

Writing for Your Audience

A. Read each pair of sentences. Circle the sentence that is better for addressing the audience of a persuasive letter.

1. No way am I paying that much money for a baseball bat!

   That baseball bat costs far too much money.

2. Buyers should be aware of these problems.

   Don't you think people should be told what's going on?

3. In the future, please make these socks in other colors.

   You really need to come out with some better colors of socks.

4. We would prefer if the campground had cabins.

   It would be really awesome if the campground had cabins.

5. You should totally let us see this movie.

   This is an important movie for everyone to see.

B. Rewrite each sentence to make it sound more polite.

1. You really should knock down those prices.

   ____

2. I don't know what's with all these new rules.

   ____

3. The directions on that game are totally impossible.

   ____

4. The popcorn at your theater is so salty that I had to spit it out.

   ____

Name: ______________________________

Giving Specific Reasons

A. Read each opinion statement. Check the box next to the reason that best supports the opinion statement.

1. **Opinion statement:** Laurel Elementary needs a school Web site.
   - ☐ **Reason:** The school could use it to share important information.
   - ☐ **Reason:** Web sites are fun to visit.

2. **Opinion statement:** We should go to Colorado this summer.
   - ☐ **Reason:** We could canoe and hike there.
   - ☐ **Reason:** The biggest city in Colorado is Denver.

3. **Opinion statement:** The library should be open on weekends.
   - ☐ **Reason:** The library has many books and magazines.
   - ☐ **Reason:** Hundreds of kids go to the library every weekend.

4. **Opinion statement:** Children under 10 years old should be able to visit the science museum for free.
   - ☐ **Reason:** It is important for all children to learn about science.
   - ☐ **Reason:** The science museum is a fun place to visit.

B. Write a specific reason in support of each opinion statement.

1. **Opinion statement:** Our family should get a dog.

   Reason: ______________________________

2. **Opinion statement:** I need swim lessons.

   Reason: ______________________________

3. **Opinion statement:** The school needs new computers.

   Reason: ______________________________

Name: ______________________________

Organizing Your Letter

A. Label the **address, body, closing, date, greeting,** and **signature** in the letter.

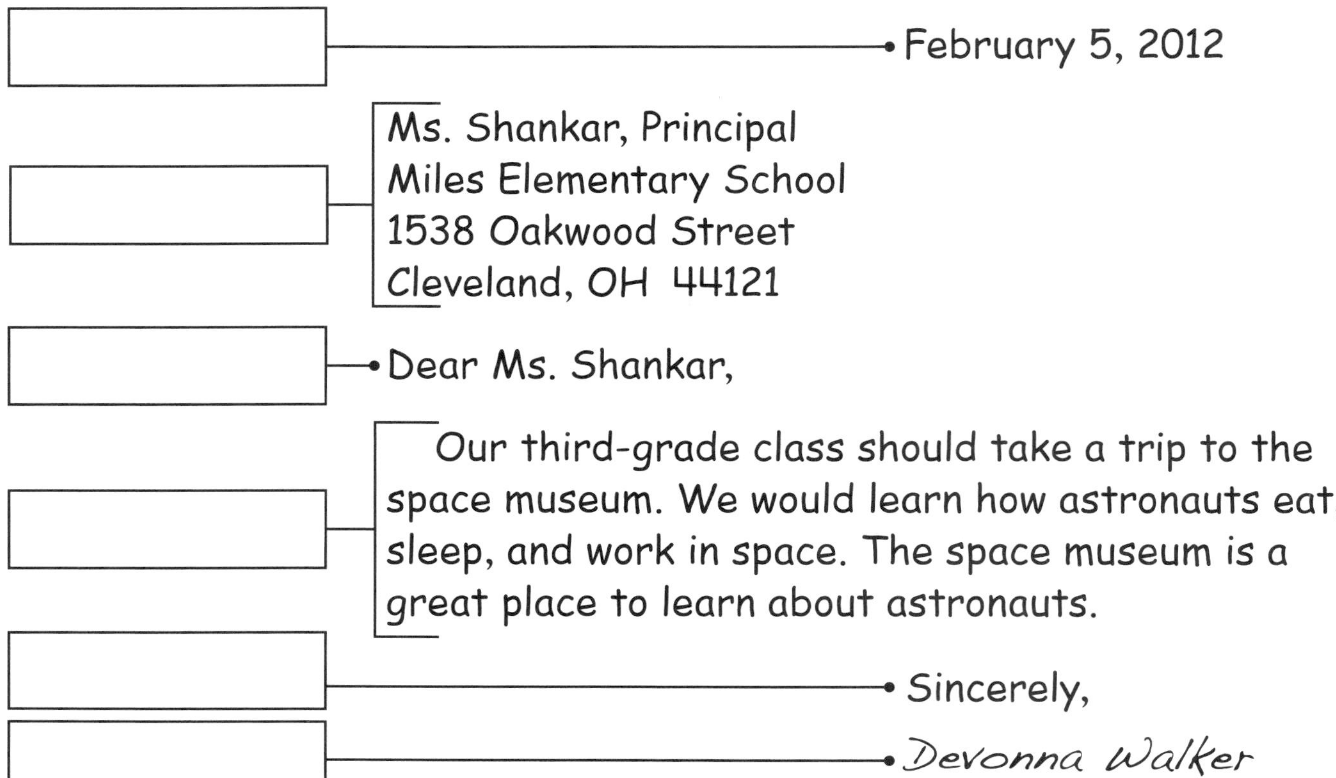

February 5, 2012

Ms. Shankar, Principal
Miles Elementary School
1538 Oakwood Street
Cleveland, OH 44121

Dear Ms. Shankar,

Our third-grade class should take a trip to the space museum. We would learn how astronauts eat, sleep, and work in space. The space museum is a great place to learn about astronauts.

Sincerely,

Devonna Walker

B. Write a concluding sentence for each persuasive letter.

1. Dear Mr. Mumford,

   You should let kids walk through your yard to get to the playground. That would keep kids from walking in the street. It will keep them safe.

   ____

   ____

2. Dear Mrs. Leotta,

   Please allow us to paint our classroom orange. Orange is a bright color. It is a color that makes people happy. Everyone in our class likes that color.

   ____

   ____

Name: ______________________________

Reviewing a Persuasive Letter

Revise this persuasive letter. Use what you have learned to make it stronger. Rewrite it on a separate sheet of paper.

Focus on:

- ✓ writing a clear opinion statement
- ✓ using the right language for the audience
- ✓ giving specific reasons that support the opinion
- ✓ including all parts of a letter

Draft

Ms. Allison Garcia
Highland Elementary School
8372 North Park Street
Bloomfield, MI 28761

Dear Ms. Garcia,

My desk is completely broken. It has been broken for one week. One leg is shorter than the others. That makes my handwriting look bad. The desk also squeaks. It's totally annoying to the other kids. Plus, I don't like the color. Please get me another desk as soon as possible.

Tina Lin

Writing a Review

Page 131 / Student Book Page 95

Name: ______________

Review

Introducing a Review

Read this example of a review.

Writing Model

The Scoop on Andy's Ice-Cream Parlor

Andy's Ice-Cream Parlor is the best place in town for ice cream. It is located at the corner of Freeman Drive and Rail Street. Andy's has 40 flavors of ice cream. Some of them are quite unusual, such as pumpkin and root beer. But all of the flavors are tasty. The prices at Andy's are not too high, and you don't even have to pay extra for a waffle cone! Andy's is open from noon to 8 o'clock p.m. every day. So go to Andy's the next time you feel like having an ice-cold treat.

Writer's Purpose: to share information and an opinion about Andy's Ice-Cream Parlor

 PERSUASIVE WRITING 131

Page 132 / Student Book Page 96

Name: ______________

Review

Telling Important Information

Choose a movie or TV show that you have seen, a game or toy that you know well, and a book that you have read. Then fill in each chart with basic information that you could include in a review.

1. Movie or TV show

Title: The Falling Stars (movie)	Length: 72 minutes
Starring: Mike Long, Katie Schwartz	About: a rock band that has only one hit song
Rating: G	Theater or TV channel: MovieTime Cinemas

2. Game or toy

Name: Super Scooter	Cost: $39.99
Company that makes it: Speedalong	Parts: a handlebar, two wheels, a footboard
Where to buy it: Toy Mart	What is special about it: folds to fit inside a backpack

3. Book

Title: The Goldstone Bracelet	Author: Catherine Soto
What it's about: a girl who wants to buy her mom a present	Number of pages: 40
Illustrations: a few realistic color pictures	Publisher: Reader Press

132 PERSUASIVE WRITING

Lesson 1 Introducing a Review

A review gives important information and the writer's opinion about a book, movie, TV show, restaurant, or product.

1. Ask students to think of books they have read, games they have played, or movies they have seen recently. Invite volunteers to complete these sentence frames:

   I like _____, because _____.

   I don't like _____, because _____.

   Explain that a good way to share information and opinions about something is to write a review.
2. Read aloud "The Scoop on Andy's Ice-Cream Parlor" on p. 131 as students follow along. Ask: **What is this review about?** (an ice-cream parlor) Point out the double meaning of *scoop*, if necessary.
3. Ask: **What is the purpose of this review?** (to share information and an opinion about Andy's Ice-Cream Parlor) Have students write the purpose on the lines provided.
4. Invite students to offer opinions about what makes this a good review. Prompt students by asking: **Does the writer tell you what he thinks about the ice-cream parlor? Does the review tell you important things you would need to know if you wanted to go there? Does the writer give reasons for his opinion?**
5. Explain that students will use the model as they practice the skills needed to write a good review.

➤ **Extend the Lesson:** Have students read book reviews posted by online children's book clubs.

Lesson 2 Telling Important Information

1. Explain that a review should include important information that the reader would need or want to know about what is being reviewed.
2. Revisit the writing model on p. 131 and ask: **What basic information does the writer include about the ice-cream parlor?** (name, location, hours, type of food, prices) Say: **That's the kind of information you would want to include when writing a review about a restaurant.**
3. Direct students to p. 132 and discuss the different kinds of information needed for a review of a movie or TV show, a game or toy, and a book.

4. Have students complete the activity in pairs. Explain that they may not know all of the information to write in the charts, and that writers often must gather information for their reviews. Ask: **How can you find the information that you need for your charts, if you don't already know it?** (e.g., look at a shopping Web site to find the price of something) Help students find the information they need.
5. Invite pairs to share their completed charts. Ask: **How would this information help you if you planned to write a review?** (It would give the facts to include in the review.)

Lesson 3 Giving Opinions and Reasons

1. Review the purpose of a review. Then explain that a review should have a sentence that clearly states the writer's opinion about the thing that he or she is reviewing. Point out the opinion statement in "The Scoop on Andy's Ice-Cream Parlor." *(Andy's Ice-Cream Parlor is the best place in town for ice cream.)* Say: **This sentence clearly tells us the writer's opinion about the place he is reviewing.**
2. Say: **When you write a review, you should give reasons to support your opinion. Reasons tell your reader *why* you did or did not like something.** Point out the first reason in the writing model on p. 131. (that Andy's has 40 flavors) Have students identify the other reasons. (The flavors are tasty; the prices aren't too high; there is no charge for waffle cones.) Say: **These reasons tell us why the writer thinks Andy's Ice-Cream Parlor is the best.**
3. Direct students to the activity on p. 133 and discuss the example. Point out how the reason supports the opinion. Then have students complete the activity in pairs or small groups. Invite them to share their answers.

➤ **Extend the Lesson:** Repeat the activity on p. 133 and have students give different examples for each category.

Lesson 4 Writing an Ending

1. Say: **A review usually ends with one last opinion about what the writer is reviewing. Sometimes the writer makes a recommendation, such as "Don't bother seeing this movie" or "I recommend this book for kids who are interested in dinosaurs." A good ending can sum up the ideas in the review.**

Page 133 / Student Book Page 97

Name: ______________________ Review

Giving Opinions and Reasons

Name something for each category. Write your opinion about it. Then write a reason that supports your opinion.

Example
A game I have played: Panda Mania
Opinion: The board game Panda Mania is confusing.
Reason: The game has too many rules.

1. A restaurant I have eaten at: Antonio's
   Opinion: Antonio's has the best spaghetti.
   Reason: It comes with lots of cheese on top.
2. A cartoon I have watched: Outback Sue
   Opinion: Kids can learn about animals by watching Outback Sue.
   Reason: The main character takes care of animals.
3. A toy I have played with: Forever Snow
   Opinion: Forever Snow is really messy.
   Reason: It gets all over everything when you play with it.
4. A movie I have seen: Rocking Rabbits
   Opinion: It's a fun movie for kids who like music.
   Reason: The music makes you dance in your seat.
5. A book I have read: Circle of Water
   Opinion: Circle of Water is a sad book.
   Reason: A whale gets lost and swims in circles.

Page 134 / Student Book Page 98

Name: ____________________ Review

Writing an Ending

Read each short review. Then write a good ending for it.

1. *Alien Babysitter* is a funny movie. It is about a babysitter from space who looks like a giant green pizza with arms! She makes silly faces and tells bad jokes. The other characters in the movie also look and act funny.

   Alien Babysitter is sure to make you laugh!

2. The new toy called Rolling Rocky is not very fun to play with. It's just a rock on wheels. It rolls only in one direction, and it gets stuck in corners.

   If you want a fun toy, do not buy Rolling Rocky.

3. Burger Barn is a great place to eat. People dining there sit on piles of hay. Each table is a big wagon wheel with a glass top. The servers wear farm clothes. Sometimes they sing and square-dance around the restaurant.

   If you want a relaxed family dinner, eat at Burger Barn.

4. Merry Mornings cereal is not very good. It gets soggy in milk. The dried berries are too chewy. Plus, it tastes like a spoonful of cardboard.

   Do not buy Merry Mornings cereal unless you like the taste of cardboard in the morning.

5. *All About Butterflies* is an interesting book. It has close-up photos of all kinds of butterflies. The book gives just the right amount of information about each one. It also tells the best places to see certain butterflies.

   Kids who like butterflies will love All About Butterflies.

134 PERSUASIVE WRITING Nonfiction Writing • EMC 6013 • © Evan-Moor Corp.

Page 135 and Sample Revision / Student Book Page 99

Name: ____________________ Review

Reviewing a Written Review

Sample Answer

Building Brix Is a Good Buy

Building Brix is a set of blocks that makes it exciting to build make-believe towns and cities. Each set comes with 200 blocks of different sizes and shapes. You can build tall towers, long bridges, high walls, and all kinds of interesting buildings. But the best thing about Building Brix is that it comes with a carrying case. So you can take the blocks anywhere! Constructor, Inc., makes Building Brix, and each set costs $19.99. You can buy it at Toy Mart. Kids who like to build things will love Building Brix.

2. Read aloud the last sentence of "Andy's Ice-Cream Parlor" on p. 131 and ask: **Does the writer think people should go to Andy's?** (yes)

3. Direct students to p. 134. Read the first review and ask: **Does the writer like the movie *Alien Babysitter*?** (yes) **Why?** (It's funny; the characters look and act funny.) **Do you think the writer would recommend this movie? If so, why?** Explore suitable endings for the review. (e.g., Anyone who needs a laugh will love this movie. I recommend *Alien Babysitter* for all kids under age 12.) Remind students that a good ending gives an opinion. Then have students complete the activity in pairs or small groups. Invite volunteers to share their sentences with the class.

Lesson 5 Reviewing a Written Review

1. Review the qualities of a good review: important information about the subject, clear opinions and supporting reasons, and an ending that sums up the main opinion.

2. Read aloud "Building Brix Is a Good Buy" on p. 135 as students follow along. Then guide students through revising the draft. Ask: **What toy is being reviewed?** (Building Brix) **Does the first sentence give an opinion?** (yes) **Does it tell the name of the product?** (yes) **Does the writer explain what makes Building Brix fun?** (no) Build background by discussing construction toys such as wooden blocks. Then ask: **What do you think would make a toy like Building Brix fun?** (e.g., You could build tall towers, long bridges, high walls, and different styles of buildings.) Work with students to turn these ideas into sentences that explain why a set of Building Brix would be fun.

3. Have a volunteer read aloud the last sentence of the review. Ask: **Does this sentence give an opinion?** (no) **How can we revise it so it restates the main opinion?** (e.g., If you enjoy building things, you should buy Building Brix.)

4. Revisit item 2 on p. 132 and point out what kind of information a writer might gather for a toy review. Then ask: **What important information is missing from the review of Building Brix?** (the name of the company and the price) Tell students that Building Brix is made by Constructor, Inc., and that a set costs $19.99. Help students add these details to the review.

5. Have students write their revisions on a separate sheet of paper. Invite volunteers to share their revised reviews.

Name: ______________________________

Introducing a Review

Read this example of a review.

Writing Model

The Scoop on Andy's Ice-Cream Parlor

Andy's Ice-Cream Parlor is the best place in town for ice cream. It is located at the corner of Freeman Drive and Rail Street. Andy's has 40 flavors of ice cream. Some of them are quite unusual, such as pumpkin and root beer. But all of the flavors are tasty. The prices at Andy's are not too high, and you don't even have to pay extra for a waffle cone! Andy's is open from noon to 8 o'clock p.m. every day. So go to Andy's the next time you feel like having an ice-cold treat.

Writer's Purpose: ______________________________

____

Name: ______________________________

Review

Telling Important Information

Choose a movie or TV show that you have seen, a game or toy that you know well, and a book that you have read. Then fill in each chart with basic information that you could include in a review.

1. **Movie or TV show**

Title:	**Length:**
Starring:	**About:**
Rating:	**Theater or TV channel:**

2. **Game or toy**

Name:	**Cost:**
Company that makes it:	**Parts:**
Where to buy it:	**What is special about it:**

3. **Book**

Title:	**Author:**
What it's about:	**Number of pages:**
Illustrations:	**Publisher:**

Name: ____________________

Giving Opinions and Reasons

Name something for each category. Write your opinion about it. Then write a reason that supports your opinion.

Example

A game I have played: Panda Mania

Opinion: The board game Panda Mania is confusing.

Reason: The game has too many rules.

1. A restaurant I have eaten at: ____________________

   Opinion: ____________________

   Reason: ____________________

2. A cartoon I have watched: ____________________

   Opinion: ____________________

   Reason: ____________________

3. A toy I have played with: ____________________

   Opinion: ____________________

   Reason: ____________________

4. A movie I have seen: ____________________

   Opinion: ____________________

   Reason: ____________________

5. A book I have read: ____________________

   Opinion: ____________________

   Reason: ____________________

Name: ____________________

Writing an Ending

Read each short review. Then write a good ending for it.

1. *Alien Babysitter* is a funny movie. It is about a babysitter from space who looks like a giant green pizza with arms! She makes silly faces and tells bad jokes. The other characters in the movie also look and act funny.

____

____

2. The new toy called Rolling Rocky is not very fun to play with. It's just a rock on wheels. It rolls only in one direction, and it gets stuck in corners.

____

____

3. Burger Barn is a great place to eat. People dining there sit on piles of hay. Each table is a big wagon wheel with a glass top. The servers wear farm clothes. Sometimes they sing and square-dance around the restaurant.

____

____

4. Merry Mornings cereal is not very good. It gets soggy in milk. The dried berries are too chewy. Plus, it tastes like a spoonful of cardboard.

____

____

5. *All About Butterflies* is an interesting book. It has close-up photos of all kinds of butterflies. The book gives just the right amount of information about each one. It also tells the best places to see certain butterflies.

____

____

Name: ______________________________

Reviewing a Written Review

Revise this review of a toy called Building Brix. Use what you have learned to make it stronger. Rewrite it on a separate sheet of paper.

Focus on:

- ✓ including important information
- ✓ giving reasons for the opinion
- ✓ writing an ending that gives an opinion

Draft

Building Brix Is a Good Buy

Building Brix is a set of blocks that makes it exciting to build make-believe towns and cities. Each set comes with 200 blocks of different sizes and shapes. You can buy it at Toy Mart. But the best thing about Building Brix is that it comes with a carrying case. Then you can take the blocks anywhere.

Writing a Personal Narrative

Page 139 / Student Book Page 101

Name: ____________________ Personal Narrative

Introducing a Personal Narrative

Read this example of a personal narrative.

Writing Model

Flying Free

Last spring, my grandpa gave me a paper kite shaped like a dragon. I couldn't wait to fly it! But I had to wait for my little sister Eva to finish her nap.

After Eva woke up, Grandpa took us to the park to fly the kite. We ran through the damp grass. Grandpa held the flapping, snapping kite. When he let go, the kite flew up. I held the spool of string while Eva whined and begged for her turn. After a while, I gave her the string and I just watched that dragon dance in the wind. Then a gust of wind jerked the kite, and Eva lost her grip. The kite started to fly away. I ran after it, but it was no use. The kite was gone.

I was angry with Eva at first. But she was already upset, so I didn't say anything. On the way home, we made up a story about the lost kite. We pretended that the dragon flew off to live in a castle. That story made me feel better. It made Eva feel better, too.

Writer's Purpose: to tell about an experience flying a kite

© Evan-Moor Corp. • EMC 6013 • Nonfiction Writing NARRATIVE WRITING 139

Page 140 / Student Book Page 102

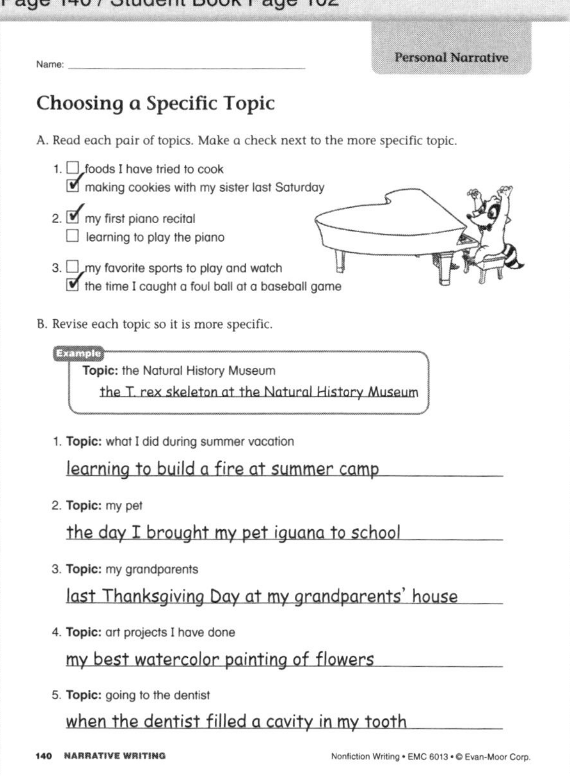

Name: ____________________ Personal Narrative

Choosing a Specific Topic

A. Read each pair of topics. Make a check next to the more specific topic.

1. ☐ foods I have tried to cook
   ☑ making cookies with my sister last Saturday
2. ☑ my first piano recital
   ☐ learning to play the piano
3. ☐ my favorite sports to play and watch
   ☑ the time I caught a foul ball at a baseball game

B. Revise each topic so it is more specific.

Example
Topic: the Natural History Museum
the T. rex skeleton at the Natural History Museum

1. **Topic:** what I did during summer vacation
   learning to build a fire at summer camp
2. **Topic:** my pet
   the day I brought my pet iguana to school
3. **Topic:** my grandparents
   last Thanksgiving Day at my grandparents' house
4. **Topic:** art projects I have done
   my best watercolor painting of flowers
5. **Topic:** going to the dentist
   when the dentist filled a cavity in my tooth

140 NARRATIVE WRITING Nonfiction Writing • EMC 6013 • © Evan-Moor Corp.

Lesson 1 Introducing a Personal Narrative

A personal narrative is writing that tells about a specific event or experience from the writer's own life.

1. Invite a few students to tell about their experiences flying kites or watching other people fly kites. Then say: **In a personal narrative, you can tell about an interesting experience such as flying a kite.**
2. Read aloud "Flying Free" on p. 139 as students follow along. Ask: **What is the purpose of this personal narrative?** (to tell about an experience flying a kite) Have students write the purpose on the lines provided.
3. Have students identify the topic sentence of the first paragraph. *(Last spring, my grandpa gave me ...)* Point out that this sentence introduces the topic of the personal narrative.
4. Invite students to offer opinions about what makes this a good personal narrative. Prompt them by asking: **Does the story tell about a specific event? Can you picture some of the details in your mind? Did the writer include thoughts and feelings about what happened? Are the details in an order that makes sense?**

➤ **Extend the Lesson:** Have students brainstorm topics for their own personal narratives. Remind them to consider specific interesting events from their own lives.

Lesson 2 Choosing a Specific Topic

1. Review the purpose of a personal narrative. Say: **A good personal narrative is about one specific event.** Revisit the model on p. 139 and ask: **What is the topic of this personal narrative?** (flying a kite and losing it) **Is this topic specific?** (yes)
2. Read aloud the directions for Activity A on p. 140 and have students complete the activity independently.
3. Read and discuss the example for Activity B. Say: **Most natural history museums have hundreds of things to look at. A museum would not be a specific enough topic for a personal narrative. A dinosaur skeleton at the museum would be a better topic for someone who saw the skeleton.** Then have students complete the activity and share their sentences with the class.

➤ **Extend the Lesson:** Have partners evaluate their topics from the Lesson 1 extension activity and decide which are specific enough for a personal narrative. Have each student choose his or her favorite topic.

Lesson 3 Adding Sensory Details

1. Say: **A good personal narrative uses details that describe things you can touch, taste, smell, see, or hear. These kinds of details help readers imagine the writer's experience.**
2. Have students underline sensory details in "Flying Free." (*kite shaped like a dragon*; *damp grass*; *the flapping, snapping kite*; *Eva whined and begged*; *wind jerked the kite*; etc.)
3. Direct students to Activity A on p. 141. Ask: **What do you see at a picnic or a barbecue?** (food cooking on a grill, people sitting at picnic benches, paper plates, etc.) **What foods might you taste?** (hot dogs, pickles, potato chips, etc.) Then have students complete the activity in pairs or small groups.
4. Have students complete Activity B independently. Invite students to share their sentences.

➤ **Extend the Lesson:** Have students brainstorm sensory details for one of the topics they selected in the Lesson 2 extension activity.

Lesson 4 Adding Thoughts and Feelings

1. Say: **A personal narrative isn't just about an event. The writer also shares his or her thoughts and feelings about what happened.** Display the model on p. 139 and read the opening paragraph aloud. Ask: **Which sentence describes the writer's thoughts or feelings?** *(I couldn't wait to fly it!)* Prompt students to find other sentences in the model that express the writer's thoughts or feelings. *(I was angry with Eva at first; But she was already upset, so I didn't say anything; That story made me feel better.)*
2. Direct students to p. 142. Read the example and ask: **Have you ever worked hard to memorize a poem? Or practiced singing a song or learning a dance so you could perform for an audience? How did you feel when you finally performed it?** Invite two or three volunteers to relate their experiences. Then read through the events on the page and provide examples, as necessary, of events from your own life. Have students complete the activity independently and invite volunteers to share their sentences with the class.

➤ **Extend the Lesson:** Have each student choose an event from p. 142 and write additional details that express what they thought and how they felt about what happened.

Page 141 / Student Book Page 103

Name: ____________

Personal Narrative

Adding Sensory Details

A. Think about going to a picnic or a barbecue. What would you feel, taste, smell, see, and hear? Write details in the chart.

I feel...	I taste...	I smell...	I see...	I hear...
mosquitoes biting, the grass tickling my feet	creamy potato salad, tart berries	smoke from the grill, roasted corn on the cob	picnic baskets full of food, squirrels running up and down the trees	birds singing, people laughing

B. Write two sentences for a personal narrative about a picnic or a barbecue, using details from the chart above.

The corn roasting on the grill smelled yummy, but the smoke burned my eyes.

A little yellow songbird sat on a tree branch near the picnic table and sang a cheerful tune.

© Evan-Moor Corp. • EMC 6013 • Nonfiction Writing — NARRATIVE WRITING 141

Page 142 / Student Book Page 104

Name: ____________

Personal Narrative

Adding Thoughts and Feelings

Think of a time when each of these events happened to you. Write about it, and tell what you thought or felt at the time.

Example
Event: when you performed something that you had practiced
At my first dance recital, I felt calm as I walked onto the stage. I knew the steps well.

1. **Event:** a time when you did something brave
The first time I jumped off the diving board, my legs were shaking. I was scared! Afterward, I felt happy.
2. **Event:** when you helped a person or an animal in need
My friend got a letter from her uncle in Mexico, but she can't read Spanish. I felt proud when I helped her read it.
3. **Event:** a time when you lost something special
I felt sad when I left my doll at the park. When I went back for the doll, it was gone.
4. **Event:** a time when you were part of a big crowd of people
I was afraid of getting lost when we went to the State Fair. I didn't want to let go of my dad's hand.
5. **Event:** when you got to do something that you had always wanted to do
I was disappointed when I went horseback riding. It wasn't as much fun as I thought it would be.

142 NARRATIVE WRITING — Nonfiction Writing • EMC 6013 • © Evan-Moor Corp.

Page 143 / Student Book Page 105

Name: ______________________ **Personal Narrative**

Organizing Details

A. Number the sentences in the correct order for this personal narrative about marching in a parade. The first one has been done for you.

7 When the parade was over, our band leader gave us sandwiches.

1 I was excited when the day of the parade was here.

4 Our band leader lined us up and gave me a banner to hold.

6 People waved and cheered as we marched through town.

3 After breakfast, Dad drove me to the place where the parade would start.

2 As soon as I woke up, I put on my marching-band uniform.

5 The band in front of ours started to play, and we all began to march.

B. Rewrite this paragraph in the order that the events happened.

My friend John and I decided to sell lemonade. We sold all of our lemonade and earned 35 dollars. All that effort was worth it! Once the lemonade was ready, we set up our stand in front of John's house. First, we picked lemons from the tree in my backyard. Then we squeezed the lemons and added sugar and water.

My friend John and I decided to sell lemonade. First, we picked lemons from the tree in my backyard. Then we squeezed the lemons and added sugar and water. Once the lemonade was ready, we set up our stand in front of John's house. We sold all of our lemonade and earned 35 dollars. All that effort was worth it!

© Evan-Moor Corp. • EMC 6013 • Nonfiction Writing NARRATIVE WRITING 143

Lesson 5 Organizing Details

1. Say: **When writing personal narratives, writers usually present details in time order, or the order in which they happened. If you write the details out of order, your readers may get confused.** Review signal words and phrases that show sequence. (e.g., *first, then, next, after that*)
2. Display the model on p. 139. Ask: **What important details happen in this story?** (The girl gets a kite, she flies it, she gives the string to her sister, the sister loses her grip, the kite flies away, the girls make up a story on the way home.) Ask: **Does the writer give the details in an order that makes sense?** (yes) Invite students to circle signal words and phrases in the model. (e.g., *Last spring, After a while, Then*)
3. Read aloud the directions for Activity A on p. 143. Have students complete the activity independently. Then review the answers.
4. Have students complete Activity B independently. Ask volunteers to read aloud the reorganized paragraph.

➤ **Extend the Lesson:** Have students organize the details they wrote during the Lesson 3 extension activity, putting the details in the order that they happened.

Page 144 and Sample Revision / Student Book Page 106

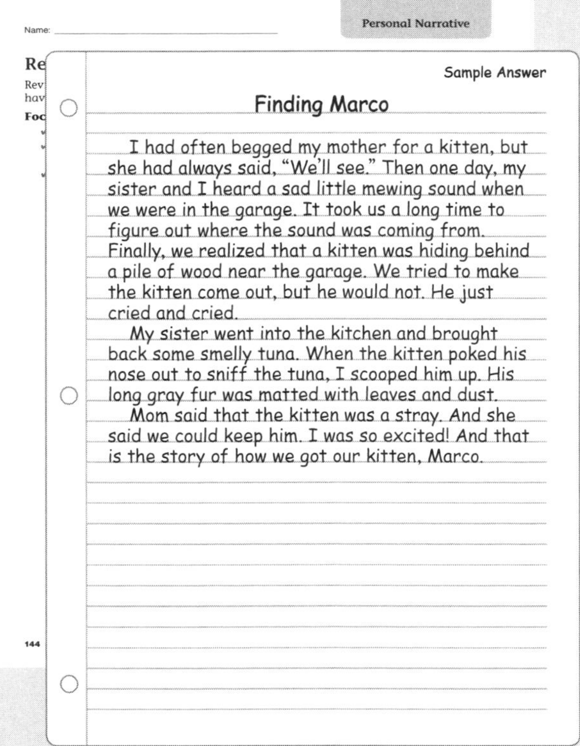

Name: ______________________ **Personal Narrative**

Sample Answer

Finding Marco

I had often begged my mother for a kitten, but she had always said, "We'll see." Then one day, my sister and I heard a sad little mewing sound when we were in the garage. It took us a long time to figure out where the sound was coming from. Finally, we realized that a kitten was hiding behind a pile of wood near the garage. We tried to make the kitten come out, but he would not. He just cried and cried.

My sister went into the kitchen and brought back some smelly tuna. When the kitten poked his nose out to sniff the tuna, I scooped him up. His long gray fur was matted with leaves and dust.

Mom said that the kitten was a stray. And she said we could keep him. I was so excited! And that is the story of how we got our kitten, Marco.

144

Lesson 6 Reviewing a Personal Narrative

1. Review the qualities of a good personal narrative: a specific topic, sensory details, thoughts and feelings about the topic, and a clear order of events.
2. Read "Finding Marco" on p. 144 as students follow along. Discuss how it can be improved. Ask: **Of all the details in this story, which one happened first?** (The writer begged her mom for a kitten.) Guide students to identify and number other details, and remind them to write the details in order when they write their revision. Then ask: **Does the writer tell how she felt when she found the kitten?** (no) **What do you think the kitten felt like when the writer picked him up?** (e.g., fluffy, dusty) **What sounds might the kitten have made?** Prompt students to add more details to describe what the writer might have seen, heard, felt, smelled, or tasted.
3. Have students work independently, writing their revisions on a separate sheet of paper. Remind them that there may be more than one way to improve the draft. Invite volunteers to share their revisions.

Name: ______________________________

Introducing a Personal Narrative

Read this example of a personal narrative.

Writing Model

Flying Free

Last spring, my grandpa gave me a paper kite shaped like a dragon. I couldn't wait to fly it! But I had to wait for my little sister Eva to finish her nap.

After Eva woke up, Grandpa took us to the park to fly the kite. We ran through the damp grass. Grandpa held the flapping, snapping kite. When he let go, the kite flew up. I held the spool of string while Eva whined and begged for her turn. After a while, I gave her the string and I just watched that dragon dance in the wind. Then a gust of wind jerked the kite, and Eva lost her grip. The kite started to fly away. I ran after it, but it was no use. The kite was gone.

I was angry with Eva at first. But she was already upset, so I didn't say anything. On the way home, we made up a story about the lost kite. We pretended that the dragon flew off to live in a castle. That story made me feel better. It made Eva feel better, too.

Writer's Purpose: ______________________________

____

Name: ______________________________

Choosing a Specific Topic

A. Read each pair of topics. Make a check next to the more specific topic.

1. ☐ foods I have tried to cook
   ☐ making cookies with my sister last Saturday

2. ☐ my first piano recital
   ☐ learning to play the piano

3. ☐ my favorite sports to play and watch
   ☐ the time I caught a foul ball at a baseball game

B. Revise each topic so it is more specific.

Example

Topic: the Natural History Museum

the T. rex skeleton at the Natural History Museum

1. **Topic:** what I did during summer vacation

   ____

2. **Topic:** my pet

   ____

3. **Topic:** my grandparents

   ____

4. **Topic:** art projects I have done

   ____

5. **Topic:** going to the dentist

   ____

Name: ____________________

Adding Sensory Details

A. Think about going to a picnic or a barbecue. What would you feel, taste, smell, see, and hear? Write details in the chart.

I feel...	I taste...	I smell...	I see...	I hear...

B. Write two sentences for a personal narrative about a picnic or a barbecue, using details from the chart above.

____

____

____

____

Name: ______________________________

Adding Thoughts and Feelings

Think of a time when each of these events happened to you. Write about it, and tell what you thought or felt at the time.

Example

Event: when you performed something that you had practiced

At my first dance recital, I felt calm as I walked onto the stage. I knew the steps well.

1. **Event:** a time when you did something brave

____

____

2. **Event:** when you helped a person or an animal in need

____

____

3. **Event:** a time when you lost something special

____

____

4. **Event:** a time when you were part of a big crowd of people

____

____

5. **Event:** when you got to do something that you had always wanted to do

____

____

Name: ______________________________

Organizing Details

A. Number the sentences in the correct order for this personal narrative about marching in a parade. The first one has been done for you.

____ When the parade was over, our band leader gave us sandwiches.

__1__ I was excited when the day of the parade was here.

____ Our band leader lined us up and gave me a banner to hold.

____ People waved and cheered as we marched through town.

____ After breakfast, Dad drove me to the place where the parade would start.

____ As soon as I woke up, I put on my marching-band uniform.

____ The band in front of ours started to play, and we all began to march.

B. Rewrite this paragraph in the order that the events happened.

My friend John and I decided to sell lemonade. We sold all of our lemonade and earned 35 dollars. All that effort was worth it! Once the lemonade was ready, we set up our stand in front of John's house. First, we picked lemons from the tree in my backyard. Then we squeezed the lemons and added sugar and water.

____

____

____

____

____

____

Name: ______________________________

Reviewing a Personal Narrative

Revise this personal narrative about finding a stray kitten. Use what you have learned to make it stronger. Rewrite it on a separate sheet of paper.

Focus on:

✓ telling the details in the order that they happened
✓ adding details that tell how something sounds, feels, looks, smells, or tastes
✓ including thoughts and feelings about what happened

Draft

Finding Marco

Marco was a stray. He was hiding behind a pile of wood near the garage and would not come out. My sister went to the kitchen and brought back some tuna. We heard the kitten when we were in the garage. It took us a long time to figure out where the sound was coming from. I scooped him up when he poked his nose out. He came out because he smelled the tuna.

This is how we got our kitten, Marco. I had often begged my mother for a kitten, but she had always said, "We'll see."

Writing a Friendly Letter

Lesson 1 Introducing a Friendly Letter

A friendly letter is a letter that tells about something personal in the writer's life. It is written to someone the writer knows well.

1. Ask students how they communicate with friends and family members they don't see every day (e.g., phone calls, text messages, e-mail). Say: **One way we can keep in touch with friends and family members who live far away is to write letters. Whether we send letters by regular mail or e-mail, their basic form and purpose are the same.**
2. Direct students to the writing model on p. 148. Read aloud the letter as students follow along.
3. Ask: **Who wrote this letter?** (Zack) **To whom did he write it?** (his cousin Colin) Explain that Colin is the writer's audience. Then ask: **What is the purpose of this friendly letter?** (to tell Colin about playing in the snow) Have students write the audience and purpose on the lines provided.
4. Invite students to offer opinions about what makes this a good friendly letter. Prompt students by asking: **Does the letter seem friendly? Is it clear why Zack is writing to Colin? Does the letter stay on topic? Are the details interesting? Does Zack share his thoughts and feelings about the topic?** Explain that students will use the model as they practice the skills needed to write a good friendly letter.

➤ **Extend the Lesson:** Have students discuss the similarities and differences between composing and sending a paper letter versus e-mail.

Lesson 2 Writing for Your Audience

1. Have students brainstorm people to whom they might send a friendly letter (e.g., a friend, a relative, an adult they know well). Then ask: **Because a friendly letter is personal, to whom might you <u>not</u> send one?** (e.g., the mayor, a business owner, a stranger)
2. Refer to the model letter and remind students of the audience. Ask: **Is playing in the snow a good topic for Zack to write about in a letter to Colin?** (yes) **Why?** (e.g., It's funny and interesting; Colin knows the people involved.) **Remind students that a friendly letter should be about a topic that the reader can relate to.**

Page 148 / Student Book Page 108

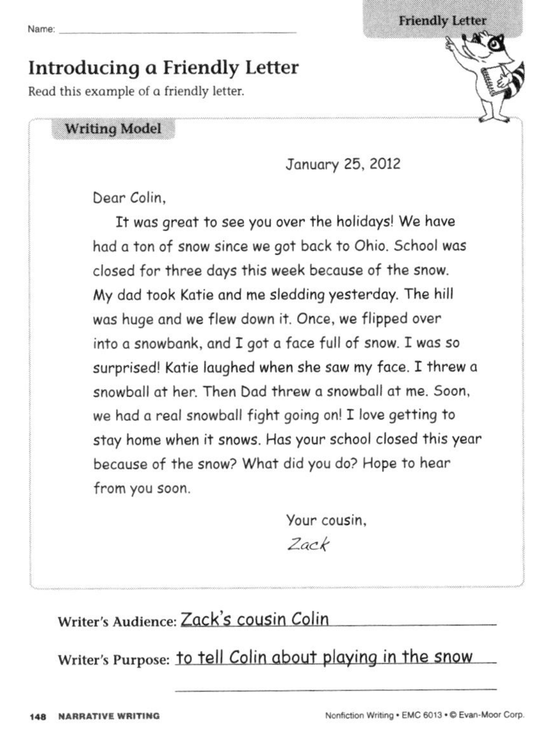
Name: ______________________

Friendly Letter

Introducing a Friendly Letter

Read this example of a friendly letter.

Writing Model

January 25, 2012

Dear Colin,

It was great to see you over the holidays! We have had a ton of snow since we got back to Ohio. School was closed for three days this week because of the snow. My dad took Katie and me sledding yesterday. The hill was huge and we flew down it. Once, we flipped over into a snowbank, and I got a face full of snow. I was so surprised! Katie laughed when she saw my face. I threw a snowball at her. Then Dad threw a snowball at me. Soon, we had a real snowball fight going on! I love getting to stay home when it snows. Has your school closed this year because of the snow? What did you do? Hope to hear from you soon.

Your cousin,
Zack

Writer's Audience: Zack's cousin Colin

Writer's Purpose: to tell Colin about playing in the snow

148 NARRATIVE WRITING   Nonfiction Writing • EMC 6013 • © Evan-Moor Corp.

Page 149 / Student Book Page 109

Name: ______________________ Friendly Letter

Writing for Your Audience

A. Read each topic. Think of someone you could write a letter to about that topic. Complete the sentence by telling why it is a good topic for that person.

1. **Topic:** the last book you read
   I could write a friendly letter about this to my friend Ben because he likes the same kind of books that I do.
2. **Topic:** a trip with your parents
   I could write a friendly letter about this to my grandfather so he will know how much fun I had visiting him.
3. **Topic:** the first day of third grade
   I could write a friendly letter about this to a second-grade student I know so she won't be scared about it next year.
4. **Topic:** your plans for the summer
   I could write a friendly letter about this to my best friend because we like to spend time together.

B. Think about a letter you could write to your best friend and another to a teacher. List three topics you could write about for each person.

My Best Friend	One of My Teachers
a great movie I saw	my science fair project
joining a softball team	acting in the school play
a Girl Scout camping trip	my new baby brother

© Evan-Moor Corp. • EMC 6013 • Nonfiction Writing NARRATIVE WRITING 149

Page 150 / Student Book Page 110

Name: ______________________ Friendly Letter

Adding Details

A. Read each friendly letter. Check the sentence that adds an interesting detail about the topic.

1. Dear Jackson,
   I helped my dad with our yard sale last Saturday. I put price tags on everything we wanted to sell.
   - [ ] This Saturday, my dad and I are going to go rock climbing.
   - [x] I also helped sell things and give people their change.
2. Dear Tia,
   Thank you! I really needed the sleeping bag you gave me for my birthday. I went camping with my friend's family.
   - [ ] My friend has two brothers and one sister.
   - [x] The sleeping bag kept me warm on a cold night.

B. Write a detail that could be added to each letter.

1. Dear Uncle Will,
   I've been riding my bike a lot. I ride it to my friend's house after school every day. Last week, I rode it on a trail behind our house.
   I'm going on a long bike ride with Dad next week.
2. Dear Ariel,
   The last time I went to the city pool was really fun! A lot of my friends were there. We took turns jumping off the diving board. We played games and had races.
   I did a cannonball off the high dive.
3. Dear Neela,
   I changed my baby brother's diaper for the first time. Mom wants me to help take care of him more often. But it was gross!
   I held my breath the whole time.

150 NARRATIVE WRITING Nonfiction Writing • EMC 6013 • © Evan-Moor Corp.

3. Read aloud the directions for Activity A on p. 149. Model using item 1. Then have students complete the activity independently. Ask volunteers to share their responses.
4. Read aloud the directions for Activity B and have students complete it independently. When finished, have students share their topics and explain why each topic might interest that person.

➤ **Extend the Lesson:** Have students name two other people to whom they could write a friendly letter, and also list topics for each person.

Lesson 3 Adding Details

1. Review the purpose of a friendly letter. Say: **In a friendly letter, you might share exciting news, describe a place you visited or something you did, or tell a story about something that happened to you. Whatever the topic is, when you write about an event in a friendly letter, it is important to include interesting details. It is also important to stay on topic so that you don't confuse the reader.**
2. Read aloud the first two sentences of the model letter. Then say: **The second sentence tells what Zack is mostly writing about in his letter to Colin.** Then read the next sentence. *(School was closed for three days ...)* Say: **This sentence tells an interesting detail. There was so much snow at Zack's house that he did not have school for three days.** Have students identify other details and explain why they are interesting. Then ask: **Are all of the details about playing in the snow?** (yes) Say: **Zack stayed on topic with his letter.**
3. Read aloud the directions for Activity A on p. 150. Have students complete the activity in pairs. Invite volunteers to share and explain their answers.
4. Read aloud the directions for Activity B. Then read aloud item 1 and say: **This letter is about riding a bike. What are some other interesting details we could add about riding a bike?** List students' ideas on the board. Then model choosing one idea and writing it as a sentence.
5. Have students complete the activity in pairs. Ask pairs to share their details.

➤ **Extend the Lesson:** Have students work in small groups to write a friendly letter to a second grader about something fun that he or she will do in third grade. Remind students to include interesting details. Send copies of the finished letters to a second-grade class.

Lesson 4 Sharing Thoughts and Feelings

1. Say: **It's important to share your thoughts and feelings in a friendly letter so the person reading it knows how you feel about the topic of the letter. Sharing your thoughts and feelings helps the reader care more and makes the letter more interesting.**
2. Direct students to the model on p. 148. Ask: **Which sentence tells how Zack felt when he got a face full of snow?** *(I was so surprised!)* Then have students look for another sentence in which Zack expresses his feelings. *(I love getting to stay home when it snows.)*
3. Read the directions for Activity A on p. 151. On the board, model completing the first web with your own thoughts and feelings about the first day of school. Then have students complete the activity in pairs.
4. Have students complete Activity B independently. Then have students share their paragraphs with each other.

➤ **Extend the Lesson:** Have students use their webs and paragraphs to write a complete letter to a friend or relative.

Lesson 5 Reviewing a Friendly Letter

1. Review the qualities of a good friendly letter: a topic of interest to the audience, interesting details that stay on topic, and sentences that express the writer's thoughts and feelings.
2. Read aloud the friendly letter on p. 152 as students follow along. Then guide students through revising the draft. Ask: **What is the topic of the letter?** (Jessie's soccer game) **Why might her grandmother be interested in this topic?** (because Jessie is playing) **Are all of the details that Jessie gives about the soccer game interesting and on topic?** (no) **Which would you take out?** (learning how to bake cookies; that blue is her favorite color)
3. Ask: **Does Jessie express any thoughts or feelings about her first soccer game?** (no) **How do you think she feels?** (e.g., nervous, excited) **What do you think Jessie thinks about the game?** (e.g., She hopes her team wins.) Model turning students' suggestions into sentences that can be added to the letter.
4. Have students write their revisions on a separate sheet of paper. Invite volunteers to share their revised letters.

Page 151 / Student Book Page 111

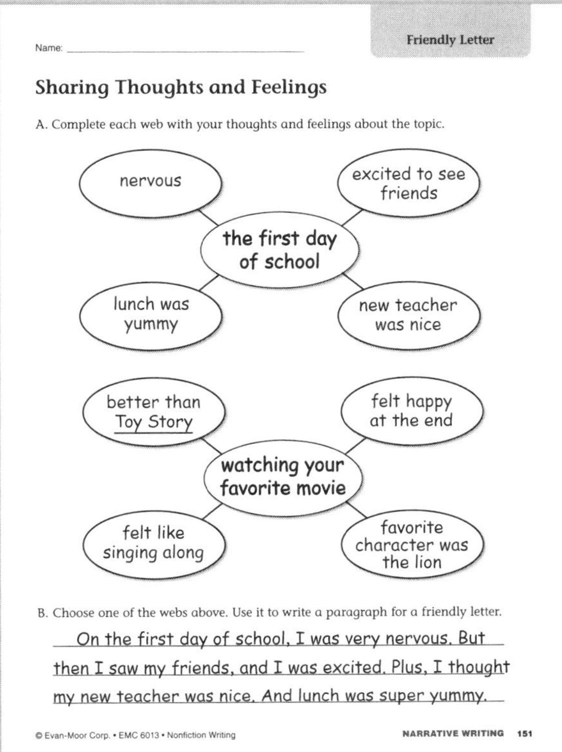
Name: ____________

Friendly Letter

Sharing Thoughts and Feelings

A. Complete each web with your thoughts and feelings about the topic.

the first day of school: nervous; excited to see friends; lunch was yummy; new teacher was nice

watching your favorite movie: better than Toy Story; felt happy at the end; felt like singing along; favorite character was the lion

B. Choose one of the webs above. Use it to write a paragraph for a friendly letter.

On the first day of school, I was very nervous. But then I saw my friends, and I was excited. Plus, I thought my new teacher was nice. And lunch was super yummy.

© Evan-Moor Corp. • EMC 6013 • Nonfiction Writing NARRATIVE WRITING 151

Page 152 and Sample Revision / Student Book Page 112

Name: ____________

Friendly Letter

Sample Answer

September 19, 2012

Dear Grandma,

I have my first soccer game this weekend. I am excited but also nervous. I have been practicing a lot. I really like soccer, and I think I'm pretty good! Mom said she will record the game so you can see it. I hope we win. I'd like to score a goal for you! We got our soccer jerseys yesterday. The next time I come to see you, I'll wear my jersey. Then I'll show you all of my new soccer skills!

Love,
Jessie

Name: ______________________________

Introducing a Friendly Letter

Read this example of a friendly letter.

Writing Model

January 25, 2012

Dear Colin,

It was great to see you over the holidays! We have had a ton of snow since we got back to Ohio. School was closed for three days this week because of the snow. My dad took Katie and me sledding yesterday. The hill was huge and we flew down it. Once, we flipped over into a snowbank, and I got a face full of snow. I was so surprised! Katie laughed when she saw my face. I threw a snowball at her. Then Dad threw a snowball at me. Soon, we had a real snowball fight going on! I love getting to stay home when it snows. Has your school closed this year because of the snow? What did you do? Hope to hear from you soon.

Your cousin,

Zack

Writer's Audience: ______________________________

Writer's Purpose: ______________________________

____

Name: ______________________________

Writing for Your Audience

A. Read each topic. Think of someone you could write a letter to about that topic. Complete the sentence by telling why it is a good topic for that person.

1. **Topic:** the last book you read

   I could write a friendly letter about this to ______________________________

   ______________________________.

2. **Topic:** a trip with your parents

   I could write a friendly letter about this to ______________________________

   ______________________________.

3. **Topic:** the first day of third grade

   I could write a friendly letter about this to ______________________________

   ______________________________.

4. **Topic:** your plans for the summer

   I could write a friendly letter about this to ______________________________

   ______________________________.

B. Think about a letter you could write to your best friend and another to a teacher. List three topics you could write about for each person.

My Best Friend	One of My Teachers
______________	______________
______________	______________
______________	______________

Name: ____

Adding Details

A. Read each friendly letter. Check the sentence that adds an interesting detail about the topic.

1. Dear Jackson,

   I helped my dad with our yard sale last Saturday. I put price tags on everything we wanted to sell.

   ☐ This Saturday, my dad and I are going to go rock climbing.
   ☐ I also helped sell things and give people their change.

2. Dear Tia,

   Thank you! I really needed the sleeping bag you gave me for my birthday. I went camping with my friend's family.

   ☐ My friend has two brothers and one sister.
   ☐ The sleeping bag kept me warm on a cold night.

B. Write a detail that could be added to each letter.

1. Dear Uncle Will,

   I've been riding my bike a lot. I ride it to my friend's house after school every day. Last week, I rode it on a trail behind our house.

   ____

2. Dear Ariel,

   The last time I went to the city pool was really fun! A lot of my friends were there. We took turns jumping off the diving board. We played games and had races.

   ____

3. Dear Neela,

   I changed my baby brother's diaper for the first time. Mom wants me to help take care of him more often. But it was gross!

   ____

Name: ___________________________________

Sharing Thoughts and Feelings

A. Complete each web with your thoughts and feelings about the topic.

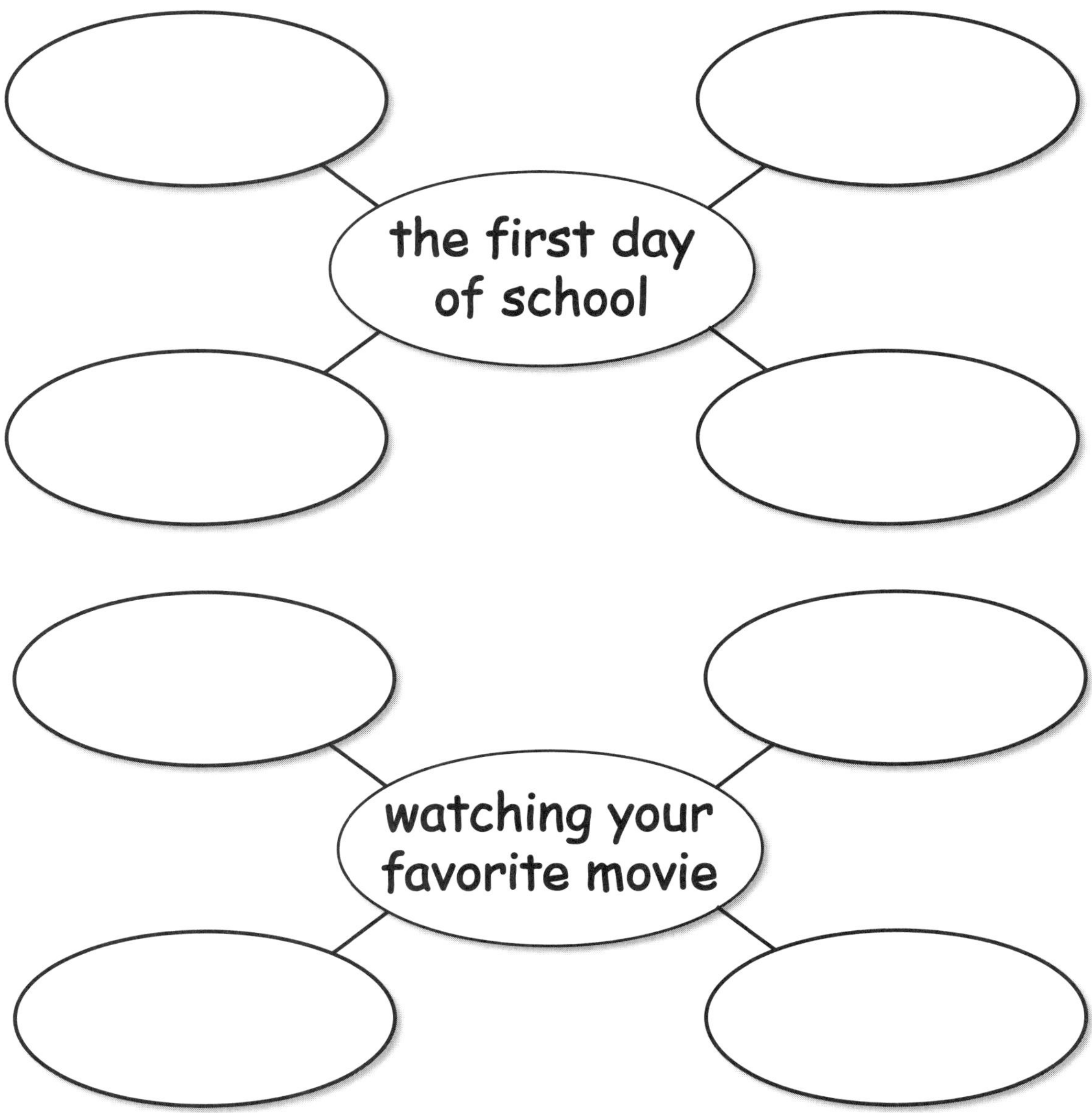

B. Choose one of the webs above. Use it to write a paragraph for a friendly letter.

____

____

____

Name: ___________________________

Reviewing a Friendly Letter

Revise this friendly letter. Use what you have learned to make it stronger. Write the letter on a separate sheet of paper.

Focus on:

✓ thinking about what the audience cares about
✓ adding interesting details about the topic
✓ staying on topic
✓ including thoughts and feelings about the topic

Draft

September 19, 2012

Dear Grandma,

I have my first soccer game this weekend. I have been practicing a lot. I've also been learning how to bake cookies. Mom said she will record the game so you can see it. We got our soccer jerseys yesterday. Blue is my favorite color. The next time I come to see you, I'll wear my jersey. Then I'll show you all of my new soccer skills!

Love,

Jessie

Writing Creative Nonfiction

Lesson 1 Introducing Creative Nonfiction

Creative nonfiction is writing that tells a true story in an interesting way.

1. Suggest a nonfiction topic such as exploring space. Say: **Many nonfiction books about exploring space just give facts. But a creative nonfiction book on this topic might give the facts by telling a story about one astronaut's personal experience of traveling into space.** Explain that writers of creative nonfiction tell about things that really happened, but reading their text is like reading a story.
2. Direct students to p. 156 and explain that the writing model is about an event that happened during the Revolutionary War. Build background as needed; if students are familiar with Paul Revere, explain that this story is similar. Then read aloud "Sybil's Midnight Ride" as students follow along.
3. Ask: **What is the purpose of this piece of creative nonfiction?** (to tell a true story about a girl who was a hero during the Revolutionary War) Have students write the purpose on the lines provided.
4. Invite students to offer opinions about what makes this good creative nonfiction. Prompt students by asking: **Does the first sentence seem like the beginning of a story? Does it hint at what the story is about? Do you think the story is true? Can you picture the events of the story in your mind?**
5. Explain that students will use the model as they practice the skills needed to write creative nonfiction.

➤ **Extend the Lesson:** As a class, brainstorm good topics for creative nonfiction. Prompt students to recall historic events and characters they've studied or read about.

Lesson 2 Writing a Creative First Sentence

1. Review the purpose of creative nonfiction. (to tell a true story in a creative way) Then say: **In creative nonfiction, the writer usually begins with a sentence that sparks the reader's imagination and gives a clue about the topic of the story.**
2. Write the first sentence of the model on the board. *(On a rainy April night ...)* Then write: *Sybil Ludington was born in 1761.* Ask: **Which of these sentences sounds like the beginning of a story?** (the first one) Challenge students to explain why. (e.g., It sets a mood; it paints a picture of the setting in the reader's mind.)

Page 156 / Student Book Page 114

Name: ______________________

Creative Nonfiction

Introducing Creative Nonfiction

Read this example of creative nonfiction.

Writing Model

Sybil's Midnight Ride

On a rainy April night in 1777, Sybil Ludington sat by the fire in her Connecticut home. Her father, Colonel Ludington, was talking about the war. He and his troops were fighting the British to win America's freedom. Suddenly, there was a knock at the door. A soaked visitor stumbled in and announced that British soldiers were burning the nearby town!

Colonel Ludington needed someone to ride through the night to gather his troops. He asked Sybil to make the 40-mile trip, even though she was just 16 years old. Sybil rode through the woods. The darkness was a black curtain around her. Her heart pounded like a drum in her chest. She called out for the troops as she rode. By dawn, the men had gathered, ready to fight.

Writer's Purpose: to tell a true story about a girl who was a hero during the Revolutionary War

156 NARRATIVE WRITING

Nonfiction Writing • EMC 6013 • © Evan-Moor Corp.

Page 157 / Student Book Page 115

Name: ______________________ Creative Nonfiction

Writing a Creative First Sentence

A. Read each pair of sentences. Choose the sentence that is more interesting and sounds more like the beginning of a story.

1. ☐ The Pilgrims held the first Thanksgiving dinner in 1621.
   ☑ It was the autumn of 1621, and the Pilgrims had gathered the harvest.
2. ☐ Riders for the Pony Express carried mail on horseback.
   ☑ Jack tied the mail pouch tightly to his saddle and sped off toward Big Sandy.
3. ☑ Young Davy Crockett packed his belongings and left his family's cabin.
   ☐ Davy Crockett was an American folk hero.
4. ☑ The Great Chicago Fire of 1871 broke out in a narrow alley one windy night.
   ☐ There was a huge fire in Chicago in 1871.

B. Read each paragraph. Rewrite the first sentence to make it more creative.

1. The president moved into the White House on Tuesday. It had been a long and difficult day. Tomorrow he would begin his job as the new president of the United States. He had many challenges ahead of him. But for now, he needed to get some sleep.

   The president lay awake in the bedroom of his new home, the White House, unable to fall asleep.

2. The runner was at the starting line. She took a deep breath to relax. She had trained hard all year for this moment. Finally, she would get her chance to win a gold medal at the Olympics.

   The runner waited nervously at the starting line as a hush came over the crowd.

© Evan-Moor Corp. • EMC 6013 • Nonfiction Writing NARRATIVE WRITING 157

Page 158 / Student Book Page 116

Name: ______________________ Creative Nonfiction

Adding Sensory Details

A. Imagine visiting the zoo a few days after a baby zebra is born. Write words to describe what you might see, hear, smell, and touch at the zoo that day.

I see...	crowds of people around a fence, dust, black and white stripes
I hear...	children shouting, zebra hoofs stomping, lions roaring nearby
I smell...	hay, the fur of wild animals, popcorn
I touch...	a cool, hard metal fence; Mom's hand

B. Read the paragraph. Add two more sentences with sensory details.

It was a warm June day at the Denver Zoo. A fuzzy baby zebra looked out at the crowd, still wobbly on his long, skinny legs. Like all baby zebras, he had brown stripes. His mother was watching him closely. A truck pulled up with a fresh supply of hay and grain. The truck kicked up dust. The smell of fresh hay filled the air.

158 NARRATIVE WRITING Nonfiction Writing • EMC 6013 • © Evan-Moor Corp.

3. Read aloud the directions for Activity A on p. 157. Then read the first pair of sentences. Ask: **Which choice uses words that help you form a clear picture in your mind?** (the second choice) Have students complete the activity in pairs. Review the answers and ask students to explain their choices.
4. Read the directions for Activity B and ask a volunteer to read the first paragraph. Build background by explaining that when a president is elected, he or she goes to live at the White House in Washington, D.C. Invite volunteers to share what they know about the White House. Read aloud the first sentence of the paragraph. Say: **This sentence hints at the topic but isn't very interesting.** Ask: **How can we change it to make it more creative?** (e.g., tell what the president is thinking or how he is feeling) Then work with students to rewrite the sentence. Repeat the process for item 2, or have students complete it independently.

➤ **Extend the Lesson:** Refer students to the nonfiction topics listed during the Lesson 1 extension activity and have them write a creative first sentence for a topic of their choice.

Lesson 3 Adding Sensory Details

1. Say: **Sensory details describe how something looks, sounds, feels, smells, or tastes. They help readers imagine the events that they are reading about.** Have students describe a sight, sound, or other sensory experience they have had recently. (e.g., the taste of cool mint ice cream, the sound of a school bus engine, the feel of a rough plaster wall)
2. Review the writing model on p. 156 and have students look for sensory details. (the rainy night, the knock at the door, the soaked visitor stumbling in, Sybil's heart pounding)
3. Read aloud the directions for Activity A on p. 158. To activate prior knowledge, invite volunteers to describe their experiences at a zoo. Then conduct Activity A with the class or have students work in small groups.
4. Read aloud the directions for Activity B. Have students complete the activity independently or in pairs, using the sensory details they brainstormed in Activity A. Invite them to share their sentences with the class.

➤ **Extend the Lesson:** Have students brainstorm sensory details related to the nonfiction topics they selected during the Lesson 2 extension activity.

Lesson 4 Using Similes and Metaphors

1. Say: **A *simile* describes something by comparing it to something else. It uses the word *like* or *as*. A *metaphor* describes something by comparing it to something else, without using *like* or *as*. Writers use similes and metaphors to describe things in a creative way.** Write these two sentences on the board: *She is graceful when she runs. She is as graceful as a dancer when she runs.* Ask: **Which sentence is a simile?** (the second sentence) **Which helps you picture the girl better?** (the second sentence) Then write: *She is a dancer when she runs.* Say: **This sentence is a metaphor. It also compares a girl to a dancer.** Ask: **How are the girl and a dancer alike?** (Both are graceful.)
2. Revisit the writing model on p. 156. Have students underline the simile *(Her heart pounded like a drum ...)* and double-underline the metaphor *(The darkness was a black curtain ...)*. Discuss the comparison in each example.
3. Read the directions for Activity A on p. 159 and discuss the examples. Review the answers after students have completed the activity. For Activity B, use item 1 to model writing a metaphor. Then have students complete items 2–5 independently or in pairs.

Lesson 5 Reviewing Creative Nonfiction

1. Review the qualities of good creative nonfiction: a creative first sentence, sensory details, and descriptive language that includes similes and metaphors.
2. Direct students to p. 160. Explain that "A Historic Journey" is meant to tell a true story about pioneers George and Keturah (ki-TOOR-uh) Belknap, who traveled by covered wagon from Iowa to Oregon in 1848. Read aloud the draft as students follow along. Then discuss how it can be improved. Ask: **Does the first sentence tell what the story is about?** (no) Help students elaborate on the time and place, and point out that the first two sentences can be combined.
3. Read the final sentence of the first paragraph and ask: **How could we describe the slow journey using a metaphor or simile?** (e.g., compare it to a snail or a turtle) **What sensory details could we add in the next paragraph?** (e.g., telling how the creek sounds or how the fire feels)
4. Have students revise the draft independently. Invite volunteers to share their revisions with the class.

Page 159 / Student Book Page 117

Name: ____________________

Creative Nonfiction

Using Similes and Metaphors

A. Read the sentences. Underline each simile and circle each metaphor.

Example

The boy's hair stood up like porcupine quills.

The moon is a big silver platter.

1. The autumn leaves were a colorful blanket on the ground.
2. The burnt toast looked like two pieces of coal on the plate.
3. The Olympic swimmer was a shark in the water.
4. The train sounded like a thunderstorm as it passed through town.
5. The boys stomped like elephants through the living room.

B. Revise each sentence to include a simile or a metaphor.

1. The spaghetti sauce is hot.
   The spaghetti sauce is lava on top of my noodles.
2. My room looked messy.
   My room was as messy as a garbage dump.
3. My guinea pig is silly.
   My guinea pig is a tiny, furry clown.
4. The wind sounded scary.
   The wind howled like a wolf.
5. The perfume smells nice.
   The perfume smells like a rose garden.

 NARRATIVE WRITING 159

Page 160 and Sample Revision / Student Book Page 118

Name: ____________________

Creative Nonfiction

Sample Answer

A Historic Journey

It was a fine spring day, and pioneers Keturah and George Belknap were heading West in their covered wagon. They had left their home in Iowa a month ago. It would take them five more months to arrive in Oregon. The journey was as slow as a snail race.

Keturah jumped down from the wagon. The tall prairie grass tickled her arms. She heard the gurgling of a nearby creek. It was a good place to stop for a rest. While George tended the horses, Keturah started the campfire and took some dried apples and a wedge of hard yellow cheese from a cloth sack. She and George would eat beside the crackling fire, tired but happy.

160

Name: ____

Introducing Creative Nonfiction

Read this example of creative nonfiction.

Writing Model

Sybil's Midnight Ride

On a rainy April night in 1777, Sybil Ludington sat by the fire in her Connecticut home. Her father, Colonel Ludington, was talking about the war. He and his troops were fighting the British to win America's freedom. Suddenly, there was a knock at the door. A soaked visitor stumbled in and announced that British soldiers were burning the nearby town!

Colonel Ludington needed someone to ride through the night to gather his troops. He asked Sybil to make the 40-mile trip, even though she was just 16 years old. Sybil rode through the woods. The darkness was a black curtain around her. Her heart pounded like a drum in her chest. She called out for the troops as she rode. By dawn, the men had gathered, ready to fight.

Writer's Purpose: ____

____

Name: ______________________________

Writing a Creative First Sentence

A. Read each pair of sentences. Choose the sentence that is more interesting and sounds more like the beginning of a story.

1. ☐ The Pilgrims held the first Thanksgiving dinner in 1621.
   ☐ It was the autumn of 1621, and the Pilgrims had gathered the harvest.

2. ☐ Riders for the Pony Express carried mail on horseback.
   ☐ Jack tied the mail pouch tightly to his saddle and sped off toward Big Sandy.

3. ☐ Young Davy Crockett packed his belongings and left his family's cabin.
   ☐ Davy Crockett was an American folk hero.

4. ☐ The Great Chicago Fire of 1871 broke out in a narrow alley one windy night.
   ☐ There was a huge fire in Chicago in 1871.

B. Read each paragraph. Rewrite the first sentence to make it more creative.

1. The president moved into the White House on Tuesday. It had been a long and difficult day. Tomorrow he would begin his job as the new president of the United States. He had many challenges ahead of him. But for now, he needed to get some sleep.

____

____

2. The runner was at the starting line. She took a deep breath to relax. She had trained hard all year for this moment. Finally, she would get her chance to win a gold medal at the Olympics.

____

____

Name: ______________________________

Adding Sensory Details

A. Imagine visiting the zoo a few days after a baby zebra is born. Write words to describe what you might see, hear, smell, and touch at the zoo that day.

I see...	______________________________ ______________________________
I hear...	______________________________ ______________________________
I smell...	______________________________ ______________________________
I touch...	______________________________ ______________________________

B. Read the paragraph. Add two more sentences with sensory details.

It was a warm June day at the Denver Zoo. A fuzzy baby zebra looked out at the crowd, still wobbly on his long, skinny legs. Like all baby zebras, he had brown stripes. His mother was watching him closely. A truck pulled up with a fresh supply of hay and grain. ______________________________

____

____

____

Name: ______________________________

Using Similes and Metaphors

A. Read the sentences. Underline each simile and circle each metaphor.

Example

The boy's hair stood up like porcupine quills.

The moon is a big silver platter.

1. The autumn leaves were a colorful blanket on the ground.
2. The burnt toast looked like two pieces of coal on the plate.
3. The Olympic swimmer was a shark in the water.
4. The train sounded like a thunderstorm as it passed through town.
5. The boys stomped like elephants through the living room.

B. Revise each sentence to include a simile or a metaphor.

1. The spaghetti sauce is hot.

____

2. My room looked messy.

____

3. My guinea pig is silly.

____

4. The wind sounded scary.

____

5. The perfume smells nice.

____

Name: ______________________________

Reviewing Creative Nonfiction

Revise this example of creative nonfiction. Use what you have learned to make it stronger. Write your revision on a separate sheet of paper.

Focus on:

- ✓ writing a creative first sentence that hints at the topic
- ✓ telling how something sounds, feels, looks, smells, or tastes
- ✓ describing things using similes and metaphors

Draft

A Historic Journey

It was spring. Pioneers Keturah and George Belknap were heading West. They had left their home in Iowa a month ago. It would take them five more months to arrive in Oregon. The journey was slow.

Keturah jumped down from the wagon. The tall prairie grass tickled her arms. There was a creek nearby. It was a good place to stop for a rest. While George tended the horses, Keturah started the campfire and took some dried fruit and cheese from a cloth sack. She and George would eat beside the fire, tired but happy.